s Cataloguing-in-Publication Data

n America : historical and critical essays /
n J. Matelski and Nancy Lynch Street.

graphical references and index.

673-4 (softcover : 50# alkaline paper)

United States— History and criticism.
res and war.   I. Matelski, Marilyn J., 1950–
Street.
5   2003
1

2003010999

loguing data are available

he United States of America

Black Hawk Down (Photofest)

mpany, Inc., Publishers
on, North Carolina 28640
andpub.com

War
in A

Historical

Edited by
and Na

LIBRARY OF CONGRES

Matelski, Marilyn J
    War and film i
  edited by Marilyn
        p.   cm.
    Includes biblic

    ISBN 0-7864-

  1. War films—
2. Motion pictu
II. Nancy, Lynch
PN1995.9.W3W
791.43'658 — dc2

British Library cat

Manufactured in t

Cover image from

McFarland & Con
Box 611, Jeffer
www.mcfa

McFarland & Con
Jefferson, North (

To Tiernan, Brittini,
Alex, Espen and Nicolay

Peace

Acknowledgments

This book represents our third joint writing venture and second coediting effort. And, as in all our projects, the final manuscript would never have come together without the cooperation and support of many colleagues and friends. Most especially, we'd like to thank Drs. Laurence Richards and Nancy Kleniewski (Bridgewater State College) for their encouragement and advocacy; Gene Neault, Rita Rosenthal, Drs. Dana Mastro, Pamela Lannutti and Susannah Stern (Boston College); our many wonderful students for their genuine interest as well as good-natured teasing during the times we never thought we'd finish; and Mary Saunders and Sharon Fortier — our administrative assistants at Boston College and Bridgewater State College — who made sure we were never sidetracked from our publishing focus. Special thanks to Bridgewater State College Center for Research and Teaching (CART) student assistants Sasha C. Link, Amanda M. Monteforte and Jenniffer P. O'Neil, who helped us weather the storms of writing while teaching. We'd also like to give special recognition to Carolyn Matelski, who has proofread each and every one of the thirteen books (as well as countless convention papers and journal articles) one or both of us have written.

Finally, we'd like to honor the hundreds of producers, directors, editors, writers and actors who have contributed invaluably to the discussion of war through their artistic work. Many of these people have shown great courage in voicing their opinions, and, as history reflects, have sacrificed dearly for their efforts. We applaud their talent; we admire their fortitude; and we are grateful to have learned from their insights. Through their "visions" we've been able to construct a much richer portrait of America — in peace and in war — than any history book could ever provide. Thank you all!

Contents

Preface

In our early discussions concerning film as it depicts, describes and often glorifies combat, we first intended to develop a collection of essays confined to the relationship of film to the Cold War culture in America. In 1999, several of our essay contributors came together for a roundtable discussion led by Drs. Donald A. Fishman and Bonnie S. Jefferson of Boston College at the annual National Communication Association convention. In addition to our mutual interest in the Cold War — living through the rivalry and enmity of it — we all either teach film studies or have a strong interest in the culture, the consequences, and the images of war as depicted through film.

As has happened in our past publishing ventures, world occurrences intervened before we were able to put together our final draft. The events in New York, Washington, D.C., and Pennsylvania on September 11, 2001, shattered our previous prism, altering (though not obliterating) our worldview. The shock waves emanating from the horror of that day's events suggested to some of us that America had been adrift since the end of the Cold War and the fall of the Berlin Wall some ten years earlier. American policies and priorities emerged from the Cold War mentality, with little concern for new realities. United States foreign affairs policies tended to unilaterally and overtly refer to the military dominance of the United States.

In the process of writing, the editors discovered that the overly simplistic view of the Cold War obscured emerging directions in world danger. We are, of course, referring to the threat of jihad and terrorism from Mullah Omar and Osama bin Laden, "weapons of mass destruction" from Iraq's Saddam Hussein, potential nuclear warfare from India and Pakistan, and North Korean Kim Jong Il's decision to resume building nuclear weapons. The essays in this book touch upon each of these dangers as they have been depicted in American and British films.

— Marilyn J. Matelski and Nancy Lynch Street

Introduction

War and Film

American films have captured the world's imagination — and war (or action) films ignite filmgoers in virtually every country on the globe, with the possible exception of those benighted countries where television and film are either prohibited or unavailable due to lack of infrastructure. Curiously enough, America's chief exports to the world are war (in its many manifestations) and entertainment. Sometimes these two products are wrapped in the same package — as in the war film. Accordingly, acceptance by the young in many countries of overtly American products — video, film, technologically superior war games and American clothing styles (as in the worldwide love of jeans) — by the young in many countries have tended to distort the feedback received in America.

Despite the warning signs of a divided perspective on the "new world order," the United States has continued to disregard signs of disaffection (i.e., escalating terrorism directed toward the United States and its allies). This disaffection has been focused primarily on the military and economic dominance of the West and in particular the United States. During the Cold War and the post–Cold War eras (including one period of "the savage wars of peace"),[1] we seemed to ignore escalating terror "events" as insignificant. Never having suffered invasion or bombs raining down upon our children, Americans believed these things couldn't happen here.

The contributors to this book take differing perspectives on various dimensions of America's love affair with war as depicted through films. Given the close relationship of Hollywood with the U.S. government during all wars, regardless of the "-ism" involved, the cultural context of each war is not ignored, nor is film as a venue for propaganda to incite fervent patriotism. This has most recently been demonstrated in *Black Hawk Down*

3

(2001) — the hero- high-tech-infused version of the "humanitarian" American presence in Somalia.

As America's war on terrorism and the search for Osama bin Laden in Afghanistan lost some of their headline status in January 2002, media reports indicated that the United States government and the military were considering interventions in other parts of the world — particularly in Somalia. One gets the idea that the timing of the release of *Black Hawk Down* was no accident. The applause of the audience at the end of the film suggests that the film may do what it was meant to do — increase the American audience's appetite for military action in Somalia even as we continue the search for Mullah Omar and Osama bin Laden. Ostensibly, we went to war in Afghanistan to bring these two leaders down. Unable to accomplish this mission in Afghanistan, the U.S. military wants to spread a wider net. More films glorifying the heroism of the American military and its Special Forces in a time when there are few heroes can be expected in the future. And these films will most likely adopt themes similar to those identified in this book.

Book Essays and Themes

In Chapter 1, "*The Bridge on the River Kwai*: The Collision of Duty and Pride," author Richard A. Kallan notes that while few would disagree with "the technical artistry of this 1957 British film, what unites the film's numerous thematic threads,"[2] remains unclear. Directed by David Lean and written by blacklisted Hollywood writers Carl Foreman and Michael Wilson, the film received seven Oscars, one of which was for its script. (Ironically, however, since the authors were blacklisted, the novel's author, Pierre Boulle, was given the Oscar instead!) Because the movie is regarded by some as an antiwar film, Kallan suggests that a "close reading of the film suggests a more complex perspective," involving duty and pride. For some, the meaning implicit in the film and others like it, e.g., *Born on the Fourth of July*, *The Deer Hunter*, or *Dr. Strangelove*, is the strong indictment of war, the madness of the enterprise which causes many to lose their moral moorings and never return home, and the insanity of those who make the rules of war and order them carried out.

In Chapter 2, "John Wayne: American Icon, Patriotic Zealot and Cold War Ideologue," Bonnie S. Jefferson explores the immense impact of three of John Wayne's films on the communist-crazed culture. The political thriller *Big Jim McLain* (1952) pairs John Wayne and James Arness as House of Un-American Activities (HUAC) investigators and has little to recommend it, except as a remnant of the blacklisting era in America in the late forties and fifties. For a look at that era in America, this film is a treasure. Continuing his "love it or leave it" message to all patriots, Wayne's *The Alamo* (1960) is the saga of the Alamo—a Western and war film. Jefferson's third Wayne film is the ultimate war propaganda film *The Green Berets* (1968), filled with clichés.

Jefferson's incorporation of these three films helps one to better understand the often-complementary relationship between the United States government and the film industry. To make *The Green Berets*, Wayne collaborated with the United States government, as filmmakers have often done during periods of war. A recent example of such a collaboration is the 2001 film *Black Hawk Down*, directed by Ridley Scott, which depicts the savage fighting in the 1993 U.S. mission in Somalia. Scenes as realistic as those in *Black Hawk Down* could have been created only in partnership with the military. Further, Hollywood makes documentaries such as *Why We Fight* at the request of the government. But when other nations do it, it's called propaganda.

In *The End of Victory Culture*, Tom Englehardt describes the way these films work:

> With their stark vision of "a free world" versus "a slave world," of "civilization against barbarism" and "good against evil," backed up by dramatic Disney-produced animated sequences, these films exuded the clarity and confidence of a country that knew its place in history. The last of them, *Know Your Enemy — Japan*, was released on the day of the atomic bombing of Nagasaki. The first, *Prelude to War*, was considered so powerful that President Roosevelt urged it be put into commercial distribution.... . In 1965, the government released its first film about the war in Vietnam, entitled *Why Viet-Nam*.[3]

One might describe the Hollywood film industry as a kind of "silent partner" to both the visible and invisible U.S. government. Through film language and images, the film industry shapes the vantage point from which we Americans see films. This is also the case in other countries. (For example, around the time of the return of Hong Kong to the mainland [July 1997], there were several films released in China depicting the scurrilous behavior of the British toward the Chinese during the nineteenth century Opium Wars.) From at least World War II to the present, America has utilized film to promote patriotism, dedication to cause, recruitment and heroism. Motifs such as "frontier justice," patriotism, victory, heroism, terrorism and propaganda are also prominent, as Jefferson and others suggest.

Chapter 3, "The Cold War: Three Episodes in Waging a Cinematic Battle," by Donald Fishman, continues the theme of patriotism discussed in Chapter 2, analyzing the cinematic depiction of patriotism in *The Fountainhead*, *Seven Days in May*, and *High Noon*. This discussion of patriotism asserts that "through time patriotism becomes marginalized as the emotional attachment of a distorted mind." The author believes that *Seven Days in May* is an important "representative anecdote" in light of the September 11, 2001, terrorist attack on the World Trade Center. Quoting *Opponents of War, 1917–1918*, Fishman says, "That attack generated an outpouring of patriotism never witnessed during the Cold War, but it was reminiscent of the jingoistic nationalism and sudden surge of patriotism during World War I."[4]

Chapter 4, by John J. Michalczyk and Susan A. Michalczyk, is entitled "Troubled Silences: Trauma in John Huston's Film *Let There Be Light*." This film, made in 1946 by John Huston, was not released until 1981. In this chapter, the authors say, "No combat film, documentary or feature, however, has ever captured the effects of trauma as searingly as (Major) John Huston's gripping 58-minute documentary, *Let There Be Light*, the third in his 'war trilogy' with the U.S. Army Signal Corps." Following World War II, "a vast number of returning soldiers with psychological problems—as many as 500,000 men—were said to have been hospitalized as neuropsychiatric cases in 1945 alone."[5] After finishing the documentary, "Huston planned to show it to a gathering of friends at the Museum of Modern Art in New York in 1946. Before the screening began, two MPs confiscated the film." The army did not want the documentary released to the public.[6] Quoting critic Charles Champlin, the authors say, "it is, by any standards, an affecting insight into the *troubled silences* after the battles and the parades."[7]

In Chapter 5, patriotism is analyzed through the dialectical tension set up when family members each have a different view of what is patriotic. In "Patriot or Pariah? The Impact of War on Family Relationships," Marilyn J. Matelski looks at the ways in which opposing patriotic views can affect families. Matelski uses two films as analytical tools—*The Way We Were* (1973), directed by Sydney Pollack, and *The War at Home* (1996), directed by Emilio Estevez. The former film highlights the disintegration of relationships when the political views of husband and wife become polarized. Challenged to give up her principles to maintain the relationship, Barbra Streisand responds to her husband (Robert Redford) by affirming that "People are their principles!" *The Way We Were* also illustrates the devastation of the blacklisting period in Hollywood.

The War at Home depicts the tension in a family whose patriotic visions differ during and after the Vietnam War. It demonstrates the anguish of the family and of the boy they sent to war who returned greatly changed. He cannot rid himself of the memories of combat—a frequent outcome of the madness of war. *The War at Home* also illustrates the decline in civility brought about by the anguish and conflict resulting from the Vietnam War.

In Chapter 6, "The Cold War, Cinema and Civility: The Top Films of 1967," Barbara J. Walkosz says, "Because cinema can both reflect and influence society, this chapter seeks to illuminate these issues through an examination of the interaction of civility, the context of the Cold War, and cinema in 1967." Walkosz analyzes the three top-grossing films of 1967 — *The Graduate, Guess Who's Coming to Dinner,* and *Bonnie and Clyde.* These films mark the beginnings of significant change in institutions, e.g., marriage and race in American culture as reflected in film, as well as the "changing nature of civil discourse in American society."

These films give insight into the turbulent sixties in America (and elsewhere), a time when the social fabric was rent by social protests and seemingly unlikely coalitions (perhaps unthinkable in the forties and fifties in America). Change was in the air — literally, as it turns out, as methods of waging war took on new configurations with advancing technology and diverse killing fields.

Chapter 7, "Top Guns in Vietnam: The Pilot as Protected Warrior Hero," by Sharon D. Downey, considers the transformation of the pilot in the Vietnam conflict, utilizing the Burkean pentad to structure the chapter. Through her analysis of film representations of the U.S. fighter pilot in Vietnam, Downey argues that "the aviator undergoes and successfully completes the archetypal hero's 'quest,' a journey made possible rhetorically by situating him within the 'context' of Vietnam, but removing him from the morally uncertain 'scene' of war."

Citing Joseph Campbell's concept of warrior as hero and a "monomyth," Downey discusses the "back-to-Nam" films, in which "the warrior has to overcome the scenic destructiveness of a corrupt bureaucracy to return to the jungles Vietnam alone where he is once again 'at home' with the terrain and where he effectively appropriates the land in pursuit of his goal." This vision is in stark contrast to the realm of the pilot-warrior, who exists in a "relatively privileged, detached, and infinite comfort zone for confrontation in a place that is at once close-up and threatening but also curiously stark and not insurmountable." Put another way, the pilot as warrior does not walk the same path as the "grunt" as warrior.

Downey also discusses the pilot-warrior's advantages over those of the ground warrior:

> First, while the warrior has always been revered in myth and lore, the
> warrior-pilot has the added advantage of triggering the universal human

dream to fly.... Second, in the larger social and political milieu framing Vietnam in the 1960s and early 1970s, the war and, by extension, the soldier participating in it may have been unpopular, but the image of the aviator remained appealing.... Third, the military pilot is a professional, an officer, and typically a career "lifer."

Thus, the pilot, in contrast to the grunt, is an elite warrior. Further adding to the mystique of the pilot-warrior in Vietnam, Downey discusses the "interrelationships among Vietnam aviator, astronaut and American POW."

She also illustrates her claims with films such as *Bat 21, Flight of the Intruder,* and *Hanoi Hilton.* The pilot-warrior image of World War II films is retained in this analysis, fusing "mythic images of the cowboy, the adventurer, the rugged individualist, the community savior, and the technological hero, all of which ideologically control past, present, and future on the ground, in the sky, and over the seas." And, as the author notes, they "later [become] the principal players of the Gulf War, and the generals and policy makers in military and government."

With the transformation of the pilot-warrior in film, Karen Rasmussen and Jennifer Asenas join Downey in Chapter 8 to argue that the ground warrior has also undergone a transformation from a "failed hero-victim into a noble social savior." Reflecting on the evolution of Vietnam imagery in films in their essay "Trauma, Treatment, and Transformation: The Evolution of the Vietnam Warrior in Film," the authors "analyze two dominant strains in Vietnam warrior films that follow the theme of restoring honor to the Vietnam veteran." These two strains include the "back-to-Nam" group of films and the "cultural savior" group of films.

In Chapter 9, "American Hero Meets Terrorist: *True Lies* and *Patriot Games* After September 11, 2001," Suzanne McCorkle investigates the series of terrorist bombings in the United States, beginning with the first bomb attack on the World Trade Center, as well as the actions of citizen-terrorist Terry McNichols,

> whose homemade fertilizer bomb killed citizens in the Oklahoma City federal building in retribution for government actions at Ruby Ridge in Idaho and the Branch Davidian fire. To this scenario add the attacks of Osama bin Laden's network on September 11, coupled with the anthrax letters, and any illusions of national invulnerability were shattered.

McCorkle examines two films with terrorist plots: *True Lies* and *Patriot Games.* She utilizes the psychological theory of terror management, which suggests that culture itself is a mechanism humans created to manage the terror of self-knowledge of one's own mortality." Applying the terror management perspective to pre– and post–September 11 viewings of *True Lies* and *Patriot Games*, McCorkle demonstrates in her analyses how the theory plays out in the films. McCorkle also sets the stage for the final chapter on *Dr. Strangelove* and *Black Sunday*.

Terrorism is not a new game in the history of conflict and war. Terrorism of one kind or another has existed for a very long time. The Luftwaffe's air raid on Guernica was an act of terror, one immortalized by Picasso. The Allied bombing of Dresden in World War II was an act of terror, as depicted in *Map of the Human Heart*. Very recently, in the book *The Fire: Germany under Bombardment, 1940–45*, Jorge Friedrich describes the horror of

> city by city, raid by raid, the razing of Germany, recording every lost architectural masterpiece, every percentage of living space destroyed, every death toll. It also depicts the human cost of the firestorm: piles of suffocated victims in Bunkers, incinerated corpses shriveled to the size of hand luggage, children boiled alive in water used to extinguish burning houses.[8]

German citizens born during World War II or after no longer suffer from the "guilt" of the war. Thus the Allies' attacks on German civilians are coming under closer scrutiny. Prior to this time, "any extended mention of German suffering during World War II was dismissed as Nazi-apologist revisionism. [Now] Germans are taking an interest in the estimated 600,000 civilians, among them some 75,000 children, killed in the Allied bombing raids."[9] For Friedrich, the idea for *The Fire* developed when he was examining the Nazi war crimes trials. He says:

> [O]ne of the military commanders accused of civilian massacres in the Ukraine asked the question, "What's the difference between lining people up against a wall and dropping bombs on them?" I tried to find an answer and couldn't, other than the fact that the one killing took place horizontally, and the other vertically.[10]

Enter *Dr. Strangelove*, where the entire world is blown up (in other circumstances, a comedic accident). The United States is one of the few nations that can destroy almost any country and its people through bombing. No longer does the United States have to engage in hand-to-hand combat, except when it miscalculates as it did in Mogadishu, Somalia (immortalized in *Black Hawk Down*). All it has to do is set its sights and drop the bombs. For the most part, Americans never know what hit the people of the other country — or who was hit. Military personnel, civilians, women and children, no matter. It's an order and a flight plan. Not looking into the eyes of the dead, the pilots simply pass over and return to base.

The air wars began with the civil war in Spain on Monday, April 26, 1937, with an attack on Guernica. German Luftwaffe Colonel Wolfram von Richthofen

> had some fifty fighter and bomber aircraft, 120 airmen, thousands of pounds of percussion, projectile and incendiary bombs, and countless rounds of ammunition at his disposal.... It was a military strike unprecedented in modern warfare: the first large-scale, deliberate airborne attack of a civilian target. The afternoon bombardment lasted 3¼ hours. Citizens fleeing the town were machine-gunned by German fighters. By nightfall in Richthofen's words, Guernica was "literally leveled to the ground...." Picasso's "Guernica" is considered by many art historians to be the most import painting of the 20th century.[11]

Dropping napalm on Vietnamese villages and civilians during the ill-fated Vietnam War was an act of terror. Suicide bombings of Palestinians in Israel are acts of terror; retaliatory attacks by Israelis upon Palestinians are also acts of terror. Suicide missions by Al Qaeda terrorists diving into the World Trade Center towers and the Pentagon are acts of terror. U.S. planes bombing women, children, villages and farmland in Afghanistan in 2001 are acts of terror. Acts of terror are perpetrated upon the innocents. They are not somehow different from conventional war or the Cold War. All rationalizations aside, whatever the label, whether terrorist event, peacekeeping missions, armed conflict or war, there are victims and perpetrators.

In Chapter 10, Nancy Lynch Street's analysis of Stanley Kubrick's *Dr. Strangelove* focuses on nuclear terrorism and the anticipatory terror of the disenfranchised, primarily women and children. When dropping bombs from great heights, as the United States has done in Afghanistan, one never has to see the victims, the fleeing children, the scattered shoes.

Dr. Strangelove provides a blueprint for the twenty-first-century terrorism threatened in 2003. Nuclear terror is a product of the Cold War era. Yet another film which needs recognition is John Frankenheimer's *Black Sunday*, which depicts the terrorism wrought by those who perceive themselves to be disenfranchised. During the time these films were made, the comedic realism of *Dr. Strangelove* and the horrific realism of *Black Sunday* converged within Cold War boundaries. In *Dr. Strangelove*, the superpowers, their managers and minions who control nuclear weapons are portrayed as crazed dolts, drunks and womanizers. Cold War paranoia over "commies" and "contamination" mixed with male sexual preoccupations and dilemmas, not to mention hubris, permeate the film, ensuring that the safeguards intended to prevent nuclear war will indeed fail.

In *Black Sunday*, both foreign and domestic disenfranchised persons team up to challenge America. Federal agents learn of a plot to bomb the Super Bowl and seek help from the Israelis, who are renowned for their expertise in dealing with terrorists (as they are today). Both films could have been instructive in limiting the effects of terrorism in this new century. Unheeded, they each became blueprints for September 11 and its aftermath. In this chapter, the author places primary emphasis on the analysis of Kubrick's *Dr. Strangelove*.

Summary

The new millennium has brought with it revised perceptions of politics, economics and technology. The "new world order" is one of free trade, democracy and globalization. Perhaps more obscure has been the evolution of war matériel and conflict and their global ramifications, especially since the 2001 World Trade Center attack by Osama bin Laden and the terrorist organization Al Qaeda. No longer do the old definitions of combat work, nor are we easily able to codify traditional notions of patriotism, terrorism, homeland defense and victory.

In this book, the essayists address the changing world of war. Using, among other methods, historical-critical, Burkean, psychological, conflict management and cultural studies perspectives, they examine war as depicted in film. Topics range from frontier justice, Cold War fervor and disarray, government-sponsored terrorism, and war's far-reaching effects on personal values, family relationships and general civility. The films in this analysis vary from epics such as *Bridge on the River Kwai* and *The Green Berets* to reflections of Cold War cultural evolution such as *The Graduate* and *Guess Who's Coming to Dinner*. Some of the essays deal with satirical films such as *Dr. Strangelove*, while others deal with openly propagandistic films such as *The Alamo* and *Big Jim McLain*. All together, however, these films form an evolving mosaic of film genres and war themes.

NOTES

1. Max Boot, *The Savage Wars of Peace: Small Wars and the Rise of American Power* (New York: Basic, 2002). Boot chronicles other small wars prior to and following the Cold War period from 1945 to 1990.

2. Quoted passages not cited in this introduction are either from the abstracts (not reproduced in this book) or actual text of the authors' chapters.

3. Tom Engelhardt, *The End of Victory Culture: Cold War America and the Disillusioning of a Generation* (Amherst: University of Massachusetts Press, 1998).

4. See H. C. Peterson and Gilbert C. Fite, *Opponents of War, 1917–1918* (Westport, Ct.: Greenwood, 1957/1986, rpt).

5. David A. Gerber, "Heroes and Misfits: The Troubled Social Reintegration of Disabled Veterans in 'The Best Years of Our Lives'" in Gerber (ed.), *Disabled Veterans in History* (Ann Arbor: University of Michigan Press, 2000), 73.

6. From Chapter 4, by John and Susan Michalczyk, in this book.

7. Charles Champlin, "Huston Wartime Films on KCET," *Los Angeles Times* (April 30, 1981): 9.

8. Jefferson Chase, "The Fire Last Time," *Boston Sunday Globe* (January 19, 2003): D10.

9. *Ibid.*

10. *Ibid.*

11. Michael C. Boyer, "Guernica: Seeing the Larger Picture: The Story of Picasso's 'Instrument of War,'" *Boston Sunday Globe* (January 19, 2003): D7.

1

The Bridge on the River Kwai: The Collision of Duty and Pride

Richard A. Kallan

"There is so much that is provocative about *The Bridge on the River Kwai* and there are so many intellectual levels on which to contemplate and analyze this film that we'll probably be talking about it and taking sights on it for years."[1] So wrote the *New York Times* prophetically nearly fifty years ago.

Beyond its commercial success and critical acclaim — winning seven Academy Awards, including top honors for Best Picture, Best Director, and Best Actor — *The Bridge on the River Kwai*[2] remains a haunting experience because of its intriguing characters and unique plot, its multiple and constantly shifting perspectives, and, of course, its somewhat ambiguous ending.

The 1957 film, based on Pierre Boulle's novel of the same name,[3] takes place in 1943 during World War II. It tells the story of how Colonel Nicholson (Alec Guinness) and his British troops, imprisoned in a Japanese POW camp nestled deep within the jungles of Burma, are asked to build a railway bridge across the River Kwai that will connect the Japanese railway between Bangkok and Rangoon. Nicholson directs the building of the bridge, but not before he and the commander of the camp, Colonel Saito (Sessue Hayakawa), engage in a month-long contest of wills over whether military officers should be required to do manual work. When Nicholson emerges victorious, he consumes himself and his troops in building a "proper" bridge. In the process, he becomes so proud of his bridge that he loses sight of how it serves enemy purposes. When a four-man British-directed commando team led by Colonel Warden (Jack Hawkins) and featuring an American, Shears (William Holden), who had escaped from the prison camp earlier, is sent to destroy the bridge, Nicholson tries to stop them. Only after two members of the commando unit (and Saito) have been killed does Nicholson realize his folly: "What have I done?" At that moment he appears to move toward the detonator, but he is fatally hit by shrapnel, stumbles, and falls (accidentally or on purpose?) on the plunger, detonating the bomb that destroys the bridge and the passing train.

Few would disagree about the technical artistry of the film: Its Oscar-winning cinematography (by Jack Hildyard) and direction seem beyond reproach. Arthur Knight notes that Lean's direction "gives the film an aura of high adventure by pacing it in the tempo of an action picture. Each incident, imaginatively staged and tersely edited, leads swiftly to the nerve-wracking finale."[4] Another critic writes: "David Lean has directed it so smartly and so sensitively for image and effect that its two hours and forty-one minutes seem no more than a swift, absorbing hour."[5] *Time* magazine even praises Lean's "dazzlingly musical sense and control of the many and involving rhythms of a vast composition."[6] Biographer Gerald Pratley aptly summarizes: "From the technical standpoint, David Lean's direction is absolutely superb, keeping every aspect of a complicated and profound human study in clear perspective. With this film, he became fully and in every sense an international artist."[7]

But what remains unclear is what unites the film's numerous thematic threads. Although many have championed it as a strong antiwar film, contending that it indicts warfare and the madness of its military leaders and their military codes, a close reading suggests a more complex perspective. This chapter focuses on the film's two key characters, Nicholson and Saito, and argues that a logic alternately informed by duty and pride shapes their actions and reactions for better and for worse and that neither Nicholson nor Saito is capable of effectively balancing and managing these competing impulses. Herein lies the downfall of Nicholson and Saito and perhaps the film's broader lesson about the nature of war and the demands of its participants.

Both Nicholson and Saito share numerous similarities, including their strong sense of duty and equally strong sense of pride. Out of duty to his men and the need to maintain his own integrity, Nicholson refuses Saito's order that Nicholson and his officers perform manual labor, believing that the acceptance of such an obvious violation of rules would only encourage Saito to commit further abuse on Nicholson's men. Yet, out of pride, Nicholson completes an enemy-aiding bridge — after asking his officers to do manual work and pressuring injured soldiers to help out — because he wants to demonstrate British superiority over the Japanese. Similarly, Saito's sense of duty is intricately linked to pride and his fear of losing honor. He dismisses the British as inferior to the Japanese, whose perceived superiority he continually derides. Saito's sense of duty coupled with his pride ensure the single-minded determination needed to convince the prisoners to heed his orders and complete the bridge. But pride also deters Saito from resolving his conflict with Nicholson sooner, which leads to a public and humiliating defeat and an undermining of Saito's credibility and authority.

A closer look at the words and actions of both characters reveals their destiny-determining mindsets.

Colonel Nicholson

As the film opens, the main character, the captured Nicholson, and his troops are making their way through the jungle to a Japanese prisoner of war camp. As the injured and hobbled soldiers enter the camp, they proudly march in formation while whistling "The Colonel Bogey March," a 1916 British military song of defiance. Once in the camp, the ragged troops continue whistling and marching in step under the watchful eye of Nicholson. Here we get the first glimpse of Nicholson's allegiance to appropriate military conduct.

Nicholson and his troops are greeted by Colonel Saito, commander of the camp, who announces that they have been selected to build a bridge across the River Kwai and that both soldiers and officers (all of whom Saito says are now "prisoners," not soldiers) will work together to complete the bridge. When Nicholson reminds Saito that the use of "officers for manual work is expressly forbidden by the Geneva Convention," a slightly smiling Saito dismisses Nicholson's authority. Nicholson, however, misreads Saito's response and believes the issue has been resolved favorably.

Later that day, Nicholson meets with his officers and Shears to discuss strategies for surviving in the camp. The scene outlines the key component of Nicholson's worldview: belief in the rule of law and the duty to obey. He tells his commanders that there will be no escape committee because any escape attempt would be futile and quite possibly an infraction of military law inasmuch as Nicholson was ordered to surrender in Singapore by command headquarters. An incredulous Shears responds, "You intend to uphold the letter of the law, no matter what the costs?"

NICHOLSON: Without law, Commander, there is no civilization.
SHEARS: That's just my point: Here, there is no civilization.
NICHOLSON: Then we have the opportunity to introduce it.

Nicholson's duty to uphold the law is consistent with his duty to his troops. The scene ends with him declaring that soldiers who believe they are commanded by their officers, not their captors, will feel they are still soldiers, not prisoners. These soldiers, one infers from Nicholson's argument, stand a better chance of survival because they will stay mentally and emotionally fit; too, they will be more capable of escaping (if escape were sanctioned by their commanding officer) and, upon their escape or release, better positioned to immediately resume their roles as wartime soldiers. Nicholson, however, never extends his argument this pragmatically. Although he is aware that nearly all previous prisoners in Saito's camp have died from disease or abuse, and although he will later note how his men have been treated better since he resumed command, he remains more concerned with broader lessons. Thus, near the film's close, when the bridge has been completed and Nicholson addresses his men for the last time, he speaks of self-worth and personal victory: "You have survived with honor. That and more. Here in the wilderness you have turned defeat into victory."

Earlier in the film, when he realizes that Saito does indeed expect all officers to work, Nicholson declares, "Since you refuse to abide by the laws of the civilized world, we must consider ourselves absolved from our duty to obey you." The standoff between Nicholson and Saito has begun.

Saito first punishes Nicholson and his men by having them stand all day in the blazing sun, after which the officers are removed to a small punishment hut. Nicholson is beaten (off camera) and dragged into the "oven," a metal-roofed sweat-box. As Nicholson's loyal troops watch him personify defiance and free will, they break into the song "For He's a Jolly Good Fellow." Nicholson has answered his captors, and, as his troops know, he has answered for them as well.

Saito escalates his battle with Nicholson when, a few days later, he sends Major Clipton, the camp doctor, to see Nicholson and tell him that the camp hospital will be closed and the sick men sent to work in place of Nicholson and his officers if they continue their defiance. Clipton pleads with Nicholson, "Wouldn't the officers be better off working than suffocating in that hole?" Nicholson replies that it is a matter of principle, but Clipton scoffs at the idea: "Sir, we're lost in the jungle a thousand miles from anywhere. We're under the heel of a man who will stop at nothing to get his way. Principle? No one will ever know or care what happens to us."

For Nicholson, the principle he is defending is inextricably linked to how his troops will be treated. "If we give in now," he says, "there will be no end to it." The implication is that the camp's conditions will worsen if he submits to Saito; hence, Saito must be defied, however great the risk to Nicholson and his officers. Nicholson's tenacity, then, stems not from blind acceptance of a principle but from the understanding of its practicality and a rational rejection of the consequences of submission. When Major Clipton tells him that prisoners were killed trying to escape, Nicholson bemoans their attempt as an irrational act. He believes instead that his troops can best survive the camp if they remain a cohesive, disciplined unit, which of course can occur only if Nicholson and his officers are allowed to command that unit. Lest his soldiers perish as so many before them had in Saito's prison camp, Nicholson must prevail over Saito.

When Saito offers to exempt Nicholson but not his officers from manual work, Nicholson refuses. Saito then offers to exempt all officers holding the rank of major and above, but Nicholson again refuses and is sent back to confinement. When Saito retrieves a withered Nicholson from the "oven" for the last time, his admiring troops salute him as he less than surefootedly makes his way to Saito. Upon hearing that Saito will no longer require officers to do manual work, Nicholson buttons his shirt, straightens up, and leaves Saito's quarters unattended. His troops rush to his side, knowing that Nicholson, armed only with principle and pride, has challenged the enemy and won.

Through his actions, Nicholson has raised the morale of his troops. Now able to command his troops, Nicholson can ensure they perceive themselves as soldiers, not slaves. Theirs is now a stronger, more self-determining position that better enables them to fulfill their duty as wartime soldiers. Unfortunately, Nicholson will never give them the chance.

Viewing the bridge site for the first time, Nicholson is appalled: "I tell you, gentlemen, we have a problem on our hands. Thanks to the Japanese, we now command a rabble. There's no order, no discipline. Our task is to rebuild the battalion, which isn't going to be easy, but, fortunately, we have the means at hand, the bridge." If Nicholson is true to his word, the bridge is but a means to achieving the noble duty of revitalizing his troops and commanding them against the enemy. But the very pride that allowed Nicholson to endure and best Saito and which he hopes to reinstill in his troops now leads him to declare that it will be a "proper bridge" because, as he explains, he knows his men and they would not take pride in anything less. What's more, "We can teach the barbarians a lesson in Western methods and efficiency that will put them to shame. We'll show them what the British soldier is capable of doing." Nicholson's belief in British superiority — voiced earlier, but never fully articulated — assumes transcendence; it will subvert all Nicholson's subsequent actions and will seal his fate.

It is not the building of the bridge *per se* that mitigates against Nicholson's upholding of his *ultimate* duty to the war effort. Rather, it his decision to build a "proper bridge" that, while meeting his *immediate* duty to his troops, would aid the enemy by providing an important link in the Japanese railway used for communications transport. When Clipton raises that possibility and speaks of the bridge as a potentially treasonous act, an astonished Nicholson reminds Clipton that prisoners of war don't have the right to refuse work and points to the improved welfare of his troops to further justify his decision.

Even in his final address to his troops, Nicholson alludes only to how the Japanese will employ the bridge to benefit prisoners of war: "You'll be glad to know that the completion of this link in the railway will enable us to transport the sick and disabled to the new camp by train." Perhaps Nicholson believes that British superiority will ensure Allied victory, thereby rendering moot the bridge's military significance, but what of the completed railway's potential to prolong the war and loss of life?

If the process of constructing the bridge functions to rebuild order and discipline within Nicholson's troops, surely a bridge building strategy that served only that end would be in order. Why build a proper bridge? Interestingly, Major Reeves, chosen by Nicholson to engineer the bridge-building, provides the perfect solution when he concludes that any bridge built on the current site "would collapse under the first train to cross it." Nicholson could set about building a perfect-looking, seemingly sound bridge that remained structurally defective. Such a plan would serve the twin goals of rebuilding his unit (immediate duty) and contributing to the larger war effort (ultimate duty). Nicholson's troops had already demonstrated the predisposition for such a mission, having repeatedly sabotaged the bridge's construction when it was under Japanese supervision during the Nicholson-Saito impasse.

As the film progresses, Nicholson becomes less concerned about the welfare of his troops — despite his proclamations and rationalizations to the contrary — and more preoccupied with demonstrating British superiority by creating a bridge that will stand as a legacy to his troops and his command. When Reeves tells him that the forest contains trees similar to the elms used in the piles of the London Bridge and that those piles lasted 600 years, Nicholson delights in the possibility: "Six hundred years. That would be quite something."

Whereas Nicholson once focused on the troop-healing process of bridge building, he now concentrates on finishing the product. Quickly, he increases the previous (Japanese-established) workload of his troops. Later, when it appears that the bridge will not be completed on time, Nicholson asks his officers to volunteer for manual labor. Still needing more help, he visits the camp hospital and asks Clipton to identify malingerers who should be working on the bridge. When Clipton asks why Nicholson does not simply ask Saito to lend some of his troops, Nicholson replies that he "wouldn't dream of it. This is our show. We must make the most of our own resources." He proceeds to cajole the sick, suggesting that "fresh air and light duties" might do them good. Heeding their colonel's call for help, nine limping soldiers come forward.

What Saito wanted — officers working alongside their troops — and what Saito threatened — injured soldiers working on the bridge — have both been effected by Nicholson. All that Nicholson once rejected out of duty and pride now comes about because of his pride and the rationalization (that Nicholson surely would make) that the process — i.e., Nicholson, not Saito, making these decisions — conforms to military code.

When the bridge is completed, Nicholson helps post a marker indicating that it was designed and constructed by soldiers of the British army under the command of Colonel Nicholson. This same pride will lead Nicholson to want to save the bridge from the commandos' attack. Only when he comes face to face with the dying Shears, who has been hit by enemy fire in his attempt to kill Nicholson and stop him from preventing the bridge's detonation, does Nicholson realize what he has done. He has mandated a feat of such malign magnitude that it has inspired the otherwise indifferent, antimilitaristic Shears to heroic action.

Colonel Saito

Saito's sense of duty and honor — and his corollary contempt for Nicholson — surfaces when he explains to Nicholson and his troops that officers and soldiers will work together because it "is only just, for it is they who betrayed you by surrender. Your shame is their dishonor. It is they who told you, 'Better to live like a coolie than die like a hero.' It is they who brought you here, not I." For Saito, duty and honor share causal connection: Performing one's duty upholds one's honor.

Saito does not believe that Nicholson has upheld his duty. Thus, when Nicholson reminds Saito that the Geneva Convention forbids officers to perform manual labor, Saito angrily denounces Nicholson's code (the

Geneva Convention) as one devoid of duty and honor. "You speak to me
of code? What code? The coward's code! What do you know of the soldier's code, of Bushido? Nothing. You are unworthy of command." Saito
believes soldiers are duty bound to resist surrender and act honorably.

When Nicholson still refuses to do manual work and Saito appears ready
to shoot him and his officers, Saito's commitment to his code is challenged
by Clipton, who rushes to Saito to ask, "Is this your soldier's code, murdering unarmed men?" Saito accedes to Clipton, demonstrating a rationality,
constraint, and openness to argument that Nicholson will never exhibit.

Nicholson and Saito subsequently engage in a protracted battle of
wills that endures for two reasons: (1) Saito cannot kill Nicholson and his
officers because he knows that to fulfill his duty to the Imperial Majesty
he needs the cooperation and leadership of Nicholson, whose troops are
sabotaging the bridge building and delaying its completion; (2) Saito cannot acquiesce to Nicholson because it would mean that Nicholson's code
of military behavior has virtue. Moreover, Saito is too proud, too superior to Nicholson to allow him to claim victory.

After nearly shooting Nicholson and then beating and confining him,
Saito turns to one final threat: shutting down the hospital if Nicholson continues to resist. Nicholson does just that, but Saito never fulfills his threat,
possibly realizing that it would be on the same plane as killing unarmed
prisoners— or maybe believing, finally, that Nicholson cannot be tortured
or intimidated successfully.

Only after Saito personally takes command of the bridge's construction and realizes that he still cannot stop the sabotaging efforts of Nicholson's troops does he try to compromise with Nicholson. Saito's sense of
duty now overtakes his pride and allows him to seek Nicholson's support.
"I must carry out my orders," he says, before offering a compromise to
Nicholson, who adamantly rejects anything less than Saito's full conces-
sion. Saito reminds Nicholson that officers all along the railway construction are doing manual work, but Nicholson replies that he has no control
over other officers' decisions, no matter how appalling.

Saito continues to plead his case to an audience whose indifference
is born of disdain:

SAITO: Do you know what will happen to me if the bridge is not com-
pleted on time?
NICHOLSON: I haven't the foggiest.
SAITO: I'll have to kill myself. What would you do if you were me?
NICHOLSON: I suppose, if I were you, I'd have to kill myself. Cheers.
[He raises his glass and drinks.]

When Nicholson subsequently goads Saito, questioning his ability to effectively command the bridge building, the proud Saito angrily surfaces: "I hate the British. You are defeated, but you have no shame. You are stubborn but have no pride. You endure but have no courage." As the scene ends, Nicholson is escorted back to the "oven," while a silent Saito knows the fulfillment of his duty appears more doubtful.

Devoid of options, Saito resummons Nicholson to his office and announces that he (Saito) has declared a general amnesty in honor of the anniversary of Japan's victory over Russia in 1905; all officers can return to their troops and will be exempt from manual labor. Nicholson emerges to a hero's welcome; a defeated and humiliated Saito has so suppressed his pride in attempting to meet his duty that he has sacrificed his honor. As the scene ends, he lies crying on his bed.

Once Nicholson takes command of the bridge building, Saito fades into the background — sometimes even literally in the artistry of Lean's direction. His character is barely present. From his speech to his gait, a diminutive and humbled Seito can only hope that Nicholson's troops will complete the bridge on time. But when they do, there will be no celebration for Saito. The pride he sacrificed to ensure the bridge's completion and the fulfillment of his duty is, paradoxically, too great to save his honor.

But what would have happened if Saito had kept his pride in check and accepted Nicholson's position sooner? Would an earlier-freed Nicholson have completed the bridge and as perfectly, or did Nicholson require a protracted sweat-box experience to motivate him to build a proper bridge and thereby prove the point he tenaciously defended (i.e., soldiers need to be commanded by their officers)?

Surely, this much seems true: Saito would not have faced the humiliation of losing to Nicholson had he not invested so much for so long only to have every threat and compromise ignored. Had the stalemate ended sooner, Saito would have lessened the appearance of capitulation. Instead, Saito's emasculation coupled with the empowerment of Nicholson places Saito in a most interesting position: In the eyes of his country, he kept his honor because he completed the bridge on time; yet, in his own eyes, honor was relinquished by his capitulation and his failure to personally direct the building of the bridge. This may account for the ambiguity of Saito's careful preparation, near the film's end, to take his own life. Has he made *the* final decision that he will soon exercise, or is he simply readying himself in case the bridge somehow fails? His stabbing death by the young Canadian commando, Joyce (Jeffrey Horne), at film's end denies us the answer. Similar to Nicholson's death, Saito's demise occurs before he is allowed the opportunity to redeem himself and achieve, finally, the balancing of duty and pride.

Duty, Pride, and the Madness of War

In exploring *The Bridge on the River Kwai*, this chapter argues that the two elements often central to the mindset of the effective wartime soldier — a sense of duty and a sense of pride — share a dynamic interplay in which they both complement and, potentially, compete with one another. They are complementary, given their obvious symbiotic relationship: Pride encourages fulfillment of duty; fulfillment of duty instills pride. A soldier concerned only with duty may lack the pride-instilled courage to confront abuse and atrocity — potentially engendering once again the now hollow refrain, "I was just following orders." On the other hand, when pride admits no constraint, duty may become subordinate to personal agenda — for which even a war hero, such as Douglas MacArthur, may be relieved of command.

The failure of Nicholson and Saito to effectively balance duty and pride leads to their downfall. *The Bridge on the River Kwai*, then, is not so much about the absurdity of military codes or renegade pride as it is about how each must temper and balance the other.

All of which is not to say that this highly complex film is lacking other messages. But it is perhaps worth challenging the popular view that *The Bridge on the River Kwai* is primarily an antiwar film.

From Marc Ferro, who referred to it as another in a long line of antimilitarist films, to Bosley Crowther, who predicted it would become a classic antiwar film, critics have viewed *The Bridge on the River Kwai* as a clear indictment of war and the military leaders who wage it.[8] This conclusion, no doubt, is fueled by the film's repetition of the idea that war incites madness. Nearly everyone in the film thinks the other is mad and says so. Nicholson calls Saito mad; Saito calls Nicholson mad; Shears thinks both Nicholson and Warden are mad; and Clipton wonders whether Nicholson and Saito are mad, or whether he himself is insane: "Are they both mad? Or am I going mad? Or is it the sun?"

By the film's climax, Clipton is sure. Surveying the carnage — the bodies of Nicholson, Saito, Shears, and Joyce amid the British-led destruction of a British-built bridge — Clipton exclaims, "Madness! Madness! Madness!"

To eschew the madness wrought by war is not necessarily to be antiwar in the sense of being categorically opposed to going to war. Indeed, acknowledging the obvious madness of war is no more ideologically telling than to say that "war is hell." Moreover, it appears that Lean is not as much interested in the madness of war as he is preoccupied with the concept of madness in general. "In several of Lean's films," Louis Castelli observes, "constant references are made to madness or insanity, either in relation to the protagonist or as description of a particular kind of behavior."[9] Lean's rather broad conceptualization of madness seems to soften the sharpness of its numerous references in *The Bridge on the River Kwai*. According to Castelli:

> Madness, for Lean, results when men or women dare to transcend their conventional roles. The protagonist seems to be labeled mad either by other characters or by himself in retrospect when he behaves in one of two manners. Either he attempts to do something that everyone in the community believes *cannot* be done or he does something that everyone in the community believes *should* not be done. Both of these conditions imply a questioning of a set of rules and regulations.[10]

Even the most antimilitaristic statement in the film, uttered by Shears, does not necessarily transform *The Bridge on the River Kwai* into an antiwar film: "You [Warden] make me sick with your heroics.... This is just a game, this war. You and Colonel Nicholson — you're just two of a kind: crazy with courage. For what? How to die like a gentleman, how to die by the rules? The only important thing is how to live like a human being!"

This indictment of military mentality is not antiwar in the pacifist sense of categorical opposition. More specifically, to truly qualify as an antiwar film, *The Bridge on the River Kwai* would need to:

1. argue compellingly that the outcome of the particular war — in this case, World War II — did not benefit society (as conceptualized in the broadest context) by either improving present and future conditions or avoiding a worsening of present and future conditions; or

2. argue compellingly how the war could have been avoided peacefully *and* with the same or better societal outcome achieved by war

The Bridge on the River Kwai — as well as many other so-called antiwar films — never posits, let alone develops, a viable alternative that would obviate the perceived "need" for war. As such, *The Bridge on the River Kwai* may be present numerous barbed references to the madness, oddity, and irony of war, but it does not present any opposing framework to war. Instead, it remains primarily a study in military character and sensibility and how noble but flawed leaders behave at their best and at their worst in the heat of conflict.

NOTES

1. Bosley Crowther, "Powerful Drama: *Bridge on River Kwai* Spans Action and Theme," *New York Times* (December 22, 1957): II-3.

2. *The Bridge on the River Kwai* (Columbia Pictures, 1957).

3. Boulle's novel, *Le Pont de la Rivière Kwai*, was first published in French in 1952. It was translated into English by Xan Fielding and published in 1954 as *The Bridge over the River Kwai*. Although Boulle was listed as the screenwriter in the film's credits, he spoke little English and, by all accounts, never worked on the screenplay. Two other writers politically blacklisted at the time, Michael Wilson and Carl Foreman, worked on the script and eventually were acknowledged and both posthumously awarded Oscars in 1985. Lean, however, has said that he and Wilson wrote most of the script and that Foreman contributed little. See Stephen Silverman, *David Lean* (New York: Harry N. Abrams, 1989), 118–119.

4. Arthur Knight, "War of Nerves," *Saturday Review* (December 1957): 23.

5. Bosley Crowther, "Screen: *The Bridge on the River Kwai* Opens," *New York Times* (December 19, 1957): 39.

6. "New Picture," *Time* (December 23, 1957): 70–73.

7. Gerald Pratley, *The Cinema of David Lean* (Cranbury, N.J.: A. S. Barnes, 1974), 141.

8. See Crowther, II-3, and Marc Ferro, *Cinema and History*, Naomi Green, trans. (Detroit: Wayne State University Press, 1988), 118.

9. Louis Castelli, "Film Epic: A Generic Examination and an Application of Definitions to the Work of David Lean" (Evanston, Ill.: Northwestern University, unpublished dissertation, 1977), 182.

10. *Ibid.*, 183.

2

John Wayne: American Icon, Patriotic Zealot and Cold War Ideologue

BONNIE S. JEFFERSON

Just weeks after the terrorist attacks on the World Trade Center, my brother-in-law sent me a political cartoon via email. It shows John Wayne in heaven. He is on his horse with his rifle at his side, trying to ride out of heaven. Three archangels are trying to stop him. The angel on the phone says to God, "Hello, Boss.... We can't stop him.... He's headin' for Afghanistan!!"

The myth of John Wayne lives on long after his death. Gary Wills, in *John Wayne's America*, noted Wayne's charisma in 1995 — more than fifteen years after his death. When people were polled on their favorite film celebrities, John Wayne bested contemporary favorites like Clint Eastwood, Mel Gibson, Denzel Washington and Kevin Costner.[1]

In short, although John Wayne died in 1979, he is still recognized as the embodiment of American patriotism, a hero to be looked to in times of national crisis. Wills speaks of the values Wayne represents:

> There is no better demonstration of the power of movies than Wayne's impact on American life. He was not like other actors, who simply hold political views.... Wayne did not just have political opinions. He embodied a politics: or his screen image did. It was a politics of large meaning, not of little policies—a politics of gender (masculine), ideology (patriotism), character (self-reliance, and responsibility).[2]

John Wayne was a larger-than-life figure. According to Mark Rahner,

> Wayne had the courage of his convictions, which were firmly red, white and blue, and anti-communist. He emerged from the public consciousness in a big way at the end of World War II as a symbol of American fighting forces. Then he also became the symbol of a cowboy. Are there two bigger heroes in America than soldiers or cowboys?[3]

Thus, John Wayne became the living symbol of American patriotism, despite the fact that his personal politics were distinctly narrow and conservative. He hated anything that threatened or belittled the institutions of American government. In 1948, for example, he was offered the lead role in *All the King's Men,* a film loosely based on the life of Huey Long. According to Roberts and Olsen in their biography, *John Wayne, American,* Wayne was infuriated by the offer. He did not want to star in a film that "[s]mears the machinery of government ... [t]hat throws acid on the American way of Life."[4] He had an equally negative reaction to *High Noon,* the 1952 Gary Cooper film. Wayne hated the film. "It's the most un-American thing I've ever seen in my whole life. The last thing in the picture is ole Coop putting the United States Marshall's badge under his foot and stepping on it."[5]

John Wayne also believed that it was his responsibility to use his power and influence to persuade the American public to adopt his perspective. As Ronald Davis states in his biography, *Duke: The Life and Times of John Wayne,* "Wayne always stated his position forcefully, disregarding the contradictions of intellectuals and Hollywood liberals. More than other film stars of his era he succeeded in integrating his politics and his profession."[6] Not surprisingly with these fundamental conservative beliefs, John Wayne, America's quintessential cowboy, would become involved in the major political battle of the late forties and early fifties, the golden era of American anticommunism.

This chapter explores the influence of the John Wayne films in the larger context of the rhetoric of the Cold War. Although the patriotic hero was central in all John Wayne movies, three examples communicate his ideological position most clearly — *Big Jim McLean* (1952), *The Alamo* (1960), and *The Green Berets* (1968). Wayne not only starred in these films but also directed two of them[7] and produced all three, involving himself heavily in the political content included. Through these examples, one can observe the consistency with which John Wayne's personal view of communism matched the prevailing notions of the Soviet Union that had emerged in the United States during the first half of the twentieth century.

Cold War Ideology

America's suspicions of communism as an evil force began as early as 1917 and the Russian Revolution. And although the United States and the Soviet Union were allied against the Germans for a brief time during World War II, traditional anticommunist feelings reappeared at the war's end. Soviets were no longer viewed as our wartime allies but as devils with world domination on their minds. Traditional anticommunist messages reemerged, declaring the existence of only one form of communism (the Soviet form), with all international communist activities emanating from Moscow. The ultimate goal of these "evil emperors" was world domination. Moreover, the Soviets were unscrupulous enemies, resorting to any means possible to achieve their goals. Thus, communists were deceitful liars who could trick unsuspecting people into converting to their cause. And once their goals were achieved, a barbaric society would arise, where family, church, and personal freedoms would cease to exist.

The belief that communism was monolithic and expansionistic led to the assumption that the United States and its democratic institutions were quite obviously the communists' ultimate target and that this dream of world domination could be achieved only through espionage. Based on this logic, it was also reasonable to assume that communists had already infiltrated U.S. institutions to meet their goals.

One of the institutions considered to be the most vulnerable (in this scenario) was the American film industry, which could serve ideally as a means for Soviet propaganda dissemination. During the 1930s, veiled insinuations of communist tendencies had already plagued some writers and directors, but by the late 1940s, the fear of communist infiltration became open and hysterical, especially when the House Un-American Activities Committee (HUAC) announced its intention to investigate the Hollywood film community.

The HUAC began to ask industry leaders to name names, people whom they could ask, "Are you now or have you ever been a member of the Communist Party?" Many of the powerful figures in the industry began to declare sides.[8] The liberals counted Douglas Fairbanks, Jr., Humphry Bogart, Melvyn Douglas, Henry Fonda, Lucille Ball and Joan Bennett among their numbers; the conservatives included Robert Montgomery, Ginger Rogers, George Murphy (who later served as senator from California), Adolph Menjou, Hedda Hopper, Gary Cooper, Ward Bond, Walt Disney and John Wayne. Before long, however, the reactionaries far outnumbered the rebels.

Accordingly, in 1944, some of Hollywood's most outspoken and influential conservatives formed the Motion Picture Alliance for the Preservation of American Ideals. They proposed to fight the "un–American ideology," pledging to "fight, with every means of our organized command, any effort of any group or individual, to divert the loyalty of the screen from free America that gave it birth."[9] Film director Sam Wood was elected as the organization's first president.[10]

Back in Washington, the HUAC committee began hearings on October 20, 1947. The first "friendly" witnesses included Sam Wood, Adolph Menjou, Walt Disney, Gary Cooper, Robert Montgomery, Robert Taylor, Ronald Reagan and George Murphy. They all discussed their perception of the foothold communism had in Hollywood. They also thanked HUAC for beginning the investigation and named names.

After the "friendly" witnesses gave testimony, those suspected of communist leanings were called. Many of these people chose to plead the Fifth Amendment rather than testify. Among them were the infamous "Hollywood Ten," who were later indicted.[11] The HUAC hearings also signaled the era of the Hollywood "blacklist," where those suspected (with or without reason) of being communist sympathizers were denied jobs, forced to change careers, leave the country or adopt pseudonyms.

During the HUAC investigations, John Wayne decided to become more active in the Motion Picture Alliance. Both he and Ward Bond became members of the executive board in 1948, and Wayne was elected president of the alliance in March 1949. Also during this same time, Wayne ended his working relationship with Republic Pictures and began his own production company with Bob Fellows— The Wayne-Fellows Production Company.[12] It was a profitable decision — at least for a short while — because of Hollywood's desire to please Washington officials.

As the HUAC hearings progressed, movie studio executives continued to grow more and more sensitive to charges that communist infiltration was rampant in the film industry. Beginning in the late forties and continuing through the McCarthy era, a series of films was produced to teach the American public about the evils of communism, thus creating a genre of Cold War films. (In fact, these films were actually a series of thinly veiled anticommunist propaganda films.) MGM was the largest major studio involved in this endeavor, but other independent producers (like the new Wayne-Fellows Production Company) saw this as an important priority as well. Adolph Menjou predicted that these films would be major hits, although most of them were financial disasters. Nevertheless, during this era many Hollywood insiders needed to be able to say that they had worked on one of these films. According to Nora Sayre, in *Running Time: Films of the Cold War*,

[F]or certain film makers, being asked to work on an anti-communist picture was like a loyalty test; if someone who was thought to be a communist refused to participate in the project it was assumed that he must be a Party member. So, for some writers, directors, and actors, taking part in a film such as *I Married a Communist*, was rather like receiving clearance — It meant that they were politically clean.[13]

The first anticommunist films appeared in 1948 with the release of *The Iron Curtain*, followed by *The Red Menace*. *I Was a Communist for the FBI* and *The Red Danube* were released in 1949. During the election year of 1952, twelve films with distinctly anticommunist messages were released, including *Big Jim McLain* with John Wayne.

John Wayne: American Patriot

John Wayne's personal anticommunist beliefs became part of this Hollywood trend in 1952. Wayne came to believe that it was his patriotic duty to use his considerable influence to make films to teach Americans about the responsibilities of patriotism and the evils of communism. To this end, he planned to use his new Wayne-Fellows Production Company to create stories to deliver these messages.

The first "message" film Wayne wanted to make was the Alamo story. As author Ronald Davis notes:

> For Duke, the battle of the Alamo was the great American story, a dramatic reminder that liberty had not been won cheaply. He wanted to recreate on film a moment from the past that would illustrate for successive generations the values on which the United States had been founded.... In Duke's mind, the time was ripe for a saga of courage and devotion to the country's founding principles. From the outset his intent was to reawaken American patriotism.[14]

While funding and production problems would delay his production of *The Alamo* until the late 1950s, Wayne did not give up on the idea of producing a film with a message. He became interested in creating movies that would not only include the staunch patriotic zeal he wanted in *The Alamo* but also teach a strong anticommunist position. A lifelong Republican, Wayne had supported Senator Howard Taft of Ohio for the 1952 presidential nomination. However, he was frustrated that Taft had done poorly at the convention, ultimately losing to Eisenhower. After Taft lost the nomination, Wayne became even more committed to producing a film with these strong messages because, as Roberts and Olson reason,

If Taft could not deliver an effective message, he thought he could. *Big Jim McLain* was the type of film Duke often claimed he hated — an open, frank, preachy propaganda film. It called on all "real Americans" to be vigilant against communism.[15]

Big Jim McLain, released in 1952, dealt directly with the Un-American Activities Committee investigations and with Wayne's growing frustration that too many communists were "getting off" by pleading the Fifth Amendment. He believed it was unfair for communists who were trying to subvert the American way of life to wrap themselves in the mantle of the U.S. Constitution.

After the completion of *Big Jim,* Wayne continued to work on the *Alamo* project. He was finally able to get enough funding to begin production in 1958, and although he had been frustrated by the delays, he still firmly believed the film had an important message to relay to the Cold War world. *The Alamo* opened in 1960, and while the story is set in the late nineteenth century (thus excluding the introduction of any communist characters), Wayne's definition of patriotism is the central theme of this film.

In the mid-1960s, Wayne began plans for his third film with the same central message of patriotism and national fervor — *The Green Berets.* Deeply disturbed by U.S. treatment of Vietnam veterans, as well as by the growing antiwar sentiment, Wayne vowed to make a pro-Vietnam film. Again he planned to produce, direct and star in the film. After Wayne consulted with President Lyndon Johnson and the Pentagon, *The Green Berets* was finally made and released in 1968.

While all three films were popular with audiences (especially *The Green Berets*) they were panned overwhelmingly by the critics. One reviewer asked, "How many loyal Americans may actually have converted to communism out of embarrassment that their county could produce such horrible films as *Big Jim McLain*?"[16] Renata Adler wrote this scathing review of *The Green Berets* in *The New York Times:*

> *The Green Berets* is a film so unspeakable, so stupid, so rotten and false in every detail that it passes through being fun, through being funny, through being camp, through everything and becomes an invitation to grieve, not for our soldiers or for Vietnam ... but for what has happened to the fantasy-making apparatus in this country.... It is vile and insane. On top of that it's dull.[17]

Wayne was furious that all three of his films had been denounced by the New York critics but dismissed their criticism because he believed the critics to be communist sympathizers.

Cold War Rhetoric

The rhetorical forms presented in the three John Wayne films were simplistic and consistent with the rhetorical forms of American anticommunism that had already been established. The American anticommunist ideology was based on two central belief systems: the "American" (a patriotic hero) and the "Un-American" (communist). Rhetorically, the Un-American was portrayed as a type of devil. In religious terms, the Christian connotation of the devil was a powerful one, believed to be the supreme evil, an enemy of God with powers to inflict bodily harm to and spiritual corruption in humans. By equating communism with the religious connotations of the devil, the anticommunist ideology was linked to a rhetorically powerful image. As scholar Harold J. Berman states, "There is a strong strain of Puritanism which tends to turn opponents into enemies, enemies into devils and devils into ugly monsters."[18]

The rhetorical structure of the anticommunist message helped to strengthen the notion of communism as evil. Richard Weaver, in *The Ethics of Rhetoric*, labeled symbols with negative connotations as "devil terms," or terms which could be depended upon to produce the desired hate response:

> A singular truth about these terms is that ... they defy any real analysis. That is to say, one cannot explain how they generate their peculiar force of repudiation. One only recognized them as publicly agreed-upon devil terms.... However one might like to reject such usage as mere ignorance, to do so would only evade a very important problem.[19]

One strength of the American anticommunist message was that all Soviet behavior could be interpreted from within the confines of the ideology and that all Soviet behavior should be interpreted as evil. As Michael Parenti states in *The Anti-Communist Impulse:*

> Any action and its opposite are treated by the anti-communist as evidence of the same inexorable demonic intent. If the communist[s] act belligerently, this demonstrates their wickedness and if they act moderately, even threatening to become downright friendly this, in turn, proves their duplicity, mendacity, and again, their wickedness.[20]

Parenti refers to the anticommunist belief system as an ideology so deeply rooted that it needn't carry with it a manifesto:

> If America has an ideology, or a national purpose, it is anti-communism.... Some ideologies have no manifesto or bible containing an explicit statement of belief. Some are so deeply rooted in the polity, so widely and imperceptibly diffused in a nation's political culture as to be rarely exposed to rational confrontation.[21]

American anticommunism was clearly defined within the prevailing belief system of good and evil. That communists were the progeny of evil and that they were as deceitful as the devil were commonly held beliefs. This message was presented continually to the American public through many media outlets, such as the popular press, newspapers, and political cartoons. Film, however, was the ultimate medium used to teach U.S. citizens the American anticommunist ideology, and given John Wayne's popularity and political prominence, he was the perfect person to teach this lesson.

The presentation of the ideological perspective of patriotism in Wayne's films is very powerful. He frequently uses traditional propaganda techniques to present his point of view; his characters often present long preachy speeches, thinly masked as dialogue and frequently accompanied by soaring patriotic music; and he often uses the double image technique so commonly found in many propaganda films.

According to Wayne, a patriotic American was someone who was willing to fight and die for his country (an ambiguous personal belief, in light of the fact that Wayne avoided military service during World War II, a time when many of his Hollywood colleagues served in the military). He also hated limited wars and believed that at times it was all right to suspend certain personal freedoms for the greater good of defeating the enemy. This is evidenced by his staunch support of Joseph McCarthy. These beliefs are well documented in Wayne's films

His films also included the other major features of the American anticommunist ideology during the Cold War. These themes were that:

1. communism was monolithic
2. communism sought world domination
3. communists were barbaric
4. communists sought to destroy the family, church and all personal freedoms
5. communism was a direct threat to the United States and its democratic institutions and would target these institutions from the inside; carefully placed spies would destroy important institutions of freedom before we could realize what had happened

Big Jim McLain

In *Big Jim McLain*, we learn that there are three types of patriotic people, all of whom have made great sacrifices for their country: first, those who have given their lives for their country in war; second, the members of the HUAC committee; and third, the brave investigators—men like Big Jim (John Wayne) and Mal (James Arness). Wayne's definition of patriotism begins in the initial roll of the credits, which are superimposed over the silhouette of a large tree. The night is dark; there is a driving rain, interspersed with lightening and thunder as well as a series of patriotic songs. (The songs include "Yankee Doodle" and "Columbia, the Gem of the Ocean," both accompanied by fife and drum.) The credits end with a bright flash of lightening and the words of Daniel Webster asking, "How stands the Union, neighbor?"

The opening credits are followed by a dissolve to the street in front of the HUAC hearing building, with the image of the capitol dome in the background. The camera pans into the HUAC hearing room, where a narrator explains that anyone who continues to be a member of the communist party after 1945 is guilty of high treason.[22] Thus, at the very beginning, we (as the audience) are set up to sympathize with the HUAC committee members, who have obviously made great sacrifices for their country. The camera then focuses on one member of the committee who asks the witness if he is now or has ever been a member of the communist party." Immediately afterward, the director cuts to a close-up of Big Jim McLain's (John Wayne's) face. We now know he is the hero of the story.

Over patriotic music, viewers begin to hear Big Jim's thoughts (John Wayne's biases)—he tells us that any intelligent person must know the witnesses on the stand to be "agents of the Kremlin." He also tells us that his buddy Mal "hates these people—they shot at him in Korea." In this brief monologue, all three types of patriotic Americans are thus established: Mal (the man who has fought for his country), the HUAC committee members (who are sacrificing time and energy for the greater good), and Big Jim (the loyal investigator).

The next definition of patriotism comes when Big Jim and Mal travel to Hawaii to root out a nest of spies. Before starting their investigation, Big Jim and Mal decide to take a boat to the *Arizona* Memorial to pay respects to Mal's dead brother. Here, the message of sacrifice is once again very clearly presented—this time, visually, as well as through Big Jim's narration. We see Mal and Big Jim arrive on the deck of the *Arizona*. Four young U.S. Navy men wearing white uniforms meet them. The wind is strong and their uniforms are billowing. A soldier with a bugle plays taps, as the flag is raised on the deck of the *Arizona*. "Anchors Away" plays in the background as the camera cuts to the plaque honoring the men who died there. John Wayne remarks:

> She is an everlasting memorial to the gallant men who died at their bat-
> tle stations, and below these decks she still carries a full compliment of
> crew: 207 officers, 1590 blue jackets and marines. They have been there
> since Sunday, Sunday 1941.[23]

The camera then pulls back to a long shot of the billowing American flag,
with a battleship on rolling seas superimposed on the flag. This scene is
heavily dependent upon the visual symbols of patriotism familiar to every
American, defining the concept of sacrifice for country.

Another dramatic scene, one that defines patriotic sacrifice, is a monologue that Big Jim gives in the morgue after Mal has been killed by one of
the spies. Big Jim stands alone in the room with Mal's body. We learn there
that communism is a monolithic threat, as Big Jim lists the varied types—
and origins— of Soviet weapons used to injure Mal during the Korean War
and notes that Mal's obituary will not tell the entire story:

> Does this tell us about a young lawyer who went into the Marine Corps,
> who lost eight feet of intestines in Korea, got shot by a grenade made in
> Czechoslovakia out of scrap and machines that had been shipped from
> the States to somewhere in Western Europe and then transshipped to
> behind the Iron Curtain? Does this give you a picture of a guy who let
> his own teeth go because his own kid needed bands on hers? OK. Mal-
> colm Baxter, 34, married, 2 children, ex-Marine. There's your obitu-
> ary.[24]

While the patriotic images developed by Wayne were powerful, other film
elements served to reconfirm negative perceptions of communism and,
more specifically, stereotypes of the Soviet spy. Communist characters have
a special "look," according to critic Nora Sayre:

> Most are apt to be exceptionally haggard or disgracefully pudgy. Occa-
> sionally, they're effeminate.... Also, more communists walk on a forward
> slant, revealing their dedication to the cause. Now and then, they're ele-
> gantly dressed equipped with canes and stickpins. But most are scruffy....
> Communists [also] never keep their promises and they're likely to go
> berserk when they're arrested. But they devote so much time to spying
> on each other that it's hard to see how they could have any free time for
> serious espionage.[25]

In *Big Jim McLain*, we see both types of communists. The leader, Sturak,
is very elegantly dressed, the cane and stickpin type. But he is a Moscovite
communist. The Hawaiian operatives, on the other hand, are pudgy and
have a slothful appearance. In addition, many of John Wayne's "communists" have evil-looking mustaches.

We first encounter the communists in *Big Jim* when Sturak arrives at
Dr. Gelster's house. He is rude and elitist and treats Dr. Gelster as a stupid underling. After they exchange a few conversational pleasantries, we

learn that (as suspected) communist infiltration goes much deeper than most Americans could ever realize. At one point, Gelster tells us that all the high-level party members are underground and that the communists that the Americans can find are only low-level ones.[26]

This assertion is repeated several times and in several different ways, especially from former communists who had "seen the light" and were now willing to testify about what life was like in the Soviet system. One prominent example is the "convert testimony" given by a spy named Namaka and his wife (who had also been a spy). Mrs. Namaka, now working in a leper colony to atone for her sinful past, imparts this carefully packaged propaganda speech to remind the audience that communists seek world domination: "After being a hard-working and dedicated communist for almost eleven years I came to my senses and recognized communism for what it is. It's a vast conspiracy to enslave the common man."[27]

In a later scene we learn that communists seek to destroy the traditional family structure as well as religious freedoms. This is revealed when Big Jim and Mal arrive at the door of an elderly couple, Mr. and Mrs. Lexiter, who are about to turn over their communist son. The son had won a trip to Russia as a prize in high school. But he liked it so much he stayed an extra year to study there. The Lexiters later learn their son is a communist. Mr. Lexiter tells Big Jim:

> Then I heard from the office where he was working that he was giving out information on the sailing and docking of ships. He was a communist. I showed him the door. I know [Mr. Lexiter is from Poland] how hard it is to reason with those heartless men, men that have turned their backs on God.[28]

The final dramatic confrontation pits patriotism against communism as Big Jim breaks into a HUAC-wiretapped communist meeting to challenge Dr. Gelster. Big Jim declares, "I wanted to hit you one punch for Mal, but I can't — you're too small. That's the difference between you people and us, I guess. We don't hit the little guy."[29]

The movie ends back in Washington, after this group of commie sympathizers (once again) gets away from HUAC scrutiny by "pleading the fifth." Big Jim laments, "We build a case and prove to any intelligent person that these people are communists and they walk out free. Sometimes I wonder why I stay."[30] The director then cuts away to a scene of young navy enlistees boarding a battleship that is getting ready to sail. As the music swells in the background, Big Jim points to the loyal men on deck and says, "Mr. Webster, there stands our Union." The film fades to closing credits, thanking the members of HUAC for their cooperation in the making of *Big Jim*. Thus ends Wayne's first major statement about American patriotism. Wayne would spend six more years preparing for the making of *The Alamo*, the story he believed to be the most important example of patriotic sacrifice in American history.

The Alamo

Since *The Alamo* is set in pre-twentieth-century America, there are no communist characters in the script. This, however, did not deter John Wayne from linking *The Alamo* to Cold War patriotism.[31] Wayne once told Louella Parsons,

> [T]he eyes of the world are on us. We must sell America to countries threatened with communist domination. Our picture is also important to Americans, who should appreciate the struggle our ancestors made for the precious freedom we enjoy.[32]

The Alamo is the traditional retelling of the siege of the Alamo during the war for Texan independence. Wayne dedicates the film to the 183 men who chose to stay behind at the Alamo, thus making the ultimate sacrifice for their country. John Wayne directs the film and casts himself as one of the lead characters, Davey Crockett.

The first half of the film is spent pulling the coalition of men together who will end up facing death at the Alamo. In the scene that is best known as the "Republic scene" we see that love of country is supreme and that a true patriot is often a simple man, not arrogant, one who does his duty without fanfare. (Incidentally, this is a common patriotic theme found in most of Wayne's films. He often chose to thumb his nose at privileged eastern liberals.) In this scene, Colonel Travis (Laurence Harvey) meets Davey Crockett for the first time. Crockett is in Texas with his Tennesseans to fight for Texan independence (although Travis does not know this yet). Travis wants to talk to Crockett about committing his men to the battle for Texas. Crockett, a wise but simple man, responds elegantly:

> Were you going to tell my Tennesseans that a good many men ... sound men ... all had a thought to ease the suffering of the people in these parts, or were you going to tell them that Steve Austin, Houston and others ... you too, Travis ... plan to declare for a Republic? To declare this the Republic of Texas? Were you going to tell them that, Travis?... Republic, I like the sound of the word. It means people can live free, talk free, go or come, buy or sell, be drunk or sober however they choose. Some words give you a feeling. Republic is one of those words that makes me tight in the throat. The same tightness a man gets when his baby takes its first steps, or his baby shaves or makes his first sound like a man.

Some words can give you a feeling that makes your heart warm. Republic is one of those words.[33]

We see another of Wayne's propaganda speeches in the scene by the river. In this scene, Davey and his love interest, Plaka (Linda Crystal), are having a picnic by a river. Plaka wants to know what's going to happen to the two of them, given the seriousness of the situation with Mexico. In the "John Wayne"-inspired speech, Davey tells her the meaning of life, the meaning of sacrifice, and what makes a man a man, an incredibly preachy speech for a scene between two lovers:

> Hit a lick against what's wrong or say a word for what's right, even though I get walloped for sayin' that word. I may sound like a bible beater, yelling up a revival at a river crossing camp meeting. But that don't change the truth none. There's right and there's wrong, and you gotta do one or the other. You do the one and you're living; you do the other, and you may be walking around, but you're dead as a beaver hat.[34]

After Davey's romantic interlude, he and his soldiers begin the standoff at the Alamo. They try to hold the fort until reinforcements arrive but soon learn that the reinforcements will not be able to get to them in time. In the "line in the sand scene" there is very little dialogue, because — in true John Wayne fashion — a patriotic act is action, not words. Travis tells the men that the reinforcements they had been expecting cannot get there in time, that the Alamo will fall, and that anyone who stays faces certain death. He tells them that he will stay at his command but that they are free to leave. He says, "But do not go with heads hung low. No man can criticize your behavior.... You are brave and noble soldiers."[35] As the music swells, Davey Crockett and his men ride toward the gates of the Alamo, then dramatically turn and come back. They all dismount and stand at Travis's side, true patriots to the death.

The Alamo concludes with the Mexican army allowing the surviving women and children to leave the fort after all the men have died in the battle. "The Ballad of the Alamo" — written especially for the film — reminds us for the final time of the noble sacrifice of the men who gave their lives for liberty. The soaring music builds as we see shots of the beautiful blue sky and as the camera tilts toward heaven for the final lines of the song.

Ironically, the mood in the United States was shifting when Wayne started filming *The Alamo*. Joseph McCarthy had lost his power after the 1954 censure; the Soviets had launched Sputnik in 1956, redirecting American political efforts toward space technology; and the infamous Hollywood blacklist was slowly beginning to erode. Despite these political climatic changes, however, Wayne was unmoved. As historians Roberts and Olsen note, "If Hollywood was a bellwether for national politics, Duke detected a shift in mood.... Wayne did not appreciate the drift. Communism remained, in his mind, as evil and malignant as ever."[36] The Vietnam War would be Wayne's next major opportunity to present his ideological perspective.

The Green Berets

In 1966, John Wayne visited American troops in Vietnam, after which, he became a staunch defender of the war. Biographer Ronald Davis writes,

> He showed draft dodgers and protesters no patience, objected to the barriers liberal members of Congress put before the military, and favored an all-out offensive in Vietnam. "Once you go over there you won't be middle-of-the-road. All those let's-be-sweet-to-our enemies" guys are doing is helping the Reds and hurting their own country.[37]

In addition to renewing his patriotic fervor, Wayne became committed to making a movie about the war, showing the importance of the war and the heroism of the soldiers, as Davis maintains:

> Duke became a man with a mission, compelled to make the first movie about America's fighting men in Vietnam. "I want to show the folks back home just what they're up against out there, their heroism against tremendous odds."[38]

Wayne also hated the protesters. He saw them as "privileged people whose lifestyles reeked of capitalism and money.... He took it all very personally.... He was determined to rally Americans to the cause of anti-communism and to support the boys going over to Vietnam to fight and die."[39]

In consultation with President Lyndon Johnson and the Pentagon, Wayne combined all these emotions and began plans for producing *The Green Berets*. The Pentagon demanded script approval but in exchange for editorial rights would provide military equipment for the shooting of the film. They also cooperated by allowing the film to be shot at Fort Benning, Georgia (not exactly an accurate representation of the Vietnam landscape, especially when the leaves began to change colors in the fall).

The representations of patriotism in *The Green Berets* begin immediately — in the introductory credits. The opening score, "The Ballad of the Green Berets," sung by Barry Saddler,[40] plays as the credits roll, superimposed on shots of helicopters in a fire fight.

The central story of *The Green Berets* is the education of George Beckwith (David Janssen), a liberal reporter who, at first, does not believe in the Vietnam War but converts to a pro-war stance as the story progresses.

We see Colonel Kirby (John Wayne) teaching Beckwith about the evils of the Vietnam War and communism itself. Kirby then challenges Beckwith to come to Vietnam to see what's really going on.

The film opens with typical Wayne preachy propaganda. It's a press conference being held in Washington, D.C. The camera zooms in on an onlooker — Colonel Kirby (Wayne) — proudly watching, as his sergeant and lieutenant enlighten skeptics about the importance of the war. First the lieutenant teaches about the barbaric nature of communism:

> If the same thing happened here in the United States, every mayor in every city would be murdered, every teacher that was ever known would be tortured and killed, every professor you ever heard of, every governor, every senator, every member of the house of representatives and their combined families, all would be tortured and killed. And a like number kidnapped. But in spite of this there is always some little fellow out there willing to stand up and take the place of those who have been decimated[41]

The skeptical Beckwith asks why the United States has to be involved in the war if it is only a war between the Vietnamese people. At this point the sergeant tells the viewers that communism is a world conspiracy:

> Let them handle it, Mr. Beckwith? Captured weaponry from Red China ... Chaicom K50 ... Chinese communists ... SKS Soviet-made carbine ... Russian communists ... ammunition, Czechoslovakian made ... Czech communists. No sir, Mr. Beckwith. It doesn't take a lead weight to fall on me or a hit from one of those weapons to recognize that what's involved here is communist domination of the world[42]

In this opening scene, Wayne begins the education of Beckwith and the film audience as well. We learn one of the tenets of American anti-communism — that communism is monolithic. In this scene, Wayne is making much the same point that he made in the scene in *Big Jim McLain* where he talks over Mal's body, listing where all the weapons were made. The sergeant reminds us that communists seek world domination. He also gives us a vivid description of the barbaric nature of the Viet Cong.

In the scene immediately following the press conference, Beckwith tells Colonel Kirby that he doesn't buy the propagandistic presentation. Kirby issues a challenge — that Beckwith come to Vietnam to see for himself. Beckwith accepts the challenge and shows up in Vietnam. In the scenes that follow, Beckwith travels with Colonel Kirby to a remote base camp, in danger of being overrun by the Viet Cong. (The base camp is ironically named Dodge City.) The men stationed here include a Vietnamese captain and his troops, the American GIs, Peterson, a scrounge and a loser, and a cute little Vietnamese orphan named Ham Chung. These characters

begin to teach Beckwith about the barbaric communists: We soon learn
(with Beckwith) that spies are everywhere and that the VC have infiltrated
the regular Vietnamese units at this location.

As the story progresses, Beckwith slowly starts to ascribe to the John
Wayne way of viewing the war. He sees that the soldiers are doing good
works—they are helpful to the local villagers, even providing them with
medical treatment. Beckwith also meets a cute little Vietnamese girl and
gives her a medal. Beckwith's conversion becomes complete shortly afterward, when he discovers that the little girl's village has been overrun by
VC, killing the old chief, many women and children, and, of course, the
cute little girl. Kirby explains that people who have not been to Vietnam
do not understand how barbaric it can be:

> It's pretty hard to talk to anyone about this country until they've come
> over here and seen it. The last village that I visited they didn't kill the
> chief. They tied him to a tree and brought his teenage daughters out in
> front of him and disemboweled them. Then forty of them used his wife.
> They took a steel rod and broke every bone in her body. Somewhere dur-
> ing the process she died.[43]

Beckwith then picks up a gun and begins dressing in fatigues and
fighting alongside Colonel Kirby and the troops. He has learned that the
VC are evil, barbaric people and that the United States is there for an
important purpose. Beckwith now believes in the war and returns to the
United States to write his story.

Kirby and his battalion are later sent to kidnap a VC colonel. During the raid to capture him, Peterson is killed. Ham Chung, the cute little orphan, had become attached to Peterson and is devastated by his death.
In the final scene Kirby places Peterson's green beret on Ham Chung's head.
With tears running down his face the orphan asks, "What will happen to
me now?" Kirby replies, "You let me worry about that, Green Beret. You're
what this is all about."[44] As the sun sets on the ocean, the "Ballad of the
Green Berets" builds. The camera pulls back and we see Ham Chung and
Colonel Kirby (John Wayne) alone on the beach. The actual Gulf of Vietnam faces east, so we see that only in a John Wayne movie is it possible
for the sun to set in the east.

Final Thoughts

All three films represent the John Wayne view of America and its
archenemy, communism. But most importantly, the messages of the film
reinforce the traditional messages of American anticommunist ideology.

While wrapped in the mantle of patriotism, John Wayne reminds us that communism is expansionistic and that a communist way of life would destroy personal freedoms. We are also clearly shown that communist infiltration into American institutions is real and that the communist threat to the United States is tangible and direct. That this message is also conveyed by many other sources makes its impact even more important. John Wayne simplistically and vividly makes a point that is completely consistent with established beliefs about the Soviet Union and does it in a highly emotional and sensationalized way. This sort of presentation gives the message tremendous appeal to the "common man" audience he tried to reach.

The enduring popularity and image of John Wayne also illustrate Wayne's ability to understand his audiences and to touch an emotional chord in them. He understood that many Americans seem to need a patriotic hero. Even today, many Americans still seem to be hungry for a John Wayne world, where all problems are black and white and where we encounter good and evil but can easily tell which is which. That we would look to John Wayne to save us in our current crisis— wishing that he could ride off to Afghanistan — is an affirmation of his lasting image.

NOTES

1. Gary Wills, *John Wayne's America* (New York: Simon & Schuster, 1997), 11.
2. *Ibid.*, 29.
3. Mark Rahner, "Beyond the Hype: John Wayne Was True Red, White and Blue," Gannett News Service (October 2, 1995) (database online); available on Lexis-Nexis.
4. Randy Roberts and James S. Olson, *John Wayne, American* (Lincoln: University of Nebraska Press, 1995), 328.
5. Quoted in Ephraim Katz's *The Film Encyclopedia* (New York: Harper, 1979), 584.
6. Ronald Davis, *Duke: The Life and Times of John Wayne* (Norman: University of Oklahoma Press, 1998), 220.
7. Wayne directed both *The Alamo* and *The Green Berets.*
8. Roberts and Olson, 329.
9. *Ibid.*, 330.
10. John Wayne was also a member of this group at the time, but he did not become politically active in the alliance until 1948.
11. The "Ten" included screenwriters (John Howard Lawn, Dalton Trumbo, Albert Maltz, Alvah Bessie, Samuel Ornitz, Ring Lardner, Lester Cole), directors (Herbert Biberman and Edward Dmytryk) and one producer, Adrian Scott. Playwright Bertolt Brecht was allowed to leave the country rather than face charges.
12. The Wayne-Fellows Production Company would later become BATJAC Productions, named after the company in Wayne's film "The Wake of the Red Witch."
13. Nora Sayre, *Running Time: Films of the Cold War* (New York: Dial, 1979), 80.

14. Davis, 220.

15. Roberts and Olson, 375.

16. *Ibid.*, 377.

17. Quoted in Davis, 281.

18. Harold J. Berman, "The Devil and Soviet Russia," *The American Scholar* (Spring 1958), 147–52.

19. Richard Weaver, *The Ethics of Rhetoric* (Chicago: Henry Regnery, 1970), 147.

20. Michael Parenti, *The Anti-Communist Impulse* (New York: Random, 1969), 8.

21. *Ibid.*, 4.

22. *Big Jim McLain*, produced by Wayne-Fellows Productions (1952).

23. *Ibid.*

24. *Ibid.*

25. Sayre, 80.

26. *Big Jim McLain.*

27. *Ibid.*

28. *Ibid.*

29. *Ibid.*

30. *Ibid.*

31. Roberts and Olson, 471.

32. Quoted in Roberts and Olson, 471.

33. *The Alamo*, produced by BATJAC Productions (1959).

34. *Ibid.*

35. *Ibid.*

36. Roberts and Olson, 471.

37. Davis, 278.

38. *Ibid.*, 279.

39. Roberts and Olson, 538

40. "The Ballad of the Green Berets" had already risen to the top of the record charts when the film opened in 1968.

41. *The Green Berets*, produced by BATJAC (1968).

42. *Ibid.*

43. *Ibid.*

44. *Ibid.*

3

The Cold War:
Three Episodes
in Waging a
Cinematic Battle

Donald Fishman

Of war films, the most difficult to understand are those that belong to a category that can loosely be called "the Cold War." The Cold War occurred between 1946 and 1991, and it created a bipolar stalemate between the United States and the Soviet Union. The war had its moments of high drama such as the 1962 Cuban missile crisis, when it looked as if the two superpowers would annihilate each other with nuclear missiles. The war also had moments of direct confrontation such as the ground battles between Soviet troops and American soldier-advisers in Afghanistan during the early 1980s. But, for the most part, the Cold War was an ideological contest. Its battlefields were the ideas, symbols, and iconography that each side utilized to bolster its virtues and to influence public opinion.

The bulk of the Cold War was fought in a rhetorical arena. This is not to dismiss the economic conflict, the various diplomatic confrontations, and the technological jousting that occurred between the two parties. All of these elements played a role in fostering what Stephen Whitfield has called "the culture of the Cold War."[1] But the war was primarily an ideological conflict whose methods stopped short of sustained, overt military action. In the realm of strategic objectives, direct military confrontation was overshadowed by the struggle to control public opinion and influence the relevant stakeholders, be they allies, neutrals, opponents, or individuals on the homefront. Thus, a rhetorical perspective serves as a useful prism to understand the longest war of the twentieth century and what Kort has called "the defining event of the second half of the twentieth century."[2] This perspective can be applied to examine the language-based or image-oriented patterns used by filmmakers to generate beliefs, attitudes, and actions.

Hollywood was conscripted into the Cold War in 1947. In May 1947, a subcommittee of the House Committee on Un-American Activities (HUAC) began to hold hearings in Los Angeles concerning allegations of infiltration by communists into the motion picture industry. From the war's onset, Hollywood's support for the government's Cold War policies was deemed crucial. Hollywood's performance during the Second World War had been spectacular. As Doherty notes, between 1941 and 1945, "the motion picture industry became the pre-eminent transmitter of wartime policy and a lighting rod for public discourse."[3] In creating enduring images of heroism and self-sacrifice, vicarious thrills of combat, and arresting scenes of death and destruction for World War II, Hollywood was able to inspire loyalty among the public at large and create a vision of the war that supported the views of policymakers in Washington. In 1947, HUAC was seeking the same type of alliance between Hollywood and Washington in fighting the Cold War. That the Cold War was a more difficult story to tell, that our former ally during World War II was now our chief adversary, and that communism was both an issue of foreign policy and a domestic political question were complications that HUAC simply ignored.

When examining the Cold War, it would be helpful if a genre existed that could be labeled a "Cold War movie." Unfortunately, no such genre exists. A genre is a class or typology of films that share similar settings, characters, and plots. "A mature genre," contends Phillip Gianos, "creates and defines a closed, self-referential universe about which much is known by the audience but in which there is room for variations provided they do not stray too far from the genre's conventions."[4] As such Extant genres westerns, gangster films, screwball comedies, and the film noir have become commonplace, they allow an audience to quickly inhabit the world that the movie projects.

Cold War movies, however, cut across existing genres. Some were westerns (*High Noon*); some were comedies (*The Russians Are Coming, Dr. Strangelove*); and some were political thrillers (*I Led Three Lives*). What the Cold War movies have in common is the desire to tell a story, directly or indirectly, about some aspect of the Cold War. Some of the movies used allegory — to conceal the political aspects of the films within a structure that deals with parallel events and personalities but at a distance removed from the Cold War setting. Others used ambivalence or personalized a story so that the political forces reflected generalized human traits and characteristics.[5] While no Cold War genre exists, it is possible to create a broad-ranging category of Cold War movies that were influential in supporting, criticizing, and advancing Cold War policies.[6]

Meanwhile, the Cold War itself defies easy discussion. The war began officially with Winston Churchill's "Iron Curtain" speech in March 1946, and the term "Cold War" was coined that same year by speechwriter and public relations specialist Herbert Baynard Swope to describe a new type of wartime atmosphere.[7] The war ended with the fall of the Berlin Wall in November 1989, but that benchmark has been revised with the failed coup of August 1991 to reestablish a communist-based Soviet Union. Even the false ending seems to reflect the slippery truths of the Cold War era. The life cycle of the Cold War includes a short period of emergence, an acute, tension-filled phase, and a longer period of thaw and disintegration. Above all, the length and complexity of the war make it difficult to study. But Kenneth Burke tells us that it is possible to select "representative anecdotes" to understand a long-term political movement or campaign.[8] These representative anecdotes provide a window to examine difficult and diffuse phenomena and help a commentator to analyze how beliefs, attitudes, and actions were generated in a controversial situation.

This chapter examines three movies to draw some conclusions about the language and imagery of Hollywood's Cold War campaign. The movies are *The Fountainhead* (1949); *High Noon* (1952); and *Seven Days in May* (1964). Each of the movies reflects a different genre and dissimilar cinematic conventions. *The Fountainhead* and *High Noon* have frequently been associated with Cold War propaganda. *Seven Days in May* is an important "representative anecdote" in light of the September 11, 2001, terrorist attack on the World Trade Center. That attack generated an outpouring of patriotism never witnessed during the Cold War, but it spurred an outpouring of jingoistic nationalism and a sudden surge of patriotism reminiscent of that during World War I.[9] *Seven Days in May* not only reflects a cynical view of the Cold War; it sets forth a paradigmatic lesson on the standards by which to judge patriotism during the Cold War era.

The Fountainhead

Between 1947 and 1954, Hollywood produced at least thirty-three anticommunist films. Films such as *The Iron Curtain*, *The Red Menace*, *The Red Danube*, and *I Married a Communist* established a framework for

movies depicting the all-encompassing threat of Soviet domination. However, all of these overtly propagandistic movies flopped at the box office.
Yet, Hollywood continued to produce anticommunist films in the aftermath of the HUAC hearings as the studios responded to allegations that
they lacked sufficient patriotism. By the late 1940s and early 1950s, the
Hollywood Ten, a group of movie-industry figures indicted for communist activities, had begun to serve their jail sentences, and Richard Nixon,
a member of the HUAC Committee, declared that "Hollywood had a 'positive duty' to make anti-communist movies."[10] Against this background,
The Fountainhead was released in 1949. The film mentioned no explicit
communist threat nor did it allude to any foreign menace in the United
States. Yet, with considerable more artistry than its overtly anticommunist counterparts, the movie depicted the evils of collective life, the nar-
rowness of communist ideology, and the lack of individual identity that a
communist society supposedly fosters. The movie quickly became one of
the most powerful statements of the anticommunist crusade.

    The Fountainhead is a film in which the ideology is more important
than the characters or the plot. The movie is based closely upon Ayn Rand's
book of the same name, first published in 1943. Rand's book glorified individualism and the workings of capitalist society, and she depicted enlight-
ened self-interest as the primary source of progress for society. Rand
envisioned capitalism as the recognition of individual rights while she
restricted the role of government to protecting individuals from those who
would use force to fulfill their own political and economic objectives. Rand,
born Alissa Rosenbaum in 1905 in St. Petersburg, Russia, came to the
United States in 1926. She had been a firsthand witness to Kerensky's failed
constitutional regime, the Bolshevik revolution, and Stalin's rise to power.
Having experienced the evils of communism, Rand vigorously embraced
capitalism and individualism in several works of fiction and philosophy.[11]

    Warner Brothers purchased the screen rights for her novel soon after
it was published.[12] The Fountainhead was on the bestseller list for twenty-
six weeks in 1945.[13] As part of her complex arrangement with Warner
Brothers, Rand volunteered to write the screenplay for no compensation
with the stipulation that no dialogue would be changed in the actual film
without her consent. In a rare move, the studio accepted this condition
and authorized Rand to write her first Hollywood screenplay. The studio
also took creative control out of the hands of the producer and director
and gave it to Rand. For instance, King Vidor, the film's director, wanted
Humphrey Bogart to play the leading character, Howard Roark. But Rand
got her first choice, Gary Cooper. The naturally reticent Cooper was an
odd casting decision to play the garrulous character of Howard Roark.

When Vidor wanted to edit part of Roark's lengthy speech to the jury, Rand objected. She asked Warner Brothers to honor her contact, and she won.[14]

THE PLOT, SETTING, AND CHARACTERS

The Fountainhead is a movie about a gifted architect who refuses to compromise his artistic vision in the face of overwhelming obstacles. Howard Roark represents the pure individualism that Ayn Rand so admires. Rand based the Roark character on Frank Lloyd Wright, the famous architect whose designs were ahead of their time but who still achieved public acclaim. Roark becomes the spokesperson for capitalism and individualism with the other characters primarily adopting opposing views.

Roark is surrounded by people who do not share his values and who are constantly pressuring him to adjust to the dictates of society. Ellsworth M. Toohey (Robert Douglass) is Roark's chief nemesis. Toohey is the architectural critic for *The Banner*, the leading tabloid newspaper in the fictional city that serves as the setting for the film. Toohey abuses his position on *The Banner* to express his views in order to shape public opinion. Like Josef Stalin, Toohey is an opportunist. He has no real interest in people; he only uses them as a tool for his own greatness. Toohey is a believer in collectivism and sees human progress as the slow, incremental movement of the masses. At one point, he states: "Artistic value is achieved collectively by each man subordinating himself to the standards of the majority." Toohey is fearful of allowing an individual the right to develop his or her own vision. His message is unambiguous: Conform or be an outcast, no matter how talented, original, or distinctive a person's ideas are.

Peter Keating (Kent Smith) represents the public. Keating is an advocate of "giving the public what it wants." He is a classmate of Roark's in architecture school, but he is an accommodationist: He submits his will to the desires of the masses. He creates buildings that easily fade into the background surrounded on all sides by similar architectural creations. Keating achieves wealth and prestige as an architect, but he lacks talent and vision.

Dominique Francon (Patricia Neal) plays Roark's love interest. She is the quirky daughter of a wealthy architect. Dominique is cold and calculating. She marries for wealth and power, but she is irresistibly attracted to Roark. She instinctively recognizes Roark's talent, but she fears the consequences of loving a man of genius. But her attraction to Roark intensifies, and she soon becomes his lover and helpmate.

The last of the main characters in the film is Gail Wynand (Raymond Massey). Wynand is the publisher and editor of *The Banner*. Wynand grew up in Hell's Kitchen, but he climbed his way to the top without integrity or moral considerations. Wynand believes in molding the public: "There is no honest way to deal with people. We have no choice but to submit or rule. I choose to rule them." Wynand eventually realizes the genius of Roark's work, and he takes a stand to support Roark. The courage of this stand is heightened by the fact that Wynand is Dominique's husband, and he is aware of the relationship between his wife and Roark. Interestingly, Wynand is the only main character in the movie to die. His suicide seems meaningless, yet it sends a message that even a sudden change of conscience and repentance cannot overcome a lifetime of unconscionable behavior. Pragmatically, his death also clears the way for Roark to end up with Dominique.

The setting for *The Fountainhead* is a purely collective society in which the individual and new ideas concerning architecture are not acceptable. Everything must be constructed in a neoclassic Gothic style. Roark is the iconoclastic architect whose designs and interests do not fit into the orthodox style. Despite pressure from other architects, and even his own mentor, to compromise his designs in order to be successful, Roark steadfastly refuses. Instead, he accepts assignments for small buildings and projects like a gas station rather than alter his designs. During a particularly difficult dry spell, he decides to work in a stone quarry rather than to compromise his beliefs. When his friend Peter Keating asks him to design a public housing project but with Keating's name on it, Roark agrees so long as his designs are not altered. When the building that he designs is changed, he and Dominique blow it up out of principle. Roark is arrested and tried as an enemy of the people.

In a lengthy courtroom scene, Roark is permitted to present his own defense. He sets forth a rambling speech on the importance of individualism and how the existing society is harmful to progress. In the end, Roark is able to convince the jurors that he did the right thing by dynamiting the building. His terrorist attack is forgiven, and he is freed to pursue his own original designs. The overarching message of the film is that individualism will prevail over socialism, communism, and all other forms of collectivism.

Rhetorical Assessment

The opening line of the film, "Do you want to stand alone against the whole world?" immediately suggests the formidable odds that the protagonist Howard Roark will confront. But the film is helped by its cine-matography. *The Fountainhead* was shot in black and white. Images of tall buildings, a forest of skyscrapers, can be seen out of every window. For instance, the panoramic view of Gail Wynand's office window displays a modernist vista, a hyper-Manhattan, but all the buildings look similar and overpoweringly tall. Moreover, all of the desks in *The Banner*'s office are set up in a similar organizational pattern. The message is bleak: Confor-mity has a harsh edge to it.

The most effective technique used to convey the communist threat is not just the repetitiveness of such scenes, but the imagery and filming techniques employed to depict the masses. This is strikingly evident in the newsroom where the reporters are packed together, in the scenes where the employees of *The Banner* go on strike and when the public openly decries Wynand's campaign to save Roark during his trial. The masses are the true source of the negative power, not a villainous individual such as Ellsworth Toohey. The masses savagely rip the newspapers away from the vendors, and they break the glass on the doors of *The Banner* building. Toohey acknowledges their power with his statement about artistic values being achieved "collectively," but he also comes to realize that he retains his own power only so long as the majority are behind him.

The masses are depicted as being part of a highly suspicious force. Their obscure faces enhance the viewer's uncertainty over whether their motivations are good or evil. In fact, Nora Sayre places *The Fountainhead* into a category of movies of the era where there is "uncertainty about the nature or location of our enemies. The communists who operate behind the scenes, the delinquents who lurk around the next corner ... seem to be part of a vast mosaic of ambiguous fears"[15] When Toohey manages to turn *The Banner* staff against Wynand, Wynand's assistant can say noth-ing but "I don't know how he did it." Roark expresses the same type of anxiety through the metaphor of the marble as he discusses the rock for-mation in a quarry: "The infiltration of foreign elements from the sur-rounding soil — they form the colored streaks around most marble." Roark explains that pure white marble is the most desirable kind.

Director King Vidor used the techniques of film noir to capture the tensions of the individual against the masses. Beverly Kelley observes that Vidor employed "the stark composition, oblique camera angles, and deeply shadowed lighting" to heighten the tensions for the audience.[16] Durgnat and Simmon contend that:

> *The Fountainhead* forges a new language, borrowing *film noir*'s angles and darkness, its paranoia, its focus on a beleaguered or tormented indi-vidual. In that sense, the *film noir* is anti-populist. Every man walks alone

down dark, mean streets ... when the masses aren't hunched over their
desks, they're rioting, egged on by tycoons of media opinion. Without
the tortured ego accessible to *noir* style, you're *One of the Mob*.[17]

Film noir techniques reflect the darkening of attitudes during and
after World War II, and they allowed for an exploration of a more "pes-
simistic and brutal presentation of American life."[18] By applying these
techniques to scenes in *The Fountainhead*, Vidor further suggests a country in peril and an ideological crisis of major proportions. In effect, the
unknown sources of motivation of the masses are intensified by film noir
techniques. They capture the vague language of political unrest, unproven
accusations, rumor, and innuendo that dominated the headlines of the
nation's newspapers during the height of the Red Scare period and serve
as the heart of the Cold War sensibility.

The most powerful enemy in the film is the public. But the media itself
is portrayed as a manipulator of public opinion, an abusive conveyor of
information, and a potential force of evil. Wynand's office wall is covered
by a gigantic map of the world, suggesting the power of *The Banner* and
propaganda machines like it. *The Banner* is also portrayed as the cause of
Roark's demise after his success with constructing Enwright House, a
highly original architectural design. Toohey immediately launches a smear
campaign against Enwright House, and letters from the masses pour into
the newspaper in support of Toohey's position. Yet, the power of the media
backfires when the masses choose not to support a cause at odds with their
fundamental beliefs as evidenced by Wynand's inability to use his own
paper to support Roark's position. In this instance, Wynand's attempt to
retake control of public opinion from the masses fails. He slowly realizes
that he had never really controlled public opinion — he could only direct
it.

In contrast to the "playing field" of communism where the scenery is
harsh, uninspiring, and repetitive, Roark is in his own element when he
can choose his working conditions. The scenes from the quarry illustrate
this point. The quarry is a place where the spaces are open and brightly lit
by the sun. The surroundings are completely natural. The ominous sense
that emanates from the masses is absent here along with the sense of chaos
and confusion that dominates modern urban life. Roark is simply a man
doing a day of honest labor of his own choice. Even his willingness to
battle the rocks seems to reflect positively on his character by "wrestling
something constructive out of Mother Earth, even at her most grudging-
hearted."[19] Roark's association with a stone quarry gives rise to imagery
that connotes his solid foundation and the strength of his character. When
he shows Dominique his understanding of the marble, Roark demonstrates

that his knowledge of architecture begins from the ground up. All in all, the setting of the quarry provides the atmosphere where Roark's credibility is substantiated as a true American hero.

The final scene of the film also illustrates that Roark works best in his natural element. Roark is high atop the Wynand Building, which he built after Wynand's suicide. Like the setting in the quarry, the imagery here is of open air and spaciousness, even though the rest of the city may be cluttered and compacted with buildings. Roark's ideology of freedom to "live for the judgment of my mind and my own sake" has finally been achieved and allegedly mainstreamed into the once-hostile city. Biskind described this scene as being filled with "a nature of absolutes— sky, space, stone — analogous to the clean, elemental simplicity of Roark's designs and antagonistic to the derivative, cluttered, ticky-tacky modifications urged upon him by small-minded, liberal arbiters of official culture."[20] The scene is bright, unlike the film noir stylization of scenes involving the masses, and it suggests that the threat of communism can be lifted. Order has been — and can be — restored by a single man committed to his beliefs. The final image of the movie is that of Roark standing on the tallest structure in the world with Dominique beside him. Roark is towering over the masses in every way. The imagery of Roark's deification reflects the ultimate glory of the capitalist ideology, in which the self is celebrated for its free-thinking qualities and its resistance to conformity.

High Noon

High Noon is probably one of the best Cold War movies ever made. It did well at the box office, and its male star, Gary Cooper, earned the Oscar for best actor for his depiction of Marshal Will Kane, the stoical, determined law enforcement officer. The theme song of the movie, "Do Not Forsake Me, Oh My Darling," earned Oscars for the best song as well as the best musical scoring. The picture also received a fourth Oscar for best editing. Produced by Stanley Kramer, directed by Fred Zinnemann, and based on a screen play by Carl Foreman, the picture had top-tier creative and administrative support and a stellar cast. Released in 1952, *High Noon* was playing in the theaters as the war in Korea reached its zenith.

But what makes *High Noon* so intriguing fifty years after it was produced is the fact that it has— and can be — interpreted in two major but opposing ways. In one interpretation, the film represents an attack on communism. While communism bolstered the power of unity and the lack of individuality in a society, *High Noon* showed that without the independent actions of key individuals in the community, a society is weak and lacks direction, and its members cannot successfully work together. Sam Girgus contends that "the strongest understanding of the film ... [is] the American hero drawing a line in the sand to oppose aggressive forces of evil and corruption."[21] In this understanding, the forces of evil and corruption are the communist outsiders, specifically the Soviets.

The second and more prominent interpretation views the film as a parable concerning HUAC's attack on Hollywood. The evils of McCarthyism are depicted indirectly in a psychological Western about a group of outlaws who threatened the livelihood of the fictional town of Hadleyville. Carl Foreman, the chief scriptwriter of *High Noon*, had been associated with the communist party during the years of the Popular Front era in the United States. Foreman openly argued that the film was a Western about Hollywood, specifically the Red Scare and the blacklist. Declared Foreman: "I used the Western background to tell a story of a community corrupted by fear, with the implications that I hoped would be obvious to everyone who saw the film, at least in America."[22] This is an extremely persuasive interpretation. But the fact that two major and opposing interpretations can easily coexist suggests the richness and the openness of *High Noon* as a Cold War social drama.

THE PLOT, SETTING, AND CHARACTERS

Unlike *The Fountainhead*, the plot, setting, and characters of *High Noon* are well known. Marshal Will Kane (Gary Cooper) retires from office after marrying his Quaker bride, Amy Fowler (Grace Kelly). Because of her religious and moral beliefs, Amy despises violence, and part of her wedding agreement with Kane was that he would retire from his position as marshal. But the happy wedding day is interrupted by the news of Frank Miller's (Ian MacDonald's) return. Kane had arrested Miller five years earlier, and Miller was coming back with a gang of three thugs to kill him. Miller, a hardened and psychotic criminal, intends to run Hadleyville. Such a prospect promises to undermine the legal and moral order that Kane had established as the town marshal.

Kane is urged by the townspeople to leave if he hopes to protect himself and his new wife. Initially, Kane does leave, but while on the road, he decides to return, explaining to his irritated wife that he refuses to run from anyone and that he will stand up to Miller and his men. Kane's wife threatens to leave him, citing a breach of his promise to avoid violence. Amy buys a train ticket to travel away from Hadleyville as her husband prepares for his encounter with Miller.

The major portion of this drama revolves around Kane's desperate plea for help in order to organize a team of men to confront Miller. His peers refuse, viewing the anticipated battle as a suicide mission. They cower at the mention of Miller's name.

There are two additional subplots to the film. The first revolves around the relationship between Kane and his young deputy friend, Harvey Pell (Lloyd Bridges). Pell refuses to support Kane and even openly opposes his efforts to take on Miller. The second subplot revolves around the tensions between Kane and Helen Ramirez (Katy Jurado), who is Kane's former mistress, Miller's former mistress, and Pell's current lover.

The only help that Kane is offered comes from a half-blind drunk and a fourteen-year-old kid. Although touched, Kane realizes that the two offers do not provide any real assistance, and he decides to take on the Miller gang alone. He writes a will in preparation for his death, and he awaits the impending battle.

The final scenes of the movie revolve around a gunfight. Kane single-handedly eliminates two of the four members of Miller's gang, but he suffers a gunshot wound during the initial scuffle. Kane tries to elude the two remaining thugs by hiding in a stable, but the two men smoke him out. The battle ends when Kane's wife, Amy, shoots and kills the last of Miller's men, and she is then taken hostage by Miller, who threatens to kill her. Amy acts quickly. She claws Miller's face and frees herself momentarily, providing just enough time for Kane to shoot and kill Miller. The film ends with Kane and his wife embracing while the townspeople come out of hiding. Dramatically, Kane throws his badge to the ground, and he and Amy ride off in a buggy.

The character of Will Kane credibly embraces both the anticommunist motif and the anti–McCarthyism interpretation. Both of these interpretations deserve to be discussed in more detail.

THE ANTICOMMUNIST INTERPRETATION

Kane represents the individual who thinks for himself and does not simply go along with the group. In theory, Kane personifies an important democratic ideal: an independent leader whose ideas are supported by the majority. Without a chance for leaders to rise and lead the majority, cohesion within society becomes impossible. While communism abhors the individual who stands out with his own independent thought, *High Noon* argues that the "greater danger stems from the absence of such individual conscience."[23] Without Kane's heroics, Hadleyville would be filled with crime and its citizens would live in fear. Kane's democratic persona is the reason for the town's salvation, and genuine leadership is a concept that was posed by Zinnemann to prove that democracy is effective and desirable.

At the same time, the townspeople of Hadleyville are presented in the film as feckless. They fear Miller, and instead of voicing their own opinion, they cower under his rule. They, in turn, surrender their independence and individuality. Their collective rationality and intelligence fall helpless in the face of their fear.[24] They move as a group, quietly and cowardly lacking the ability to voice an opinion for the majority to follow. In effect, the citizens of Hadleyville represent the members of a communist society. When Kane searches for a team of people to assist him, he encounters individuals who know that what he is doing is right, but they refuse to join him because of fear. In this conundrum, communism is framed as a force that weakens society.

The subtle framing of communism as a destructive force is one of the masterful feats of the film. When Miller was in jail, Hadleyville was peaceful. Symbolically, democracy creates a peaceful and productive society. When Miller returns, chaos is reborn, and the people live in fear, giving up their identity as independent, thinking men and women. Communism is related to these feelings of vulnerability, and the message of the film is that communism corrupts and destroys a healthy, functioning society. Miller represents communism, and he presents an evil persona. Arguing on behalf of this anticommunist motif, Girgus contends that "in *High Noon*, Zinnemann and Cooper dramatize a world in which one man of inner-direction ... confronts a society of other-directed conformists [communists] who are morally crippled by fear and helplessness."[25]

THE ANTI-MCCARTHYISM INTERPRETATION

Auster and Quart not only describe *High Noon* as a parable of HUAC's attack on Hollywood, but they claim that the central message of the film is that "evils such as McCarthyism must be resisted and could no longer be rationalized or evaded."[26] Not only did the scriptwriter and producer of the film have proleftist backgrounds, but the symbolism of the movie underscores its strong critique of blacklisting and the exaggerated fears of the Hollywood community.

Within an allegorically based plot, the anti–McCarthyism and anti-blacklisting interpretation are evident without the film openly drawing parallels between the Western motif and the political occurrences in Hollywood. Will Kane represents a blacklisted individual. He is opposed by Miller and pressured to leave town. The film depicts Kane standing up to

the opposition, symbolically fighting the war against the officials responsible for the exaggerated accusations—the blacklisters themselves and,
specifically, Senator McCarthy. The people in the film responsible for the
blacklist are represented by Miller and his gang. He comes to destroy
Kane—just as the blacklisters were attempting to destroy left and liberal-
thinking people in Hollywood. The townspeople represent the public, the
people who know Miller and his criminal ways but who refuse to fight
because of fear. Symbolically, these are American citizens who refuse to
attack McCarthy's unfair exclusions because they are afraid of being stig-
matized as communists themselves.

Amy represents the Hollywood industry. Her marriage to Kane is a
metaphor for the loyalty and link that the people of Hollywood should have
for each other. Just as Amy deserts her husband when he decides to stand
up against Miller, the Hollywood community deserted those individuals
who were blacklisted. One line that implies the injustice of the blacklist
occurs when Kane is explaining to his wife why he must return to
Hadleyville to face Miller. He tells her, "I've got to go back, Amy.... They're
making me run. I've never run from anybody before." This simple dialogue represents a telling criticism of McCarthyism: McCarthyism forces
people to run away from their beliefs by instilling fear in them whereas a
true democracy is supposed to allow citizens to voice their opinions freely
and not worry about whether their political affiliations coincide with popularly held opinions.

Another reference to the venality of blacklisting occurs later in the
film. Kane encounters Percy Mettrick (Otto Kruger), the judge who sen-
tenced Miller. Mettrick tells Kane to leave town, and when Kane refuses,
the judge attacks his decision: "Why must you be so stupid? Have you forgotten what he [Miller] is? Have you forgotten what he's done to people?"
The judge tells Kane to leave because Miller has hurt people and is a dangerous person. Symbolically, this warning is what an average person might
say to someone who would attempt to do battle with the injustices of
McCarthyism. Mettrick presents Miller as an unbeatable foe and says that
Kane should save his own neck and accept what is happening. With regard
to about McCarthy and his power to ruin a person's career, it is possible
to ask the same question that Mettrick asks Kane about Miller: "Have you
forgotten what he is?"

Another reference to the blacklisting occurs when Amy is waiting in
the hotel lobby for her train to arrive. She is angry with her husband about
his decision to fight Miller. Amy converses with the hotel clerk (Howard
Chamberline) about a variety of topics. When he tells her that "There's
plenty of people around here think he's [Kane] got a comeuppance com-

ing," he is emphasizing the public's fearfulness, even hostility, toward alleged do-gooders. The clerk does not explain why the towns people want to see Kane defeated. He simply did not know — just as the public did not know — the specifics about those who were on the blacklist. This suggests another characteristic of and parallel with McCarthyism: unsubstantiated accusations based upon reckless generalizations.

The symbolism of blacklisting manifests itself in still another crucial scene in the film. During a conversation between Kane's former mistress, Helen Ramirez, and his wife, Helen advises Amy to stand by her man: She asks Amy, "What kind of woman are you? How can you leave him like this?" She goes on to tell Amy that if Kane were her husband she would get a gun and fight. Taken literally, this interaction focuses attention upon Amy's loyalty to, and her relationship with, her spouse. Symbolically, it takes on a different meaning. Amy represents the Hollywood community; she is close to Kane and has a special bond with him that demands loyalty. Amy's leaving Kane is similar to the Hollywood actors and actresses who allowed blacklisting to ruin their peers because they were afraid to speak out. Just as Kane was harassed by Miller, the Hollywood community was being victimized by the excesses of McCarthyism; unless the people of the community join in the fight, McCarthyism would be unstoppable.

Above all, *High Noon* serves a vehicle to express the feelings of a Hollywood community that was afraid to speak out against injustice. Through the use of metaphor, symbolism, and indirect connections between the common themes in the Old West and America during the late 1940s and early 1950s, *High Noon* offers a powerful political statement. *High Noon* carefully packaged its anticommunist and antiblacklisting motifs in nonthreatening ways. Equally important, *High Noon* combines the two interpretations into a single message. The film suggests that the Hollywood community should fight against communism but not at the expense of innocent people who need to work there. Moreover, the movie implies that those who are falsely accused should be supported by their fellow Hollywood members, even at the prospect of a temporary risk to their own well-being. In essence, *High Noon* argues that by banding together, by having the courage to speak out, and by remaining true to your conscience, communism eventually will be defeated and unfair practices such as blacklisting and McCarthy witch-hunts will be eliminated.

RHETORICAL ASSESSMENT

As a genre, the basic outline of any Western focuses directly upon a primal clash between civilization and savagery, producing a series of conflicts until the climactic confrontation or the showdown becomes inevitable. The Western is a good format to tell the story of blacklisting. Gehring maintains that "[t]he Western is tied more directly to social and historical reality than virtually any other film genre."[27] Buscombe contends that "[n]o other genre in cinema delineates so precisely the details of every-day life."[28] But because the Western is such a flexible genre, and because the depiction of good and evil are expected conventions of the genre, high-lighting the venality of Miller's gang as a substitute for McCarthyism does not appear to strain the film's depiction of evil. The Western genre actu-ally warrants such a depiction.

The filming of the screenplay for *High Noon* in black and white also tends to highlight the good versus evil contrasts. The starkness of the char-acters reinforces the desperation that the hero faces as well as the savagery of the villains. The black-and-white coloration also seems to reflect the black-and-white newspaper headlines on the major developments of the Cold War, especially during the Korean War era.

Rhetorically, the use of the concept of time is a key strategy in the nar-rative sequence of the film. Basinger, Scorsese and Rossellini declared that in *High Noon*, "the theme of time is present in that the past dominates all characters and their decisions ... and a past grudge is the motivation for the villain's actions."[29] The emphasis on the concept of time also identifies another criticism aimed at blacklisting. Those who were blacklisted were often accused of criminality because of opinions that they had held in the past. Kane was being pursued by Miller because of his role in arresting the criminal. What he was doing presently did not matter. Similarly, many of those who were blacklisted were convicted because of their past opinions, even though they might have changed their thinking. The concept of time was employed to show how foolish it was for blacklisters to use a person's past while ignoring their current beliefs.

Finally, Fred Zinnemann, the director of *High Noon*, also contributed to the film's widespread acclaim and its Oscar for best editing. Zinnemann breathed life into the film by manipulating the cinematography in such a way that the end product exhibits tension-packed but realistic qualities. Filmed in real time, each minute that passes brings the audience closer to the final confrontation between Kane and Miller. Images of clocks con-tinually flash on the screen and serve to heighten the tension. The final shoot-out is a gripping, edge-of-your-seat scene. Shifts in camera angles force the audience's perspective to move from looking around the corner of a building to looking down at the enemy from the top of a barn loft while never knowing where or when the next shot will be fired. Spectac-ular directing and effective acting make these scenes entertaining. Moreover, Zinnemann's specialty is his ability to frame issues of good and evil. From *High Noon* and *From Here to Eternity* to the 1966 classic *A Man for All Seasons,* Zinnemann showed an ability to deftly personify and humanize evil. And the forces of civilization and savagery that the Western fluidly conveyed were precisely the tensions that the audience faced in the early 1950s as they watched *High Noon* with communism, the Korean War, and McCarthy's Red Scare campaign in the background.

Seven Days in May

Seven Days in May is a political thriller that focuses upon the military's attempted takeover of the United States government in the aftermath of president's having negotiated a nuclear disarmament treaty with the Soviet Union. Adapted by Rod Serling from the best-selling novel of Fletcher Knebel and Charles W. Bailey, the movie was inspired by the far-right ramblings of General Edwin Walker, the surge of support for right-wing views during the early 1960s, and the "better dead than red" mentality that dominated 1950s America. Interestingly, during the Cold War, advocates of the political Right believed that civilian leaders from both the leading political parties were selling the country out. This led them to see political decision making as a vast conspiracy wherein secrecy and betrayal were the staple elements. The Goldwater forces during the early 1960s adopted a modified version of this militant outlook, but they still adhered to the view that Democrats and centrist Republicans had colluded to hurt the American public. Moreover, Joseph McCarthy's great skill as a propagandist during the 1950s was in his mainstreaming of the communist conspiracy argument and in legitimizing the political position that the United States had been betrayed from within.[30]

The storyline in *Seven Days in May* reflects the conspiracy-film genre that its director, John Frankenheimer, first employed in the 1962 political thriller *The Manchurian Candidate* and that Oliver Stone would continue to celebrate during the 1980s and 1990s. During the 1960s, Frankenheimer produced a trilogy of psychologically suspenseful political thrillers. All drew upon the anxieties of the Cold War to fuel the tensions in the movies. Frankenheimer's *Manchurian Candidate* (1962) and his *Seconds* (1966) were separated by the 1964 release of *Seven Days in May.*

Seven Days in May, although a popular film, is a political potboiler. It has an excellent cast and the tense pacing of a television documentary and presents realistic but highly dramatized scenes from the White House and the Pentagon. What makes this movie an important exemplar — a representative anecdote — is its treatment of patriotism, and this depiction reflects a more generalized view of patriotism during the Cold War era.

THE PLOT, SETTING, AND CHARACTERS

The plot of *Seven Days in May* revolves around the activities of General James Matoon Scott (Burt Lancaster), the charismatic chairman of the Joint Chiefs of Staff, who believes that the liberal-leaning President Jordan Lyman (Fredric Marsh) is soft on communism because he supports a nuclear disarmament treaty. Scott and his military allies fear that this treaty will trigger a Soviet sneak attack. The public also reacts negatively to the treaty, and the Gallup Poll indicates that the president's approval rating has dropped to twenty-nine percent. Both the treaty and the president are highly unpopular. To protest Lyman's signing of a disarmament treaty, protest marches occur in front of the White House. These marches with protesters and counterprotesters have the look and feel of the civil rights demonstrations that occurred at the White House during the early 1960s.

The film opens with a picture of the U.S. Constitution with blood running from the top of the page to the bottom, slowly smearing each of the enumerated articles of the document. The point of view that the film immediately presents is that of a constitutional crisis triggered by a military junta. The camera and the script follow closely the action of the president, but he is depicted as a steady but weak figure. The most powerful and determined character in the movie is General Scott.

General Scott believes that the Soviet Union will violate the provisions of the nuclear disarmament treaty and that the treaty will result in the destruction of the United States with a hundred million casualties. Scott argues that "There's not a single piece of paper in history that's ever served as a deterrent to a Pearl Harbor. Every twenty years or so we pick ourselves up bleeding off the floor and forget that. Mistakes which are delivered to us COD by peace-loving men and are bought and paid for by peace-loving men — men in uniform." Scott's thesis is that a "peace on paper, whether a treaty or constitution is worthless to guard the national security."[31] Only strong actions supported by an uncompromising outlook will preserve the United States. Thus, Scott begins to plot a coup.

Scott's plan is not only plausible but also clever. He has created a secret military base outside of El Paso, Texas, where 100 officers and 3600 enlisted men are being trained in prevention and seizure tactics in case of a national emergency. The military base is called E-Com-Con which stands for Emergency Communications Control. Scott's plan is that strategic use of military force plus control over the chief mechanisms of communication will allow him to succeed in a complete governmental takeover. Several U.S. senators support him. As chairman of the Joint Chiefs of Staff, Scott has scheduled a "military alert" for the following week. The alert is allegedly designed to concentrate efforts upon protecting the communication mechanisms in the United States. Many people know about the alert. What they do not know is that the alert is really a pretext for a military coup.

Scott has organized support among key leaders of the military. Almost all of the Joint Chiefs of Staff have allied themselves with him, but only a select few of the enlisted men know the true purposes of the alert. Not all of the people close to General Scott have been trusted with the news or details of the coup. One of those who begins to suspect that the alert is a cover story for a more nefarious operation is Scott's assistant at the Joint Chiefs of Staff, Colonel Martin "Jiggs" Casey (Kirk Douglas). Colonel Casey informs President Lyman of the emerging plot.

President Lyman is now aware of the disenchantment of General Scott, but he cannot act until he gathers concrete evidence against the conspirators. The efforts by President Lyman to uncover the rumored takeover are blocked by "political protocol, human error, and accidental death."[32] Lyman is forced to rely heavily upon the person who first uncovered the plot, Colonel Casey. The dramatic action in the film centers upon Casey's efforts to stop a takeover that is allegedly scheduled to occur in fewer than seven days. Casey is helped in his efforts by presidential aide Paul Girard (Martin Balsam), U.S. Senator Ray Clark (Edmond O'Brien) and Scott's former girlfriend and Washington socialite, Eleanor Holbrook (Ava Gardner). A web of intrigue occurs as Casey tries to provide proof to the president that General Scott is actually planning a coup d'état.

Through a series of fortuitous developments, Casey assembles evidence about the coup. This evidence eventually forces some of Scott's military allies on the Joint Chiefs of Staff to resign, and it stops the plot in progress. The movie ends with the president at a nationally televised press conference touting the virtues of democracy and a constitutional form of government. It is a legalistic type of love of your country, he claims, but it is the only realistic option that we have.

The ending of the movie is abrupt, even unsatisfactory. The audience can only imagine what will happen to Scott; whether the president's poll ratings will improve; whether Colonel Casey will begin a romantic relationship with Eleanor Holbrook; and whether the nuclear disarmament treaty will succeed in reducing the brinkmanship that the president has decried. In potboiler fashion, the film is incapable of answering these questions.

With no clear-cut answers, the film has focused on a small part of the puzzle: the dramatic military actions by General Scott to implement a military takeover. At one point, President Lyman states the real enemy of America is the age that we live in with its "impotency, weakness, and desperation." The enemy is the hysteria of the times, and this film has no answer for that hysteria. Instead, it can only exploit that hysteria to tell the story that it presents to the audience.

RHETORICAL ASSESSMENT

Seven Days in May is set during the height of the Cold War when nuclear war and massive destruction seemed a likely occurrence. The movie is extremely entertaining. The relationship between a rogue general, members of the Senate, and right-wing television commentators make the sequence of events both plausible and intriguing. The film's effectiveness is also enhanced by five rhetorical strategies.

First, like *High Noon,* this film returns again and again to the date and the clock. Frankenheimer focuses on a large clock in the Pentagon, and the audience is left with a vivid impression that time is slipping away. Second, the black-and-white cinematography adds to the suspense, creating the feeling of watching a television docudrama. Third, the minimalist, militaristic score with its frequent use of a drumbeat reinforces the stark visual images. This is music designed to highlight intrigue, swift action, and quick cuts between one scene and another. Fourth, the dialogue is very well written. Serling and Frankenheimer have combined to make the characters sound real as they discuss political and military events. For instance, one of the best speeches in the films is given by Senator Ray Clark, who is an amiable alcoholic but a close and trustworthy friend of the president. Clark cogently explains to the president why the public is disappointed with the treaty and hostile to the president's sponsorship of it:

> We've been hating the Russians for a quarter of a century. Suddenly we've signed a treat that says they're to dismantle their bombs and we're to dismantle ours. We all ride to a peaceful glory. This country will probably live as if peace was just as big a threat as war.

In addition, the dialogue and interaction between the key characters, especially Lancaster and Douglas, and Douglas and Gardner is riveting and emotionally moving. These microhuman interactions carry with them great impact, and they appear to exist independently of the film's inability to answer the searing macroquestions that it poses. Fifth, the film makes excellent use of television sets as artifacts and mechanisms to convey realism. People who speak on the telephone in the White House and the Pentagon appear on the other end of a television set as if videotelephones existed. The president and General Scott give political addresses on television, and the movie audience watches part of each address via a television set. The ever-present portrayal of television in its news-making function adds a docudrama quality to the movie and enhances the film's status as political thriller.

The Question of Patriotism

This film makes frequent references of Pearl Harbor, a sneak attack against the United States in 1941 that resulted in massive deaths and suffering. But the deaths and destruction at Pearl Harbor seem small in light of the September 11, 2001, terrorist attack on the World Trade Center. Civilians, not military combatants, were the victims of that attack, and the number of deaths was staggering. In the aftermath of that September 11 attack, what emerged in the United States was an outpouring of patriotism not seen since World War I. In the September 11 tableau, the best faces of patriotism were government workers: fire fighters and police officers; members of the Federal Emergency Management Agency who provided rescue supplies; and local and national politicians who supported the rescue and relief efforts.

Signs of a newfound patriotism were widespread. Suddenly, stickers with the American flag and the slogan *United We Stand* appeared on cars and buses. Patriotic concerts with popular and legendary rock stars were given in New York. Funds were raised to help the victims of this disaster. All of this authentic feeling — the heightened emotionality and the expressions of love for the country — had been missing during the Cold War era. Patriotism was not a popular feeling among the cold warriors. It was muted, legalistic, and, at its best, much like the patriotism that President Jordan Lyman offers the public in the closing speech of *Seven Days in May.* This outlook made authentic patriotism difficult to foster. This is not to say that patriotism was totally absent during the Cold War. But its scope and intensity were far different from what Americans had experienced during World War I and World War II.

Because it placed the issue of patriotism at the center of its social drama, *Seven Days in May* offers us an insight that goes beyond the film. Robert L. Scott has observed that ambivalence was one of key characteristics of the Cold War.[33] By definition, a "cold war" meant stopping short, or truncating, not only military action but patriotic feelings as well. In fact, the patriotism in *Seven Days in May* is viewed as a distorted feeling spearheaded by megalomaniacs who really did not understand what America represents.

General Scott and his military supporters claim to be acting in the name of authentic patriotism. But Scott's patriotism is at odds with the Constitution, and it encompasses removing a president by terrorist actions and placing control of the government in the hands of the military. It is a patriotism that knows no boundaries and that is not anchored in the American experience. The most patriotic figures in the *Seven Days in May* are willing to trample over the legal and moral order of the country.

The movie frames an interesting dilemma. Both sides in the conflict wish to see themselves as patriots, persuaded that the righteousness of their principles justify the actions that should be undertaken. President Lyman's side views the best prospects for peace emerging from taking an initial step to begin disarmament. General Scott's side believes that peace can be accomplished only by military strength because of the treachery of the Soviet Union. It is not clear who is right or wrong, but the film argues that those who wrap themselves in hyperpatriotism are the greatest enemies of the United States. Their patriotism embraces a bizarre and untruthful love of their country.

With few exceptions, the best of the Cold War movies did not strengthen patriotism. Movies such as *The Fountainhead* and *High Noon* emphasize the role of the individual. They weaken the belief that the group is right, casting doubt on this principle because the uncritical love of the masses suggests the concepts associated with communism. Most Cold War movies avoided the sanctification of the masses because they could not draw a convincing distinction between communism's blind support for the masses and democracy's support for a republic-like form of government. This, in turn, led to an emphasis by Cold War films on the individual.

The principle suggested here is that the Cold War movies did not engender or strengthen patriotism. The Cold War rhetoric was limited and truncated whereas patriotism requires an uninhibited emotional outpouring, a faith in government officials, and a willingness for all elements of society to express their commitment to the vague but stringent requirements of a patriotic call. The Cold War was never able to arouse that type of emotional commitment.

If anything, patriots of the Cold War were depicted as extremists, zealots, or individuals with a distorted sense of reality. *Seven Days in May* is a good representative anecdote to provide insight into an important interpretation of what devotion to one country meant or implied during the Cold War.

Conclusion

Kenneth Burke tells us that by clustering a subject we can acquire a better sense of "symbolic mergers" and gain insight into a topic even though we have not examined the full range of a category.[34] This approach may be of assistance as we look at selected films of the Cold War.

By and large, Hollywood had difficulty in telling the story of the Cold War. This type of war lacked the scenes of physical combat and images of people on the homefront eagerly waiting for news of how their loved ones were faring abroad. Instead, this variant of war placed a premium on rhetorical and psychological combat—creating the winning image and strengthening the will to survive. In addition, the more openly propagandist films such as The Red Menace (1949) and My Son John (1952) were dull and inartistic endeavors.[35] These and other hyper patriotic films had difficulty seeming credible. To be sure, there were many exceptions to these generalizations, and over the course of a forty-five-year period, several first-rate films emerged that were influenced by a Cold War sensibility. But the number of outstanding Cold War movies is disproportionately low given the time span of the hostilities.

The three movies discussed in this chapter on the Cold War share some commonalties. All three were shot in black-and-white film despite the increasing use of color film in the years after World War II. All three employed cinematic innovations, and the editing of each of these films stands out for its originality. High Noon, for instance, is a film that exemplifies the Western's transition from the classical style of straightforward action to psychological intrigue and social consciousness. Most importantly, all three of the films focus upon the struggle between good and evil. But what makes these movies effective is that all three have found a vehicle to humanize the struggle between good and evil.

The best of these Cold War movies is High Noon. High Noon speaks to the Cold War in two major ways. First, it assures the public that America's attack on communism is justified because communism is a force of unambiguous evil. Second, the film speaks on a different level when it criticizes McCarthyism and blacklisting. McCarthy's aggressive form of blacklisting was portrayed as the wrong way to combat communism — making accusations about people based on their past. Kane, for instance, should not have had to run away from his beliefs or explain his past to those who questioned his stance against Miller. High Noon tells the viewer that by only banding together, by having the courage to be express your views, and staying loyal to your community will communism and the evils that it engenders be pushed out.

In addition, the Western genre serves as a powerful instrument to highlight a story of good versus evil. The conventions of the Western allow for the storyline to concentrate on the venality of the villain. The well-written script, the superb acting, and the cinematography make this an instructive as well as entertaining movie. *High Noon* requires one to think about its subject matter, and only after such an examination does one realize the searing criticisms of the Cold War that the film presents.

On the other hand, *The Fountainhead* received mixed reviews. Its attempt to deal with broad philosophical issues such as individualism versus conformity, democracy versus the masses, and the strength of capitalism make it didactic and preachy. Moreover, there is a lack of realistic dialogue between the script and the characters. *The Fountainhead* is very blunt, probably too blunt about its political stance, even though there are no explicit political references in the film. But political ideology is the driving force behind this film. Yet the cinematography is superb, and the film noir techniques that director King Vidor employs makes this an engaging story.

Finally, *Seven Days in May* is the most underrated of the three films. It has a superb cast, a well-written script, and fast cuts between the scenes. The audio and video portions of the films also seem perfectly in harmony. This was the only film script that Rod Serling ever wrote despite his years of success in writing for television. But the pacing of the film has a television drama-like quality. In terms of cinematic artistry, Frankenheimer's film of two years earlier, *The Manchurian Candidate,* is probably the superior work. But the lasting value of *Seven Days in May* is its depiction of patriotism as a distorted and bizarre force at work in society. This film offers an insightful portrait of patriotism that arguably speaks to the cynicism and excesses of the entire Cold war era.

NOTES

1. Stephen J. Whitfield, *The Culture of the Cold War,* 2nd ed. (Baltimore: The Johns Hopkins University Press, 1996).

2. Michael G. Kort, *The Cold War* (New York: Columbia University Press, 1998), 3.

3. Thomas Doherty, *Projection of War: Hollywood, American Culture and World War II* (New York: Columbia University Press, 1993), 5.

4. Phillip L. Gianos, *Politics and Politicians in American Film* (Westport, Conn.: Praeger, 1999), 7.

5. Rhetorical theorist Robert L. Scott contends that the term *Cold War* is an oxymoron. "Can a war be cold?" he asks. According to Scott, what is essential for Cold War rhetoric is words and actions that stop short of outright military conflict and that "stopping short is essential to the meaning of cold war. Ambivalence is built into the concept." See Robert L. Scott, "Cold War and Rhetoric: Conceptually and Critically," in *Cold War Rhetoric: Strategy, Metaphor, and Ideology,* edited by Martin J. Medhurst, Robert L. Ivie, Philip Wander, and Robert L. Scott (East Lansing: Michigan State University Press, 1997), 4.

6. The author has a list of Hollywood films from the 1940s to 1991 that fall into the category of the "Cold War movie." The list is available upon request.

7. Gianos, 133.

8. Kenneth Burke, *A Grammar of Motives* (Berkeley: University of California Press, 1945/1974, rpt.), 59–61.

9. See H. C. Peterson and Gilbert C. Fite, *Opponents of War, 1917–1918* (Westport, Conn.: Greenwood, 1957/1986, rpt.).

10. D. Leah, "I Was a Communist for the FBI: Anti-communist Films of the 1950s," *History Today* (database online); available from Lexis-Nexis.

11. James Thomas Baker, *Ayn Rand* (Boston: Twayne, 1987), 66.

12. O. S. Fern, "Fairy-Tale Start for Capitalist Ayn Rand." *The Straight Times* (March 6, 1999): 13.

13. Baker, 51.

14. Raymond Durgnat and Scott Simmon, *King Vidor, American* (Berkeley: University of California Press, 1990), 268.

15. Nora Sayre, *Runningtime: Films of the Cold War* (New York: Dial, 1982), 26.

16. Beverly Kelley with John Pitney, Craig R. Smith and Herbert E. Gooch III., *Reelpolitik: Political Ideologies in '30s and '40s Films* (Westport, Conn.: Greenwood, 1998), 143.

17. Durgnat and Simmon, 259.

18. Thomas G. Schatz, *Hollywood Genre: Formulas, Filmmaking, and the Studio System* (Philadelphia: Temple University Press), 112.

19. Durgnat and Simmon, 268–69.

20. Peter Biskind, *Seeing Is Believing: How Hollywood Taught Us to Stop Worrying and Love the Fifties* (New York: Pantheon, 2000), 322.

21. Sam B. Girgus, *Hollywood Renaissance: The Cinema of Democracy in the Era of Ford, Capra, and Kazan* (New York: Cambridge University Press), 140.

22. *Ibid.*, 139.

23. *Ibid.*, 142.

24. *Ibid.*, 149.

25. *Ibid.*, 144.

26. Al Auster and Leonard Quart, *American Film and Society since 1945* (New York: Praeger, 1984), 49–50.

27. Wes D. Gehring, *Handbook of American Film Genres* (New York: Greenwood, 1988), 85–86.

28. Edward Buscombe, *The BFI Companion to the Western* (New York: Atheneum, 1988).

29. Jeanine Basinger, Martin Scorsese, and Isabella Rossellini, eds., *American Cinema: One Hundred Years of Filmmaking* (New York: Rizzoli, 1994), 51.

30. Donald Fishman, "Joseph R. McCarthy: Historiography and Rhetorical Strategies Revisited," in *Arguing Communication and Culture*, vol. 2, G. Thomas Goodnight, ed. (Washington, D.C.: National Communication Association, 2002), 452–453.

31. Dragan Antulov, "Seven Days in May (1964)" (database online) available from http://www/us..imdb.com/Reviews/309/30904.

32. Hal Erickson, "Seven Days in May," *All Media Guide* (online); available from http://www.allmovie.com/cg/avgdll?p=avg&sql=A43837.

33. Scott, 4.

34. Kenneth Burke, *Attitudes toward History* (Boston: Beacon, 1937/1959, rpt.), 232–234.

35. See Thomas Doherty, "Hollywood Agit-Prop: The Anti-Communist Cycle, 1945–1954," *Journal of Film and Video* 40 (1988): 15–27.

4

Troubled Silences: Trauma in John Huston's Film *Let There Be Light*

JOHN J. MICHALCZYK AND
SUSAN A. MICHALCZYK

The war was won, the heroes cheered, the parades ended. Yet there were further burning issues for America to deal with in order to be restored, to be at peace with itself. Wounds, both physical and mental, had to heal in order for the country to be whole once again. John Huston's documentary film *Let There Be Light* would address these issues in 1946, but the film would not see the light of day until 1981, after a stirring controversy over its raw images of trauma.

Many war films portrayed the physical casualties of combat whether dealing with World War I (*Johnny Got His Gun*), World War II (*The Best Years of Our Lives*), or the Vietnam War (*Born on the Fourth of July*). No combat film, documentary or feature, however, has ever captured the effects of trauma as searingly as (Major) John Huston's gripping 58-minute documentary, *Let There Be Light*. This film, the third in his "war trilogy" with the U.S. Army Signal Corps, placed him in the prestigious ranks of other wartime directors such as Frank Capra, William Wyler, John Ford and George Stevens.[1] For Huston, it was the culmination of a series of many combat experiences in filming, as well as the beginning of a more profound understanding of the human psyche.

The Background

Huston initiated his three-part series by documenting the preparations for war in *Report from the Aleutians,* then capturing the chilling combat scenes in his graphic work *Battle of San Pietro,* fought from December 8 to December 15, 1943. This film, however, contained images that were too realistic and "would demoralize the young draftees," according to Huston in his interview with Peter Greenberg.[2] The documentary was therefore censored by the U.S. War Department. General George Marshall intervened to have the film shown, but it was still not released until May 21, 1945, after VE Day.

Following the end of the European campaign, Huston found himself still working for the Signal Corps. In his documentary film production during World War II he had already looked combat straight in the eye and then confronted its horrifying aftereffects. He truly felt himself a "veteran," although his "shooting" was done with a camera and not with an M1 rifle. In undertaking to film a third documentary for the Signal Corps, he was unaware that this production would change his worldview, his personal understanding of our fragile humanity.

As the war was winding down, the U.S. government continued to feel strongly about its responsibility to care for the veterans, wounded in body and spirit. In the latter case, it had to provide for those suffering mentally from their combat duty and had them sent for psychiatric care to specialized hospitals. Following their treatment, the government further wanted to assure future civilian employees, not unlike those seen in *The Best Years of Our Lives,* that the returning veterans were qualified to be hired.[3] The government wished to get rid of the stigma of the shell-shocked soldier as undesirable for employment. It also wanted to inform potential employers that the impaired mental condition of these veterans was just a temporary setback, that they were not madmen, and that they were now on the road to full recovery. With a clean bill of health and the blessing of the government, these men were now ready to reenter civilian life with a positive future ahead of them and should therefore be hired.

The civilian population, however, had long been kept unaware of war trauma. The myth of the returning war hero, courageously defending the weak and victimized against the forces of evil, left no place for exposure of the soldier's own vulnerability. The fear of victims returning as "psychological cripples," "undesirables," or "mental cases," flooding the streets of America after the war created an atmosphere of secrecy and denial, as the government attempted to "fix" as quickly and as quietly as possible the traumatically wounded of World War II.

In late 1945, once again, the psychological scars of war took on a sense of immediacy as veterans' symptoms vaguely reminiscent of World War I cases started filling the hospitals. The tragic shadow of Virginia Woolf's character Septimus, a World War I veteran in her novel *Mrs. Dalloway* lingers on, and we are reminded of the toll war takes on every man, as we witness his throwing himself out of an upper-floor window and falling to his death on the wrought iron fence and cement below.

During World War I, the illness was called "shell shock," and it afflicted countless American soldiers who had battled in the bloody trenches of France. During World War II, the name was changed to "battle fatigue," and finally after years of treating Vietnam War veterans, doctors diagnosed the new illness as *Post Traumatic Stress Disorder* and listed it in the *Diagnostic and Statistical Manual* of the American Psychiatric Association of 1980. The symptoms first described by psychiatrist Abram Kardiner in 1941 in his text *The Traumatic Neuroses of War* are threefold — hyperarousal, constriction, and intrusion — and serve as a coping mechanism. It is the result of the human body's attempt to survive the unsurvivable, a human response to endure that which is inhumane.

Recognizing the vast number of returning soldiers with psychological problems — as many as 500,000 men were said to have been hospitalized for neuropsychiatric disorders in 1945 alone[1] — the U.S. government attempted to alleviate a probable negative social impact with aggressive psychiatric treatment. *Let There Be Light* clearly documents the effectiveness of a variety of treatment programs — from medication to hypnosis and from individual to group talk therapy. The patients display a wide range of symptoms, all telltale signs of their traumatic wartime experience.

The steps toward healing and the amazing programs documented in Huston's film illustrate the remarkable resilience of the human spirit as well as the strides made in the understanding of "mental illness." The soldiers-patients in the documentary exhibit to a high degree the symptoms of Post Traumatic Stress Disorder — hyperarousal, constriction of feelings, and the intrusion of memories through flashbacks and nightmares. Through therapy, these symptoms diminish, and ideally over time the traumatic wartime memories are integrated into the veteran's life, permitting a return to a normal, routine existence.

Although the method sounds straightforward, the path to healing is anything but that, as it twists and turns, often spiraling in upon itself as new memories flood the patient's thoughts, while old ones continually play on the rerun channel. Unable to process the trauma witnessed during the war, these veterans suffer from intensive memories, flashbacks, amnesia, nightmares and panic attacks. Huston's documentation of the initial stages of this arduous healing process attempts to clarify the response of the U.S. government to a serious problem often ignored and misunderstood in nineteenth- and early twentieth century society. "Neuropsychiatric disability also raises more immediate fears, for it is associated with a direct physical threat to the observer and to society ... in fact, societies have long been haunted by fears of the violent potential of veterans with unpredictable mental states."[5] Keeping this tension in mind, one can see the dilemma facing the U.S. government. It needed to address the overwhelmingly large number of psychiatric casualties and offer a plausible reason for effective treatment, as well as provide successful results, so as not to tarnish the image of the courageous soldier triumphantly returning from battle. "In the hopes of finding a rapid, efficacious treatment, military psychiatrists tried to remove the stigma from the stress reactions of combat. It was recognized for the first time that any man could break down under fire and that psychiatric casualties could be predicted in direct proportion to the severity of combat exposure."[6]

The key then was to convince the society at home that the returning veterans, although stressed during the trauma of the war experience itself, were now safe and sound at home. The course of therapies used in *Let There Be Light* illustrated this point perfectly, and yet the government feared a skeptical, judgmental response from the audience, not a sympathetic one.

Ironically, as had occurred with the previous interest in the psyche of veterans returning from World War I, so too, after World War II did the initial fervor about healing the soldier of the traumatic effects of war and studying the long-term effects soon die down. Once soldiers had been "cured" and returned to their units while the war was still going on, or once "cured" at a Veterans Administration Hospital such as Mason General in a short number of weeks, the men were returned to society and their war experiences, regardless of the intensity of their trauma, were put to rest. Sadly, it would not be until the Vietnam War that the staggering long-term effects of Post Traumatic Stress Disorder would emerge, and the truth that such a devastating psychological trauma would never be forgotten. The experiences of World War II — witnessing death and destruction, fearing for one's own life, killing other human beings, forsaking all rules of civilization and morality — permanently shattered the soldiers' vision of the world, down to the very core of their existence. Life went on for these returning veterans, as we see in *Let There Be Light*, yet it was irrevocably altered, tinged with an awareness of the evil that can strike out at any time in an otherwise peaceful existence.

The Film

Situated somewhere between an information film and a propaganda documentary, John Huston's film, first titled, *The Returning Psychoneurotics,* was commissioned by the U.S. Army on June 25, 1945. John Huston visited several army hospitals before choosing the army psychiatric center, Mason General Hospital, located in Brentwood, Long Island. He settled on this hospital since it was the largest on the East Coast and also because of the cooperation and sympathetic guidance of the doctors and officers there. Every week, two groups of seventy-five patients would arrive at the hospital for an eight-week intensive therapy program. For almost three months, day in and day out, Huston and his cameramen, including the well-known Stanley Cortiz (*Magnificent Andersons*), would shoot hundreds of hours of film as they followed one group of men through their program. They would eventually shoot 375,000 feet of film, or a ratio of 72 to 1 based on the one-hour final version of the film. The camera would attempt to get into the psyche of the patients to record their evolution during their treatment at the hospital.

In preparation for the film, Huston had to understand some basic psychiatry and the whole hospitalization process, line up the two camera positions on interviewer and interviewee, and then get the permission of the veterans to film the intensely personal interviews and procedures. He also had to view the film *The Enchanted Cottage* (1945) to get a grasp of the nuances of wartime trauma.[7] Throughout this process, Huston worked closely with Charles Kaufman on a script that would honestly reflect the situation of these victims of combat. In encountering the hidden emotions of these men Huston came to grips with the essence of combat neuroses, far beyond the limited parameters of any textbook on modern psychology.

The film poignantly frames the human longing for home. It begins with the soldiers returning to the United States from combat duty at the close of the war. Then, as the film concludes, it is hoped that they are ready to return home to their loved ones.[8] The prologue to the film appears on the screen:

> Almost 20% of all battle casualties in the American Army during World War II were of a neuropsychiatric nature. The special treatment methods shown in this film, such as hypnosis and narco-synthesis, have been particularly successful in acute cases, such as battle neuroses. Equal success is not to be expected when dealing with peacetime neuroses which are usually of a chronic nature. No scenes were staged. The camera merely recorded what took place in an Army hospital.[9]

The voice of narrator Walter Huston accompanies the images of the soldiers broken in spirit as they pass across the screen. A cortege of soldiers leaves the ship, some in stretchers, others supported by nurses, and a few blinded ones led by another soldier evoking an image of John Sargent's painting of World War I casualties, *Gassed* (1918):

> The guns are quiet now; the papers of peace have been signed and the oceans of the earth are filled with ships coming home. In faraway places men dreamed of this moment, but for some men, the moment is different from the dream. Here is human salvage, the final result of all that metal and fire can do to violate mortal flesh.

Although the soldiers who arrive at Mason General Hospital do not have bandages or crutches, they, too, are wounded, for they are "the casualties of the spirit, the troubled in mind, men who are damaged emotionally." As the ambulances bring the soldiers to the army hospital, the narrator remarks, "Every man has his breaking point, and these, in the fulfillment of their duties as soldiers, were forced beyond the limit of human endurance." The camera pans the faces of the men broken by combat, some plagued with tics and trembling, others with absent stares or paralysis. We are told that these men suffer from fear and apprehension, a sense of impending disaster, and a sense of hopelessness and isolation — all characteristic of trauma induced by wartime experiences, as noted earlier. The common thread in their pain and anguish appears to be death and the fear of death.

Of the seventy-five soldiers that the film highlights, twelve patients initially reveal their anxieties to the interviewing doctors. A wide range of traumatic effects is recorded by the medical staff. A soldier confesses guilt about his friend being shot, while another expresses intense fear of dying while facing a bombing attack. There are other soldiers who stutter, tremble, feel "mixed up." Still others have problems sleeping, still reliving their harrowing days of combat. Two of the twelve soldiers poignantly demonstrate the effects of trauma upon their lives. One soldier says simply, "I got tired of living," and the last one admits, "I took off because I saw too many of my buddies gone. A man can just stand so much."

Part of the therapy is to reconnect these men with their earlier home lives. They are first allowed to make a free long-distance phone call to their families after their months or years of silence. At the same time, the soldiers will start to make a temporary "small home" for themselves in their hospital wards for the next eight to ten weeks.

Very dramatically, the restless night of the traumatized soldier unfolds. "Now in the darkness of the ward emerge shapes born of darkness: terror of things half-remembered, dreams of battle, the torments of fear, uncertainty and loneliness." Caring nurses sensitively allay their fears.

Following reveille and ward inspections, the narrator notes: "Modern psychiatry makes no sharp division between the mind and body. Physical ills often have psychic causes, just as emotional ills have a physical basis." Gone are the clear Cartesian distinctions of body and soul. The Rorschach blot tests and electroencephelograph tests help determine some of the physical and mental causes of the soldiers' neuroses.

At the heart of the film are several diverse cases of trauma. The first of these is a soldier brought in to the doctor by two nurses. His legs are paralyzed. One would think that his is a physical problem, and we are assured that this paralysis is as real as if it were caused by a spinal lesion. It is, however, purely psychological in origin. In this powerful scene, the doctor administers sodium amytal inducing a type of hypnosis. This produces a shortcut to the unconscious mind to find the emotional conflict disturbing the patient, and it will remove the symptoms that impede his recovery. In a hypnotic state, the patient is asked why he feels anxiety. He suggests that he has problems with his sick mother, as well as his overly anxious father, and just wishes the war would be over. The doctor then tells him that he can walk. On screen, with emotional music in the background, the soldier miraculously takes some halting steps and then begins to walk normally. The narrator cautiously warns: "The fact he can walk now does not mean his neurosis is cured, but the way has been opened for therapy to follow."

A second soldier's plight is confronted through hypnosis. The young man experienced amnesia following a shell burst, and he cannot now recall even his own name. In an emotionally charged scene, the soldier enters into a deep sleep and "returns" to Okinawa, where he was under fire. He physically and emotionally relives the bombardment, anxiously trembling as he recounts to the doctor what he senses. He awakens and peacefully recalls his name — the start of his journey toward wholeness.

A third soldier's healing is even more emotional. From battle tensions while in combat in France, he developed a serious but not chronic case of stuttering. After an injection and the soothing words of the doctor, the soldier finds that his tongue is freed. Emotionally he cries out, "I can talk! I can talk! O God, listen, I can talk!" After "the cure," the doctor attempts to find out the cause of the soldier's stuttering and learns that it was an embarrassing scene on the boat going over to Europe. For some reason he did not pronounce an "s" properly, and other soldiers laughed at him. It appears that he later connected this shame with the hissing sounds of the German 88mm shells which terrified him. Now he can continue in therapy to deal with the underlying symptoms of his stuttering, most likely confronting his fear of death for the first time.

Interspersed with these "miraculous" cures is another method of healing — group interaction. Through art, mechanics and carpentry, the soldiers learn to relate to each other and their work in a positive manner. Group sports such as basketball and baseball help them to get out of their isolation and adjust to the company of others.

The group therapy session is very revealing. The patient learns the basic cause of his distress and the need for inner conflicts to be resolved. The lecturing doctor highlights the experience of safety and notes that this goes back to childhood safety. Soldiers open up and confess their inner feelings and earlier experiences during their adolescence. A man who never spoke until age seven, one who stuttered, and another who was very sheltered frankly confront their past.

As the men listen to music, enjoy visitors, and attend classes such as one on starting a small business, the shock and stress of war wear off. Fortunately for these men suffering from trauma, "they are blessed with the natural regenerative powers of youth." They slowly heal and begin to think of the future.

The doctor in a second group therapy session in the film tries to assuage the soldiers' fears of the stigma attached to war neuroses. He puts them at ease by admitting that "All of us have our so-called breaking points" and that the public must get rid of its stereotyped notion of these men as "madmen," as one soldier expressed. In this session, a young man remarks that someone coming to visit him thought that he was going to see something like Bellevue (Mental Hospital), where everyone from the last war would be a maniac. The doctor reassures them, concluding by saying that "You have nothing to hide, nothing to be ashamed of."

While the men return somewhat to normalcy, the signs of their anxiousness to return home become evident, especially in their view of less than ideal food and movies at the hospital. As their therapy is nearing its conclusion, the narrator observes: "No longer is a man shut up within the lonely recesses of himself. He is breaking out of his prison into life, the life that lies ahead, offering infinite possibilities for happiness and sorrow." The doctor in the group therapy session quotes from the Bible, "Man does not live by bread alone," implying there are other elements that are needed in life. He points out that children do not grow up well without safety and confidence, a recurring theme in the sessions. And if these ingredients are missing in their lives, how do you supply them? The doctor's closing advice is meant to penetrate deep in the hearts and minds of the patients. The soldiers are urged to find someone with whom they can find safety and feel accepted and cherished, someone with whom they can sense that they are worthwhile and important. In this way, the veteran who is temporarily healed of his combat neuroses can have the required continuity of feeling secure.[10]

The film comes to a close with images of group sports. Some of the soldiers whose cases were presented in the film play a game of baseball. We see flashbacks to earlier interviews: The stuttering soldier becomes an articulate umpire at the game, while the soldier with paralyzed legs runs the bases with great speed. The narrator cautiously inquires: "How complete is their recovery? Are they well enough to be discharged? It is up to the doctors to decide."

As the soldiers line up to receive their discharge papers, the band symbolically plays "When Johnny Comes Marching Home Again." These soldiers will now return to their homes, their families and friends. The discharging officer encourages them, emphasizing that the responsibility for the postwar society is on their shoulders. As the soldiers leaving on the bus joyously wave back to the nurses and doctors who helped in their healing, we are left with the closing of one bitter chapter of their lives and the opening of another more hope-filled one.[11]

The Critics

Several critics point out the intensity of the material in this documentary. Richard Jameson calls it an "emotionally luminous vérité document about the rehabilitation of shell shock victims."[12] In *The People's Films*, Richard Dyer MacCann comments, "there is gained through watching these tortured men, with their torn memories and their longing for safety, a new awareness of the damages of war and the strange paths some men must walk when they return to peace."[13] David Denby of *New York Magazine* sees parallels here to the brutally honest sixties' documentaries of Fred Wiseman and Allan King but also compares some of the images to the forties' wartime films: "Polite, angelically innocent, beautiful, but not handsome, the men are guilt-ridden versions of those boundlessly eager proletarian heroes in the feature films of the period. Seeing them break down is almost unbearable."[14]

When John Huston finished editing the film, he planned to show it to a gathering of friends at the Museum of Modern Art in New York in 1946. Before the screening began, two MPs confiscated the film. The U.S. War Department and the U.S. Army felt that the "warrior" image of the U.S. soldier should be maintained, as Huston once pointed out.[15] A film like *Let There Be Light* was diametrically opposed to this image, revealing veterans shattered by combat. The decision was made by the War Department not to release the film to the general public for fear it would give the wrong impression of the army. Lawrence Grobel comments on this decision: "It was too unsettling, it opened a whole Pandora's box of the evils of war and the effects on not only the vanquished but also the victors."[16] The U.S. Army felt that the public was not ready for these shocking images of the soldiers in varying stages of trauma. This act of censorship, in a sense, was seen by Huston and others as a "corporate denial" of the effects of war.[17] Huston, as quoted by David Desser, interpreted the ban as follows: "What I think was really behind it [the banning of the film] was that the authorities considered it to be more shocking, embarrassing perhaps to them, for a man to suffer emotional distress than to lose a leg, or part of his body. Hardly masculine, I suppose they would say."[18] Huston further noted in an interview in 1973, "Some of the brass said that there was a question of invasion of the privacy of the men shown as patients in the film. The men themselves, however, after they recovered, said that they as a group were all in favor of the film being shown."[19] Richard Dyer Mac-Cann reflects how important it would have been to show this film to an American audience in 1946:

> That it was not shown widely at a time when many young men were returning from experiences of terror is a thing to be regretted, for its spirit of compassion is such as to leave almost any audience chastened and changed."[20]

The film and its therapeutic message nonetheless would lie dormant without an audience for almost thirty-five years.

The Reopening

In 1980, there was a campaign spearheaded by the documentary's producer, Ray Stark, Jack Valenti of the Motion Picture Association of America, and Vice President Walter Mondale to release the film. The film was finally released and screened at the Los Angeles County Museum on November 8, 1980, and then shown on KCET-TV (Los Angeles) to very favorable reviews, as part of the war trilogy with commentary interspersed by Huston. The commercial release took place on January 16, 1981. In May of that year, it was screened at a small theater at the Cannes Film Festival.[21] At its public release, the film revealed a very intense and historical insight into the nature of psychiatry and trauma studies in a postwar America.

This film was important to Huston in several ways. He felt it gave him an insight into the fragility of the human psyche and human behavior, and it also helped him understand Freudian analysis in great depth.[22] It would also make a profound impact upon him. He says in a 1973 interview with Gene Phillips, "To me it was an extraordinary experience — almost a religious experience."[23] In his memoir, *An Open Book*, published in 1980, Huston still called it a "religious experience" and elaborates on it: "It made me begin to realize that the primary ingredient in psychological health is love: the ability to give love and receive it."[24] The new title, itself drawn from the poetic narrative of Genesis, would harken back to the dawn of creation: "And God said, 'Let there be light,' and there was light" (Genesis 1:3). As with birth and rebirth, the production became for him one of the most hopeful and optimistic experiences he had had in filmmaking. His very positive conclusion after filming for three months the seared souls of the returning soldiers was that there *is* life after trauma. Despite human frailty, there is resurrection. However, on a cautionary note, Huston would still assert that although wounds heal, deep emotional scars may still remain.

Charles Champlin, in his review, wisely assesses the power of the film:

> It is, by any standards, an uncommonly subtle and dramatic motion picture, an affecting insight into the *troubled silences* (authors' emphasis) after the battles and the parades.[25]

These haunting silences on the part of the patients and the unwarranted silence brought on by government censorship have thus made this intriguing film a milestone in both documentary filmmaking and the study of trauma.[26]

NOTES

1. For a solid discussion of the genre of the war film, *see* Thomas Doherty, *Projections of War: Hollywood, American Culture, and World War II* (New York: Columbia University Press, 1993).

2. Peter S. Greenberg, "Saints and Stinkers: The *Rolling Stones* Interview" in *John Huston: Interviews*, Robert Emmet Long, ed. (Jackson: University Press of Mississippi, 2001), 116.

3. Gary Edgerton, "Revisiting the Recordings of Wars Past: Remembering the Documentary Trilogy of John Huston" in *Reflections in a Male Eye: John Huston and the American Experience*, Gaylyn Studlar and David Desser, eds. (Washington, D.C.: Smithsonian Institute, 1993), 44.

4. David A. Gerber, "Heroes and Misfits: The Troubled Social Reintegration of Disabled Veterans in *The Best Years of Our Lives*, in *Disabled Veterans in History*, David A. Gerber, ed. (Ann Arbor: University of Michigan Press, 2000), 73.

5. Gerber, "Introduction," 7.

6. Judith Lewis Herman, *Trauma and Recovery: The Aftermath of Violence — From Domestic Abuse to Political Terror* (New York: Basic/Harper Collins, 1992), 24–25.

7. David Desser, "The Wartime Films of John Huston: *Film Noir* and the Emergence of the Therapeutic" in *Reflections in a Male Eye*, p. 27. The film *The Enchanted Cottage*, with Dorothy McGuire as a simple young woman and Robert Young as the returning soldier, provides a melodramatic view of the psychological repercussions of the veteran's facial disfigurement. This film would be one of Dory Schary's RKO and United Artists features about various physical and mental casualties of war—*I'll Be Seeing You* (1944–1945), *They Dream of Home* (1945), and *Till the End of Time* (1946). The most realistic of the period is still *The Best Years of Our Lives* (1946), where Harold Russell, without hands, plays a returning GI, disabled during the war.

8. Lesley Brill, *John Huston's Filmmaking* (New York: Cambridge University Press, 1997), 115. Brill emphasizes the theme of "home" in *Let There Be Light* and reflects on how it dominates Huston's opus.

9. For the full text of *Let There Be Light*, see Robert Hughes, ed., *Book 2: Films of Peace and War* (New York: Grove, 1962), 205–33.

10. The soldiers who are being released after their eight-week program will be quite different from the more psychotic cases which would require more serious treatment. Not included in the film are intense shock therapy sessions which, John Huston noted, in the 1940s were very violent to body and mind. In *Open Book* (New York: Alfred A. Knopf, 1980), p. 23, he describes how several staff members were needed to hold down the soldier's body as it arched from the shock treatment.

11. For a solid discussion of recent views of the aftereffects of war, see Patrick J. Bracken and Celia Petty, eds, *Rethinking the Trauma of War* (New York/London: Free Association, 1998).

12. Richard T. Jameson, "John Huston" in *Perspectives on John Huston*, Stephen Cooper, ed. (New York: G. K. hall, 1994), 50.

13. Richard Dyer MacCann, *The People's Films: A Political History of U.S. Government Motion Pictures* (New York: Hastings House, 1973), 170.

14. David Denby, review, *New York Magazine* (January 19, 1981): 44.

15. Huston, *Open Book*, 25.

16. Lawrence Grobel, *The Hustons* (New York: Avon, 1989), 273.

17. Brill, 112.

18. Desser, "The Wartime Films," 29. Desser also suggests that this film initiates Huston's rethinking and revisioning of traditional modes of masculinity and male behavior.

19. Gene D. Phillips, "Talking with John Huston" in *John Huston: Interviews,* 38.

20. MacCann, 170.

21. I viewed the film there and recalled feeling like a voyeur, most uncomfortable in watching the neuroses of the soldiers play out. I remember feeling very sympathetic toward these young men who were placed in the line of fire and who were then considered as "basket cases" by the less than politically correct society of two decades ago, a time when Post Traumatic Stress Disorder was being studied more seriously in light of the returning Vietnam veterans.

22. From his experiences with psychiatry at Mason General Hospital and his discussions with the very helpful medical staff, Huston later went on to create his portrait of the pioneer of the field in *Freud* (1962).

23. Phillips, 38.

24. Huston, *An Open Book* (New York: Knopf), 125.

25. Charles Champlin, "Huston Wartime Films on KCET," *Los Angeles Times* (April 30, 1981): 9.

26. We acknowledge our gratitude to Ronald Marsh and Paul Schutz for their invaluable assistance with the research.

5

Patriot or Pariah? The Impact of War on Family Relationships

MARILYN J. MATELSKI

In the last several decades, patriotism in America was often seen as more a mixture of romance and sentimentality (shown at World Series games and Independence Day celebrations and in Arnold Schwarzenegger films) than a fusion of fear, sacrifice, honor and potential death. On September 11, 2001, this quixotic worldview took a radical turn. Americans faced potential attacks by nameless and faceless terrorists (halfway around the world or perhaps in their own backyards), congressional calls for the restoration of mandatory military conscription, and a very real threat of world war and mass destruction. The definition of patriotism has now become more somber and dangerous. More Americans are exploring what love of country really means. For some, it may mean fighting a war thousands of miles from home, and for others, it may mean challenging the very concept of marching to war. At both ends of the spectrum, strong patriotic arguments can be made.

Not surprisingly, however, when opposing views collide, bonds are often broken — tragic enough for friends and acquaintances, but utterly devastating when occurring within a household. This chapter examines the ways in which opposing views — both patriotic — can fracture family relationships. Two movies serve as reference points for analysis — *The Way We Were* (highlighting America's political polarity during the Red Scare of the late 1940s and early 1950s) and *The War at Home* (dramatizing the visceral strife in many American homes during the Vietnam era).

At first glance, *The Way We Were* and *The War at Home* seem to be an "odd couple" of comparative films. First, they are at opposite ends of the money spectrum — *The War at Home* was shot with a $4.2 million budget (barely enough to cover the stars' salaries in *The Way We Were*, even in 1973). Second, one was a major theatrical release, marketed heavily with two of the most popular stars at that time; the other, while featuring highly respected actors, was introduced at regional film festivals, barely making it on the marquee before moving to the video stores. Third, *The Way We Were* spans several decades of war; *The War at Home* takes place during a four-day Thanksgiving weekend. And finally, one has become a romantic classic while the other is hardly ever mentioned in most movie or video guides.

Despite the marketing and financial differences, there are some striking artistic similarities between the two films. Both were adapted from another source (*The Way We Were* from a book; *The War at Home* from a stage play). Both have "A" stories that focus on relationship, with war serving as the background ("B") story. Most importantly, both discuss issues of morality, honor and patriotism. Katie Morosky (*The Way We Were*) and Jeremy Collier (*The War at Home*) — the protagonists in each drama — love their country but object vehemently to its policies against those who oppose them at home and abroad. Their families and friends view them as odd and perhaps even brainwashed but definitely unpatriotic. Rather than criticize the U.S. government, both Katie and Jeremy are chided to either go along with the existing national sentiment (because nothing will really change anyway) or back the government's stand (right or wrong).

The most important similarity between *The Way We Were* and *The War at Home*, however, is the issue of family communication — how each member of a family (or marriage) copes (or not) with conflicting perspectives on war and love of country.

Family Relationships and Balance

Among the earliest and most studied topics of interpersonal communication is cognitive consistency — the internal need for balance (or homeostasis) in a person's life. Fritz Heider was one of the first scholars to study this aspect of communication and his balance theory has been credited as the touchstone for later research in this area.

Heider's model concentrated on the relationship between two individuals when confronted with disparate views on a particular topic or person. He postulated that the need for balance in the relationship would almost always supercede the point of conflict. In short, the relationship was more important than the issue, and the psychological tension caused in an unbalanced relationship "becomes relieved only when change within the situation takes place in such a way that a state of balance is achieved."[1]

One of the problems with Heider's paradigm, however, was its black-and-white perspective on the relationship vis-à-vis the issue. There were no degrees of agreement or disagreement; all issues were seen as equal, not prioritized as in the real world. To address these concerns, C. E. Osgood (along with others) developed a congruity theory. While this was quite similar to balance theory, Osgood created a model that could predict not only degree of change, but possible direction. Using his semantic differential to measure the amount of a person's liking of another (or of the issue), he could predict how much that person might change attitudes to maintain continuity with the other. Later, Osgood teamed with Percy Tannenbaum to include media as "the other" in their research.

Around the same time as Osgood and Tannenbaum's work in congruity theory, Leon Festinger presented his work on cognitive dissonance — concentrating more on the intrapersonal dilemma of resolving conflict. Festinger postulated that a person would make one of three choices while trying to achieve consonance: either (1) pretend that the dissonance did not take place, i.e., ignore it; (2) see the dissonance as an exception to the norm and, therefore, discount it; or (3) change his or her attitude to some degree. Festinger also suggested that "in addition to trying to reduce it the person will actively avoid situations and information which would likely increase the dissonance."[2]

These theories are important to consider when addressing the issue of balance in interpersonal relationships. They seem to address homeostasis (or the lack of) from an individual standpoint — choices possible for one person when confronted with unfamiliar or contradictory information. These choices become much more difficult and limited when the individual is part of a couple or family unit, as demonstrated in both *The Way We Were* and *The War at Home*. Still, they are useful in describing both the overall gestalt and individual mindsets of the characters in adversarial situations.

The Way We Were *and Family Dissonance*

Written by Arthur Laurents,[3] directed by Sydney Pollack,[4] and produced by both Pollack and Ray Stark,[5] *The Way We Were* is the story of doomed lovers at opposite ends of the political spectrum amidst the backdrop of antiwar protest, government blacklisting and Cold War fervor. In the opening scenes of the movie, college student Katie Morosky (played by Barbra Streisand) immediately reveals her political passion as she leads a campus peace movement in 1937. Her speech, interrupted from time to time by WASP hecklers, nonetheless draws enthusiasm and applause by students like Hubbell Gardner (portrayed by Robert Redford).

Hubbell and his friends "JJ" (Bradford Dillman), Judianne (Susan Blakely) and "Carol Ann" (Lois Chiles) characterize the typical upper-middle-class, "privileged" college students in pre–World War II America—living their lives within the protective bubble of campus pranks, fraternity parties and formal dances, while ignoring the significant world events taking place around them. But they are not unreachable, as Katie Morosky proves when she appeals for a campuswide rally:

KATIE: What are you scared of? The Russians don't want anybody in Spain but the Spanish. Is that scary? They're communists, yes, but they want total disarmament now. Is that scary? Hitler and Mussolini are using the Spanish earth as testing ground for what THEY want — another world war. Is that scary? You're darned right it is! There's only one thing to be scared of ... and it's not me ... not the Young Communist League ... and it's not the Red bogeyman. You be scared of anybody, any place who will not stand up for world peace now! (*applause*)

You're really ... uh ... really something. You're really beautiful. No, I mean it. You're really beautiful. You're the best, the brightest, the most committed generation this country has ever had. And that's why you're here today striking for peace. Why they're striking on almost every single campus in this country! They're taking that pledge now — so share your solidarity by taking it with them. I refuse to support ... c'mon, c'mon ... I ref ... c'mon EVERYBODY ON YOUR FEET! I refuse to ... c'mon ... that's right — on your feet ... c'mon ... EVERYBODY!

The students follow her lead, ending the rally with thunderous applause.

Hubbell Gardner is clearly moved by Katie's passion at this event and later reveals both depth and acumen in a creative writing course they both take. Katie is attracted not only to Hubbell's looks— he also seems to have a good mind, considerable talent and a political conscience unknown to his other friends. Hubbell, on the other hand, admires Katie's drive, determination, and independence of thought. Though from two totally different worlds— an upper-middle-class, WASP majority and a working-class Jewish minority — the couple form a bond of friendship and, later, love.

But politics always lurks in the background, creating constant ten-

sion and trouble in their relationship. Times are turbulent, both eco-
nomically and socially, in the United States (as well as the world) during
the 1940s and 1950s, and the characters' tempers often flare over political
events. Katie and Hubbell are often at odds—she joining political groups
to change the world while he goes out with his old college pals to "remember the good old days." With each tumultuous episode, their relationship
gradually loses its fragile balance, even when the couple is seemingly
unified over an event such as mourning the death of a president.

When Franklin Delano Roosevelt died, many Americans mourned a
great leader, but some celebrated the end of his socialist ideals. Katie Morosky
encounters this reaction when she attends an informal gathering with
Hubbell's old college pals, and they hear the news that the president has
passed away. JJ, Judianne and Carol Ann even try to lighten the atmosphere
by making fun of Eleanor Roosevelt, but Katie will have none of it.

Katie continues to challenge Hubbell's complacency after they move
to Hollywood, where he gives up his career as a fledgling novelist to become
a screenwriter. Not only does this decision intensify the personal conflict
between the couple as time goes on, but it also becomes highly political,
as tensions mount over suspicions of communist infiltration in the movie
industry. Being a vocal Jewish liberal brings Katie Morosky—and by association, her husband, Hubbell—under the scrutiny of the House Un-
American Activities Committee (HUAC).

HUAC AND HOLLYWOOD

In post–World War II (and Cold War) America, anyone professing
(or sympathizing with) Marxist ideology was viewed as potentially trai-
torous to American democracy, especially those who were influential in
areas of mass communication. In *Nightmare in Red*, author Richard M.
Fried writes:

> The mid-century Red Scare targeted ideas as well as people. Critics
> feared that it had spawned "thought control" and conformity and fed
> deep springs of anti-intellectualism. Commentator Elmer Davis warned
> that "many 'local movements' constituted a nationwide 'general attack'
> not only on schools and colleges and libraries, on teachers and text-
> books, but on all people who think and write ... in short, on the free-
> dom of the mind." Many purveyors of ideas were charged with having
> communist or front connections, indoctrinating the young with alien
> principles, or holding views that aided the communist cause or con-
> tributed to forms of moral decay associated with the advance of com-
> munism. As part of the counteroffensive, many Americans labored to
> eliminate noxious sorts of entertainment, thought or culture—and
> thinkers and performers.[6]

At first, anticommunist talk seemed ludicrous, as illustrated in *The Way We Were* during a backyard barbecue conversation at the estate of Hubbell's studio colleague George Bissinger (played by Patrick O'Neal):

> GEORGE: Can you believe that this village band of Hollywood intellectuals is plotting to overthrow the government? Oh, they couldn't overthrow Louella Parsons!
>
> RHEA: Yet in '37, in Munich, Hitler was a joke, too.

With time, the fear of foreign espionage grew incrementally; as such, communist sympathizers were seen as much more invasive than Hitler's storm troops. "Fellow travelers" (as they were often called) could hide easily because they looked and spoke like other Americans. But they represented the devil incarnate, threatening mass extinction through their alleged commitment to help build the Soviet Union's secret nuclear bomb arsenal. In one scenario (broadcast in the early 1950s), host (and then Screen Actors Guild president) Ronald Reagan spoke to his television audience of impending doom:

> In the traditional motion picture story, the villains are usually defeated. The ending is a happy one. I can make no such promise for the picture you're about to watch. The story isn't over. You in the audience are part of the conflict. How we meet the communist challenge depends on you.[7]

As viewers watch the characters in this drama face almost certain extinction with the impending communist takeover, a narrator comments (over a clock ticking down for atomic bomb detonation): "Fortunately, we can move the clock back. The time is not yet. Let us pray that it never happens."[8]

The threat of a potential communist takeover in the United States became so great in 1947, a congressional committee (HUAC), under the leadership of New Jersey Republican J. Parnell Thomas, was formed to investigate potential un-American activities and associations. HUAC's domain included organized labor movements, potential Soviet infiltration within the federal government and insidious propaganda within the film industry. Hollywood was perhaps hit most deeply because of (1) the tremendous popularity of movies during this time, providing potential for massive anti-American messages, and (2) the number of Jews in Hollywood known for their social activism and Marxist sympathies.

To be fair, some members of Hollywood's movie-making system may have been communist sympathizers, contributing to the party during the 1930s; however, most fears of subversive activity were completely groundless. The lack of evidence did not seem to matter. In September 1947, chairman Thomas and his committee subpoenaed 41 witnesses (19 of who were deemed "unfriendly" for their refusal to disclose their political affiliations). Eleven were asked specifically about membership in the Communist Party. One of these, German émigré Bertolt Brecht, left shortly after being brought before the House Un American Committee, resulting in a final count of the infamous "Hollywood Ten," who refused to testify by reason of the First Amendment.

At first, the HUAC hearings were closed, but within months, people were called to testify in open proceedings. As documented in *Blacklist: Hollywood on Trial,* many popular celebrities (like director George Bissinger in *The Way We Were*) eagerly volunteered to reflect on "rampant" communist influences in the film-making community, including:

ROBERT TAYLOR (actor): I think in the past four or five years specifically, I've seen more indications which seem to me to be signs of communist activity in Hollywood and the motion picture industry.... I suppose the most readily determined field in which it could be cited would be in the preparation of scripts, specifically in the writing of those you read to us. I have seen things from time to time which appeared to me to be slightly on the "pink" side, shall we say.

ADOLPH MENJOU (actor): I have seen things that I thought were against what I considered good Americanism.... I've seen pictures I've thought shouldn't have been made. This is a foul philosophy, this communistic thing. I would move to the state of Texas if it ever came here because I think the Texans would kill them on sight.

GARY COOPER (actor): I've never read Karl Marx and I don't know the basis of communism beyond what I've picked up from hearsay. From what I've heard, I don't like it because it isn't on the level.

In *The Way We Were*, Katie Morosky's friend Rhea Edwards (played by Allyn Ann McLeary) describes the insanity of these times when she discusses the House Un-American Activities Committee in the safety of her kitchen. Almost everyone in Hollywood seen as an "unfriendly witness" before the committee risks being fired and put on an official blacklist. In short, Rhea says, "It's an open season for witch hunters and ... umm ... stool pigeons. Now, the problem is how to convince the public that a stool pigeon is a hero."

And things continued to worsen. By 1950, Senator Joseph McCarthy had replaced J. Parnell Thomas, and within two years, the HUAC hearings became even more surrealistic, forcing witnesses to identify persons thought to be "suspicious." Most claims of subversive behavior in the film industry were often more fanciful than factual, as authors McGilligan and Buhle suggest in their book, *Tender Comrades: A Backstory of the Hollywood Blacklist*. They trace the metamorphosis of HUAC (under McCarthy's leadership) into a certifiable "hanging party," indicting screenwriters for one or two lines in a script. One of the committee's most infamous actions taken was against Dalton Trumbo for one line in the 1943 film *Tender Comrade*: "Share and share alike — that's democracy!"[9] Further, the film title — assumed by McCarthy's House Un-American Activities Committee to be part of a Communist Party code for fellow travelers — was actually taken from Robert Louis Stevenson's affectionate description of his wife.[10]

Thankfully, McCarthy's witch-hunt finally ended in 1954, after his flaming paranoia discredited his office as well as the entire blacklisting furor. But the damage was done. Some writers, directors, producers and actors falsely accused of communist subversion were deprived of rewarding careers for decades, if not permanently. Some died penniless and in oblivion, while others fled the country and lived anonymous lives in Europe. Friendly witnesses like Elia Kazan (thought, by some, to be the basis for the character of George Bissinger in *The Way We Were*) were later ostracized in Hollywood for aiding and abetting a group of crazed politicians in ruinous accusation and ultimate censure.

In *The Way We Were*, this enigma is best illustrated by a fiery argument between Katie and Hubbell after Hubbell rescues her from a mob scene during a demonstration in support of the Hollywood Ten. The couple mirrors the conflict between many former friends, lovers and professional colleagues about truth, justice and integrity, especially during times of political crisis. Hubbell starts the argument by voicing his anger over Katie's need to "tell off the world." Katie counters by saying that it's not a matter of telling off the world, it's an issue of integrity — of standing up for one's beliefs. Hubbell doesn't buy her argument:

KATIE: Hubbell, you are telling me to close my eyes and to watch people being destroyed so that you can go on working. Working in a town that doesn't have spine enough to stand up for anything but making a blessed buck!

HUBBELL: I'm telling you that people — PEOPLE — are more important than any goddamn witch-hunt. You and me. Not causes. Not principles.

KATIE: Hubbell, people ARE their principles.

At this point in their marriage, Katie and Hubbell are unable to balance their feelings of love, given the dissonance of their opposing views of who they are as individuals. Their political differences have always been in the background. More importantly, they are polar opposites when it comes to defining what it means to love one's country. Katie interprets patriotism as critiquing her country when she feels it's in the wrong. Hubbell, on the other hand, doesn't want to rock the boat — that the best way to be loyal to one's country is to weather each political storm as it happens and then to wait for life to return to normal. After years of debating each other's political philosophies, they discover that their differences are too great to maintain their marriage. The result is devastating ... but necessary to achieve some sort of balance in each of their lives.

THE WAY WE WERE AND COGNITIVE CONSISTENCY

Katie and Hubbell provide a perfect prototype for the cognitive consistency theories discussed earlier in this chapter. Heider's balance theory — the decision to compromise on issues to maintain a homeostatic relationship — works for most of the film. After Hubbell moves to Hollywood, becomes a "mouthpiece" for the studio system, and grows increasingly troubled by Katie's protests against the HUAC hearings, he decides that the issue of his wife's social activism overshadows their relationship. To achieve balance in his life, he must choose to give up the marriage, rather than face more distress in his otherwise orderly life (with his professional "family").

Relatedly, using Osgood and Tannenbaum's congruity continuum, neither Hubbell nor Katie is likely to be persuaded to change or alter their political views. In fact, as the movie develops, they move farther away from each other, not closer. As Osgood and Tannenbaum have asserted, persons who are on opposite ends of a specific belief spectrum can rarely, if ever, be persuaded to move to the other end or even to a more compromising, neutral position. Thus, the story of star-crossed lovers, doomed from the start by opposing world views is both legendary and genuine. For a time, other factors (e.g., physical attraction, romantic interludes and mutual friends) may blur the blemishes of the relationship, but sooner or later, these dissipate, creating a reflective mirror that must be scrutinized.

Once acknowledged, several possibilities emerge to regain balance in the relationship. According to Festinger, Katie and Hubbell would have had several choices: (1) to ignore their continued conflicts; (2) to characterize each argument as an exception to their otherwise blissful relationship; or (3) either change the relationship or end it.

In *The Way We Were*, Katie and Hubbell seem to go through all three stages. In the opening scenes, Hubbell minimizes Katie's social activism as coinciding with monumental world events as well as her youth and economic class. He later tries to move her into a new geographic area and social milieu; but discovers (much to his disappointment) that Katie will not change her political convictions or her sense of social justice — even if it means Hubbell's loss of face and potential employment. He no longer feels that love is enough and, to regain his own perceptual balance, must end the relationship.

Katie, on the other hand, loves both Hubbell and political causes, and believes that if he can give up his WASP college friends, his social conscience will emerge. Her faith in Hubbell's potential, created through her admiration of his reflective written work, is soon challenged by his decision to move to Hollywood's celluloid world. She follows him with little question, denying that the move represents Hubbell's true ambition. Even after building frustration over nasty encounters with Hubbell's college chums, Katie discounts these experiences as exceptions to Hubbell's basic character — as a socially responsible, politically active adult. While Hubbell behaves innocuously at several points during the Soviet-American friendship activities during World War II, hearing of President Roosevelt's death and responding to initial threats of the 1950s' communist witch-hunt, he still seems (to her) open to independent thought and different worldviews. Unfortunately, her fantasy world of romance comes to an abrupt end when she discovers his affair with an old college flame — and more significantly — during their all-too-frequent arguments about people and principles. At this point, Katie can no longer deny or minimize the couple's philosophical and political differences. Her only choice is to agree with Hubbell that the relationship should end. After a painful divorce, the couple meet years later (while Katie is conducting an antinuclear protest) — both sad at the failure of their marriage but relatively content with the balance in their lives and new mates.

The War at Home *and Family Dissonance*

The War at Home picks up familial discord and the historical timeline where *The Way We Were* ends, with the U.S. entry into Vietnam amid a Cold War backdrop. Based on a true story, the film takes place in November 1972 (over the Thanksgiving weekend) in a small Texas town. Jeremy Collier, a Vietnam vet, returns to celebrate the holiday with his parents— Bob, a car salesman (Martin Sheen), and Maurine (Kathy Bates), a ditzy religious, born-again Southern Baptist homemaker — and his younger sister, Karen (Kimberly Williams). But the mood is hardly celebratory. In fact, the Colliers bicker over who stole Maurine's homemade peanut brittle, how to dress for dinner, and why Jeremy refuses to say grace at breakfast. These seemingly petty arguments evolve into something much more visceral and frightening, however, as Jeremy battles demons from Vietnam as well as his father's inability to relate to his horror of combat or the reality of war.

At first (and in accord with Festinger's cognitive dissonance theory), most of the family ignores Jeremy's "bad" behavior — Bob busily finds pictures to give to an aunt for a collage, and Maurine bustles around, fussing about whether to serve Jeremy a Coke or a Dr. Pepper, whether he's too hot or too cold, whether he should get a good night's sleep, and so on. Karen, who is a bit more realistic about her brother's apparent posttraumatic stress, tells her parents about a recent symposium on Vietnam vets. She raises concerns about returning military personnel who are having trouble readjusting to their life at home. But she barely touches upon the topic before Bob, her father, tells her to stay out of trouble and to keep their family problems to herself.

This is far from the end of a perfectly awful weekend. As the holiday progesses, Jeremy's bitterness and resentment — always present — continue to erupt without warning. His mother, Maurine, becomes one of his first victims on Thanksgiving morning when she tries to create a holiday mood by singing Bible songs to rouse her family for a special breakfast. Maurine's incessant juvenile chatter as well as her shrill chiding to "wakey up" (reminiscent of Edith Bunker on *All in the Family*) irritates everyone, but Jeremy is especially aggravated. He tries to control his anger, but he is barely seated at the table before Maurine brings up what turns out to be an explosive topic: her missing peanut brittle. Within moments, this seemingly inane question turns into a full-blown argument over Jeremy's integrity. Maurine then wisely decides to drop the topic, justifying this incident (in keeping with Festinger's cognitive dissonance theory) as an anomaly to Jeremy's otherwise cheerful demeanor.

While humorous to the film audience, this breakfast scene suggests a more serious tone to the film. Jeremy wants his family to see that he's been ruined, mostly because of being forced by his father into accepting the military draft, rather than being helped (or even allowed) to live in Canada. After entering the service, he was then forced to go to Vietnam and to return to a life he hates. But no one seems to be listening.

Several painful incidents later in the film, Jeremy's bitterness toward Bob becomes more ugly, visceral and frightening as he recounts his experiences in Vietnam and his return as a "damaged" veteran, all the while threatening to shoot his father:

JEREMY: I know how to do things I don't want to do. See, I've done all this before but you weren't there. That's how I know how, see. It was O.K., sort of, but I didn't think it was THEN. But he'd already killed four of us. While we were on patrol. It turned out he was just trying to scare us off. But he made the sergeant mad so it didn't work. You don't even know what I'm talking about, do you?

(Jeremy then tells the horror story of murdering a Viet Cong.)

(To Bob) You killed those people. With your f**king duty and your f**king embarrassment.

BOB: You — that's not fair —

JEREMY: No, it's not f**king fair. That's just what I said. It's not fair, you shit. And he got up on his knees, and he said, it's not fair, and I blew your f**king brains out all over the top of that hill. I killed you. I killed you over and over again just to survive, man, I killed you everywhere I could find you. And here I am, I get home, and here I am and you're still here. Here you still are. Kicking me out of my own house with a couple of thousand bucks and a word about what is right for me to do. I killed those people over there for nothing. It was for nothing. Nothing. Nothing. All the time I thought I was doing it, it was only you I wanted. It was you. It was you.

No one in the Collier family can deny the rift anymore. As Festinger's work on cognitive consistency would suggest, Bob, Maurine and Karen must reconstruct their family relationship, which means cutting Jeremy out of their lives in order to return to some semblance of domestic harmony.

But who was the patriot? Who was the pariah? An interesting dilemma emerges. Jeremy insists that he is the most honest, truthful and perhaps patriotic person in the family because he loves his country enough to resist when he feels it has been led into senseless combat. Bob, on the other hand, believes in "my country, right or wrong." Ironically, however (as Jeremy points out), Bob has never had to participate in a controversial war — Jeremy was the one forced to live by Bob's notion of patriotism.

The Vietnam War at Home

The battle between Jeremy and Bob mirrors many family clashes during the Vietnam conflict. Those who went to fight overseas felt betrayed by those who demonstrated against U.S. intervention. Protesters, however, felt they'd seen the bigger picture and were exercising their democratic right — and duty — to dispute a political policy that seemed imperialistic and unwise. Both sides felt they were true patriots, and each felt the other was disloyal. Caught in the middle of these two disparate positions were many "neutral" family members as well as some returning Vietnam veterans, who had participated in the horror and hopelessness of military intervention, only to return as injured (sometimes), drug addicted, psychologically damaged misfits — hardly the hailed, heroic figures they'd expected to become (like their fathers and grandfathers). To these vets, Vietnam had taken away their pride, their sense of honor, and (perhaps most importantly) their innocence. They had failed in their mission overseas and had become an embarrassment at home.

Indeed, Ronnie D. Lipschutz, in *Cold War Fantasies: Film, Fiction and Foreign Policy* notes that one of the defining differences between the Vietnam conflict and the wars that preceded it was the emotional reality of the war versus its political legitimacy, which, in turn, leads to a sort of bipolarism in its retelling:

> From the American perspective, the Vietnam War did have a great deal to do with psychology, as opposed to politics, which might be one reason why it remains so traumatic today (especially for those who aspire to the presidency). In a curious fashion, moreover, both films and novels seem to contain what is almost an air of accusation *against* the (South) Vietnamese, who are made to seem as somehow having *enticed* the United States into the morass of Southeast Asia.[11]

In point of fact, Vietnam, like many other Cold War conflicts, was a commitment made by the United States in the waning days of World War II. At the Potsdam summit, American, Russian and British leaders all agreed that after the Japanese surrender to Allied Forces, Vietnam (then called French Indochina) would first be divided at the sixteenth parallel — with Chinese occupation to the north and British occupation to the south — and later returned to the French. France returned to reclaim its colony in 1946, but almost immediately, civil war ensued between the Vietnamese nationalists (known as the "Viet Minh") and the French army. By year's end, the entire country was enveloped in a conflict known as the First Indochina War.[12]

Three years later — in 1949 — fear of Soviet atomic power, along with the rise of communism in China under Mao Zedong and growing tensions in Korea, caused the United States to invest more resources (both military and economic) into Southeast Asia. American commitment grew steadily for several years as the First Indochina War continued. By 1954, the French were driven out of Vietnam, but by now, the United States was much more fully obligated to stay in the region to protect what had become its own interests. While maintaining its presence in the South, American diplomats continued to try to negotiate with North Vietnamese leader Ho Chi Minh. But the situation was hopeless. Twenty years of unresolved conflict followed, fomenting a mindset removed from reality. Lipschutz contends:

> Vietnam, as a "syndrome," has little to do with the actual war. Instead, it has become an indicator of faith in America's "exceptionalism" as well as a question of loyalty to that ideology. Inasmuch as the North could not have defeated the Americans via raw military power, the loss must have been the work of "traitors" to the faith, in Washington, and the body politic at large.... Had everyone kepth the faith, the United States could not have lost the war.[13]

Vietnam, as former CBS television correspondent Bernard Kalb has described is "shrapnel in our hearts—inoperable and irradicable. Impossible to move. There to stay."[14] And the ones who suffer most from the wounds are those who have lost relationships, in addition to the people they loved.

Final Thoughts

As both *The Way We Were* and *The War at Home* demonstrate, the effects of war can often be devastating, especially on family structures where members do not share similar — or even neutral — perspectives. No matter how much a mother, father, sister, brother, husband or wife may love one another, the heated interpersonal exchanges during times of political upheaval can be heartbreaking, ultimately leading to permanent alienation and perhaps total dissolution of the relationship. Clearly, there are more casualties in times of war than the victims of combat, which may explain why so many films are made in this genre.

NOTES

1. Fritz Heider, *The Psychology of Interpersonal Relations* (New York: John Wiley, 1958), 180.

2. Leon Festinger, *A Theory of Cognitive Dissonance* (Stanford: Stanford University Press, 1957), 3.

3. Arthur Laurents was the primary writing force behind the picture, having adapted the screenplay from his original novel. Writers David Rayfiel and Alvin Sargent also assisted in the final draft. Laurents's other writing credits include *Rope* (film,

1948), *Home of the Brave* (play, 1949), *Anna Lucasta* (film, 1949), *Caught* (film, 1949), *Summertime* (film, 1955), *Anastasia* (film, 1956), *Bonjour, Tristesse* (film, 1958), *West Side Story* (play, 1961), *Gypsy* (film, 1962), *The Turning Point* (film, 1977) and *Anastasia* (animated children's film, 1997). He also produced 1977's *The Turning Point*.

4. Pollack has been both an actor as well as a producer and director in many of his films, including *The Slender Thread* (1965), *This Property Is Condemned* (1966), *The Scalphunters* (1968), *Castle Keep* and *They Shoot Horses, Don't They?* (both in 1969), *Jeremiah Johnson* (1972), *The Yazuka* (1975), *Three Days of the Condor* (1975), *Bobby Deerfield* (1977), *The Electric Horseman* (1979), *Absence of Malice* (1981), *Tootsie* (1983), *Out of Africa* (1985), *Havana* (1990), *The Firm* (1995), *Sense and Sensibility* (producer only, 1996), *Sabrina* (1996), *Random Hearts* and *A Civil Action* (1999), and *Changing Lanes* (2002).

5. Stark has produced dozens of hits, including *The World of Suzie Wong* (1960), *Night of the Iguana* (1965), *Oh, Dad, Poor Dad, Mama's Hung You in the Closet and I'm Feelin' So Sad* (1966), *Funny Girl* (1968), *Funny Lady* and *The Sunshine Boys* (1975), *The Goodbye Girl* (1977), *Murder by Death* (1978), *The Electric Horseman* (1979), *Annie* (1982), *Brighton Beach Memoirs* (1985), *Peggy Sue Got Married* (1986), *Biloxi Blues* (1988), *Steel Magnolias* (1989), *Lost in Yonkers* (1993), and *Random Hearts* (1999).

6. Richard M. Fried, *Nightmare in Red: The McCarthy Era in Perspective* (New York: Oxford University Press, 1990), 29–30.

7. *Time Machine: The Un-Americans*, videocassette (British Broadcasting Corporation, 1993).

8. *Ibid.*

9. Patrick McGilligan and Paul Buhle, *Tender Comrades: A Backstory of the Hollywood Blacklist* (New York: St. Martin's Griffin, 1997), xiv.

10. *Ibid.*

11. Ronnie D. Lipschutz, *Cold War Fantasies: Film, Fiction and Foreign Policy* (Lanham, Md.: Rowman & Littlefield, 2001), 119.

12. *Ibid.*, 121.

13. *Ibid.*, 144.

14. "1968 Remembered: Ghosts of Vietnam," Voice of America radio report (aired June 30, 1998).

6

The Cold War, Cinema, and Civility: The Top Films of 1967

BARBARA J. WALKOSZ

From expressions of road rage to fights on television talk shows to the contentious nature of political campaigns, the growing lack of civility in America has been identified as a threat to democracy. In response to this threat, school boards have instituted antibully programs, universities have rewritten their codes of conduct, and national and local governing groups have brought in consultants to learn better methods of deliberation. Scholars such as Stephen Carter, Deborah Tannen, Robert Forni, and Kathleen Hall Jamieson have also written about what constitutes civility in a postindustrial society.[1] To be clear, contemporary concerns about civility are neither nostalgic nor a yearning for the "good old days," but rather seek to establish a framework for a public discourse grounded in civil communication.[2]

The word *civility* derives from the Latin *civitas* or *city* and shares its roots with *citizen* and *civic*. Thus, civility is connected to the development of norms of communication, deliberation, and shared decision making of good citizens and good neighbors.[3] Civil discourse is required for a democracy to function to its maximum potential because, without civil interactions, self-governance and the honest debate and deliberations that make democracy work cannot occur. Democracy is built on mutual trust and cooperation among strangers.[4]

The sources of contemporary incivilities have been attributed to things such as a decline in trust in the political system, the increasing adversarial nature of the media, a sense of isolation created by technology, and urban and suburban environments that separate rather than unite communities.[5] Although these reasons are valid, I suggest that a historical perspective can expand an understanding of the pervasiveness of contention and argument and lack of civil discourse in our culture. An important link exists between unique historical moments and the discourse of an era, and attention to those moments can facilitate the development of new models of civil communication.[6] Civility is rooted in particular societal conditions, and it is possible that through the study of different sets of conditions the circumstances connected to the rise or decline of civility can be identified. The late '60s, a paradigm of extreme social and political change, provide a significant historical context from which to examine the construct of civility. During this time, a myriad of American traditions began to crumble. The Vietnam War, the Civil Rights movement, the Free Speech movement, and a cultural revolution began to redefine America, and the shared vision that had once tied the culture together fragmented.[7]

Because film can both reflect and influence society, I examine the interactions between civility, the events of the Cold War era at the close of the '60s, and cinema as a means of understanding changes in the nature of public discourse. I believe that such an exploration can identify the possible foundations of contemporary incivility and provide a path for solutions. To accomplish this goal, I define civility and distinguish it from politeness and courtesy, detail important social and political events of 1967 that impacted civility, and analyze three of the top-grossing films of 1967, *The Graduate, Guess Who's Coming to Dinner,* and *Bonnie and Clyde.*[8]

Definitions of Civility

Definitions of civility include concepts such as courtesy, politeness, respect, compassion, love, trust, generosity, union, diversity, and community.[9] Although some definitions of civility are inclusive of all of these concepts, many limit civility solely to politeness or courtesy. To differentiate civility from politeness and courtesy is important, however, because such minimalist and superficial approaches to the term can mask oppression by the dominant culture and silence authentic concerns of the marginalized.[10] Peter McClelland clarifies the distinction between politeness and civility: "If courtesy is a treatment of others with respect and deference it overlaps with civility; but when courtesy becomes mere attention to the etiquette of a given society, it can prove to be profoundly uncivil."[11]

A society characterized by "diversity, change, and difference"[12] requires a different approach to definitions of civil interactions. I prefer a definition of civility as "an approach to life, a way of carrying one's self and of relating to others—in short, living in a way that is civilized."[13] Civility "requires consciousness of one's self, consciousness of the other person, and consciousness of the larger system."[14] Civility entails every-day expressions of equal respect, recognition, and even love for one another that have important social and political implications[15] and is "the recognition of the full humanity of both one's self and the other; the awareness of one's interdependence with the other; and the desire to make common cause with the other."[16] It is the "sum of all sacrifices that we are called to make for the sake of living together"[17] and a "welcoming of all parties to the debate that fosters the dignity of all participants."[18] Arnett, Arneson, and Wood summarize this view of civility:

> Dialogic civility is ultimately a reminder that life is best lived with concern for self, other, and sensitive implementation with the historical moment, while consistently reminding ourselves that our communicative actions have public consequences that shape the communicative lives of many people.[19]

Driven by increasingly complex and volatile events, less-than-civil communication characterized the late '60s.

The Context: 1967

> *This confused war has played havoc with our domestic destinies.*
> *Despite feeble protestations to the contrary, the promises of the Great*
> *Society have been shot down on the battlefield of Vietnam. The pur-*
> *suit of this widened war has narrowed the promised dimensions of*
> *the domestic welfare programs, making the poor — white and Negro —*
> *bear the heaviest burdens both at the front and at home.*
> (Martin Luther King, Jr., April 15, 1967)

Both at home and abroad, for the United States, 1967 was an extremely turbulent year. The Civil Rights movement, the war in Vietnam, détente, the war in the Mideast, and the growth of the counterculture movement combined for a tumultuous environment. To illustrate, while Congress increased appropriations to fight for democracy in Southeast Asia, blacks were denied their basic civil rights at home.[20] In Detroit and Newark, riots erupted as protestors clashed with police following incidents restricting civil rights to black citizens. Eighty-three people died (26 in Newark and 43 in Detroit), and thousands were wounded.[21] Standing in the smoke and rubble of Detroit, a black veteran said, "I just got back from Vietnam a few months ago but you know, I think the war is here."[22] Martin Luther

King declared that the United States was the "greatest purveyor of violence in the world" and suggested that the ties between the civil rights movement and the antiwar protests be strengthened.[23]

The Vietnam War was escalating as the United States began using B-52s to bomb the military bases near Saigon. By the end of the year, there were 486,000 troops in Vietnam; a total of 15,000 soldiers had been killed in the war, and 60 percent of them died in 1967.[24] The American public was increasingly dissatisfied with the war, with 46 percent of Americans declaring that U.S. military involvement in Vietnam was a "mistake."[25] This disagreement was manifest in growing antiwar protests as over 200,000 people joined marches in New York and San Francisco. This year of increased dissension culminated with a protest at the Pentagon joined by Dr. Benjamin Spock, a famous children's doctor and icon to parents, which resulted in the arrests of over 600 antiwar protestors.[26]

To compound matters, the situation in the Middle East and the nuclear arms race were creating strained relations between the United States and the Soviet Union. The United States supported Israel, while the Soviet Union supported Egypt, Syria, and Jordan. The Six-Day War, fought between Israel and the Arab nations of Egypt, Jordan, and Syria, resulted in Israeli control of all Jordanian territory west of the Jordan River, the Golan Heights of Syria, and the Sinai Peninsula.[27] When President Johnson and Soviet Premier Kosygin met in Glasboro, New Jersey, to discuss the reduction of tension in the Middle East, a discussion about intercontinental ballistic missiles also occurred. The Russians were committed to building an antiballistic missile (ABM) system to defend against the American missiles. At the same time, American scientists were developing multiple independently targeted reentry vehicles (MIRVS) that would allow one missile to carry as many as ten warheads. The development of the MIRVs meant that the Soviets would be placed in the position of increasing their new ABM defense system tenfold.[28] This newest escalation of nuclear armaments added fuel to the already volatile political context.

Simultaneously, the emerging youth counterculture challenged social norms: "Music, dress, language, sex, and intoxicant habits changed with breathtaking speed."[29] Approximately 75,000 youth poured into the Haight-Asbury district of San Francisco for the Summer of Love in 1967, and the Monterey Pop Festival that year headlined the Grateful Dead and Janis Joplin. The first issue of *Rolling Stone* magazine appeared, and the Corporation for Public Broadcasting was initiated.[30] *Time*'s cover asked, "Is God Dead?" as society demonstrated a growing disillusionment with outmoded authorities and searched for new spiritual voices and new moral values.[31]

An explosion of violence was also occurring in all sectors of American life, and violence itself became inescapable; in fact, no element of culture seemed untouched by the excesses of violence that were evident in 1967.[32] The youth culture confronted the values of the Cold War, which included military imperialism externally and racism internally.[33] Pluralistic views regarding American policies were developed, particularly among American youth: "[S]ome went to Vietnam, some became conscientious objectors, some went to Canada, some marched with Dr. King, and some became Black Panthers."[34] Against this complex social backdrop, Americans went to the cinema to see films that both reflected and created social norms.

Civility and the Cinema in 1967

Media scholars contend that films both create and reflect society's values. Thus, while films cannot be viewed as identical mirrors of society, they do have value in that they can reveal something about the "cultural conditions that produced them and attracted audiences to them."[35] The '60s reflected a shift in the normative discourse of American society from politeness, acceptance, and courtesy to discursive practices that challenged the status quo. A parallel move occurred in cinema as well. During this time, as the film industry faced a number of changes including an economic breakdown of the Hollywood studio system, the aesthetic influences of the European art house, and the creation of a new film ratings system, a "New American Cinema" developed.[36]

Although *Dr. Strangelove* was released in 1964, it broke new ground for the emergent films of the late '60s. *Dr. Strangelove* was called "the first break in the catatonic cold war trance that had for so long held our country in its grip."[37] The historical significance of *Dr. Strangelove* and the other films of the decade was that viewers were finally provided with a diversity of opinions that allowed them to make more discriminating judgments about social, political, and personal issues, resulting in important conversations and dialogues.[38] It was in this historical context of Hollywood that *The Graduate, Guess Who's Coming to Dinner,* and *Bonnie and Clyde* were produced.

Although these films do not directly address the social and political changes occurring during 1967, their themes articulated the zeitgeist,[39] and they provide a pathway to understanding contemporary instantiations of civility. I argue that this connection can be established through an examination of the norms of discourse as politeness, uncivil acts, and enactments of civility in each film. To elaborate these points, I discuss how politeness was the dominant discourse that reinforced and often masked the beliefs, both civil and uncivil, that underpinned the characters' actions. Next, I demonstrate that the behaviors that rejected the status quo were often constructed as uncivil acts that paralleled the social changes occurring in 1967. Further, I contend that these uncivil acts of the '60s, often grounded in political and social change, may have actually provided the foundations of contemporary incivility. Finally, I illustrate examples of civility that foreshadow postindustrial definitions of civil communication.

The Graduate

The Graduate is the story of Ben Braddock, a recent graduate of Harvard, who returns to his family's upper-middle-class home in California to plan his future. Ben soon discovers that he is unable to identify with his parents' affluent lifestyle, and his once-crystal-clear future as a graduate student becomes muddied as the summer progresses. To complicate matters, he has an affair with his father's business partner's wife, Mrs. Robinson, and then falls in love with the Robinsons' daughter, Elaine, against the wishes of her mother.

The Graduate echoed a growing societal dissatisfaction with the traditional values of capitalism. The youth culture's rejection of their parents' plastic existence was based on a belief that the older generation lived a life devoid of personal and professional standards. In *The Graduate,* American youth, for perhaps the first time, perceived an onscreen image of themselves that they could both identify and emulate: that of a generation seeking its own unique cultural identification. As dissatisfaction with the war in Vietnam escalated, the anarchic mood of *The Graduate* was a perfect fit for the times as it combined humor and satire to comment on social and sexual customs.

Characteristic of the midsixties, the polite discourse in *The Graduate* demonstrates the characters' inability to engage in authentic conversations regarding the nature of their relationships and their positions on social and personal issues. To illustrate, at the start of the film, Ben violates a social code as he retreats to his room rather than joining the guests at his graduation party. His father follows him upstairs, asking:

MR. BRADDOCK: What's the matter? The guests are all downstairs, Ben. They're all waiting to see you.

BEN: Look, Dad—could you explain to them that I have to be alone for awhile.

MR. BRADDOCK: These are all of our good friends, Ben. Most of them
have known you since — well — practically since you were born.
BEN: I'm just ...
MR. BRADDOCK: ... worried?
BEN: Well ...
MR. BRADDOCK: About what?
BEN: I guess about my future.
MR. BRADDOCK: What about it?
BEN: I don't know. I want it to be ...
MR. BRADDOCK: ... to be what?
BEN: ... Different.
(Mrs. Braddock enters the room.)
MRS. BRADDOCK: Is there anything wrong?
MR. BRADDOCK: No! No— we're just on our way downstairs!
MRS. BRADDOCK: The Carlsons are here.
MR. BRADDOCK (to Mrs. Braddock): They are?
(to Ben): Come on.
MRS. BRADDOCK: They came all the way from Tarzana.[40]

In this interaction, the family members remain very polite to one
another, but they fail to explore the reasons why Ben wants his future "to
be different" from that of his parents. The topic is masked by the
announcement that the Carlsons have arrived from Tarzana, a fact alone
that is seen as an adequate reason for Ben to join his guests.

An additional example of these discursive norms is illustrated in one
of the most memorable exchanges of the film. Ben is taken aside by a family friend who gives him a word of advice about his future:

MR. MCGUIRE: I just want to say one word to you — just one word.
BEN: Yes, sir.
MR. MCGUIRE: Are you listening?
BEN: Yes, I am.
MR. MCGUIRE (gravely): Plastics.
BEN: Exactly how do you mean?
MR. MCGUIRE: There's a great future in plastics. Think about it. Will
you think about it?
BEN: Yes, I will.
MR. MCGUIRE: Shh! Enough said. That's a deal.[41]

Following this exchange, Ben again retreats to his room realizing that
he is disconnected from a world in which individuals' worth is measured

by their success.[42] Plastics is the perfect metaphor for an older generation, whose defining characteristics are portrayed as materialism, scotch, barbecues, and rigidity. Ben consistently seems to lack the courage or the skills to challenge or break away from the pretentious middle-class lifestyle and polite conversation that surrounds him. He remains polite, trying to be "personable and genuine in a hypocritical society."[43]

Ben even continues to call his lover "Mrs. Robinson," implicitly recognizing the distance between them in age and experience.[44] The first time Ben and Mrs. Robinson go to a hotel, the following exchange occurs:

BEN: Mrs. Robinson — I can't do this.
MRS. ROBINSON: You what?
BEN: This is all terribly wrong.
MRS. ROBINSON: Ben — do you find me undesirable?
BEN: Oh no, Mrs. Robinson, I think — I think you're the most attractive of my parents' friends. I just don't think we could possibly —
MRS. ROBINSON: Are you afraid of me?
BEN: No — but look — maybe we could do something else together — would you like to go to a movie?[45]

While Ben's politeness may be a manifestation of his discomfort at having an affair, the discourse inhibits him from getting to know Mrs. Robinson and further positions her as a stereotypical seductress masking the underlying reasons she has chosen this unconventional relationship.

A theme of alienation develops as Ben retreats into his own world, spending his days floating in his parents' swimming pool. In one scene, Ben dons scuba gear and views a barbecue party from the vantage point of the bottom of the pool, underscoring his distance from the "real world."[46] At the same time, his affair with Mrs. Robinson — an act of sexual rebellion — continues. Ben's summertime malaise is interrupted when he discovers his one true love in Elaine, the Robinsons' daughter. Ben not only reveals to Elaine his feelings of disconnection from the world around him, but as they grow closer, he also tells her of his affair with her mother. Learning of the unlikely relationship, Elaine cuts off her relationship with Ben and returns to school.

In the second half of the film, Ben follows Elaine to Berkeley to try to win her back. During these times, Ben remains polite and courteous, positioning himself outside of what is occurring in society, especially on the Berkeley campus. For example, when his landlord asks him if he is one of those "outside agitators," Ben responds: "Oh — no sir." However, a series of events leads Ben to make an overt break with the status quo. He soon discovers that not only is Elaine engaged but also that he has been betrayed by Mrs. Robinson. She has told Elaine that there was not an affair but that Ben had raped her. While Ben tries to explain the affair to Elaine, she screams repeatedly, resulting in Ben's eviction from his room. His landlord tells Ben he just "doesn't like him." Elaine ultimately rejects Ben's proposals and decides to proceed with her marriage to another man.

At the end of the film, Ben carries out an uncivil act when measured against upper-class society norms.[47] In what are now considered classic scenes, Ben rushes to the church to stop Elaine's wedding. The dramatic tension increases as Ben cannot enter the church and watches the marriage vows from the glassed-in balcony, serving as a metaphor for Ben's "glassed-in" nonexpressive existence. Ben tries to break through as he pounds on the glass, screaming Elaine's name. He makes his way to the vestibule and grabs Elaine's hand, and they escape the church and leap onto a bus. The audience, expecting to see the couple joyous in their love, is instead introduced to the "brave new world." Ben and Elaine do not embrace when they get on the bus but rather take the back seat and look at each other, stunned and out of breath as they move toward an unknown future. As the scene closes, the bus pulls away, and Ben and Elaine stare straight ahead. Simon and Garfunkel sing the "Sounds of Silence," implying that Ben and Elaine may not have found the solution to contemporary alienation. Mike Nichols, the director, stated that the final scene demonstrates that Ben and Elaine had many choices open to them; however, he later remarked that he believed that Ben and Elaine would become their parents within the next five years.[48]

In *The Graduate*, authentic dialogue about issues of alienation, betrayal, love, and compassion are denied by the norms of politeness and courtesy. Although uncivil acts provide temporary solutions to problems, the characters of *The Graduate* may have had more options had an alternative model of problem solving, based in respect and honesty, been available.

Guess Who's Coming to Dinner

Guess Who's Coming to Dinner was Hollywood's attempt to deal with the issue of race in America in the '60s via an onscreen interracial relationship. Like *The Graduate*, the context is the upper-middle-class society of the '60s. In the film, the Draytons (Matt and Christine), a white liberal couple, must come to terms with the fact that their daughter, Joanna, wishes to marry John Prentice, a black man. The film positions

John, played by Sydney Poitier, as a physician whose own upper-middle-class status mitigates any problems that might arise because of his race.

The dramatic tension revolves around approval of the marriage, primarily by the Draytons, played by Spencer Tracy and Katherine Hepburn. John informs them he will not marry Joanna without their support. He states that the lack of approval from Joanna's family is an obstacle that he is not willing to try to overcome on top of all of the other societal issues that the couple will be facing.[49] The film tests the viability and hypocrisy of white liberalism with its commitment to integration as a means of achieving equality for blacks.[50] The white liberals in the film are not the only ones facing a challenge, however; John's father is also opposed to the union and must face the generational differences of the construction of race in the face of changing times.

Critics have charged that *Guess Who's Coming to Dinner* lacks the capacity to make a serious political statement because of the "romantic comedy style" in which the story is told.[51] The claims of the film's inadequacies are also based on the construction of John Prentice as such an unbelievable character that his perfect persona undermines the significance of the plot.[52] Director Stanley Kramer responded to this criticism by stating

> We took special pains to make Poitier a very special character in this story ... respectable, yes. And intelligent. And attractive. We did this so that if the young couple didn't marry because of their parents' disapproval, the only reason would be that he was black and she was white.[53]

Perhaps Hollywood was not capable of anything more direct in 1967 and the film emerges as a compromise between "the desire to make a politically significant statement about interracial romance and a realistic assessment of the obstacles posed to such a project by a racist film industry and society."[54]

In *Guess Who's Coming to Dinner*, politeness also exemplifies and dominates the discursive acts of the characters. An understanding of the nature of these exchanges can be illuminated by the work of historians who, when writing about interactions between the races prior to the '60s, note that "there existed an elaborate code of conduct for relations between whites and blacks ... such as eye contact, pedestrian behavior and forms of address that were all strictly regulated in order to reinforce white supremacy and black submission."[55] Elizabeth Lasch-Quinn writes that one of the goals of the civil rights movement was not only to bring about equality but also to eliminate the racial protocols for daily interaction and that this film sits at the intersection of the old and new rules regarding interaction and race.[56] Thus, while members of the older generation struggle with their interactions, members of the younger generation "demonstrate a relaxed and even sensual and uninhibited norm of communicating."[57]

In the beginning of the film, politeness and courtesy prevail when Joanna introduces John to her parents. In fact, they utilize politeness to cover up their shock at the announcement that Joanna and John plan to marry. While Christina Drayton's facial expressions reveal her disbelief, she politely asks permission to say "my goodness!" In this interaction, John acknowledges her condition by assuring her that he can provide her with medical assistance if needed. Yet, Christina does not overtly discuss any concerns she may have about the interracial relationship; rather, her courtesies take the group out to have tea sandwiches on the patio. Matt Drayton is also quite polite when he meets John and even when he learns of the impending marriage. However, following a conversation with John, Matt places a call to "check up" on Prentice's credentials, suggesting that Matt does not trust John. In fact, courtesies dominate Matt's interactions, but these acts mask his resistance and growing disapproval of the marriage.

Politeness also dominates the scene when Mr. and Mrs. Prentice are greeted at the airport by John and Joanna. John greets his parents by telling them that there is this "one thing" he should have told them. The Prentices are shocked to learn that the "one thing" is that Joanna is white. Joanna reassures them that her parents were shocked, too, but she suggests that the shock was from the fact that she wanted to get married at all, not necessarily that the relationship is interracial. Mr. Prentice breaks the code of courtesy when he suggests that the couple is acting like a "couple of escaped lunatics."

Both sets of parents engage in very civilized and stiff conversation upon meeting, detailing several times the nature of the flight from Los Angeles to San Francisco. Joanna suggests that they talk about another flight — the one to Geneva, where she and John planned to be married. Her comment allows a change in the nature of the discourse from a polite discussion about the weather and travel to deliberations about the viability of the impending marriage.

In *Guess Who's Coming to Dinner*, the break from the traditional is the marriage of Joanna and John. The primary incivilities in this film are the explicit and implicit racist reactions to the couple. From the disproving look on their cab driver's face as Joanna and John exchange their only onscreen kiss to the implicit disdain of Hillary, Christina's employee at her gallery, racist attitudes of the '60s are revealed.

An exchange between Christina and Hillary provides Hillary with an opportunity to demonstrate her racism further. She purposefully visits the

Draytons' apartment to determine what John is doing there. When she finds out about the marriage, she unsuccessfully attempts to camouflages her racist reaction with politeness as she expresses her sympathy to Christina. Christina's response is to tell Hillary to go back to the gallery, write herself a check for $5,000, and pack up her things and leave. This is the first time in the film that Christina overtly responds and expresses her support for the couple. This act is unlike the behavior of Matt, who has decided, in a racist and uncivil act, that he will not give his blessing to the wedding.

The Prentice family is not without their concerns either. John decides to confront his father about his resistance to the marriage. In several parts of the conversation, John does not empathize with his father or demonstrate compassion regarding the sacrifices that his father, a mail carrier, had made to ensure that John received the best education. Rather, John informs him that times have changed:

JOHN: You listen to me. You say you don't want to tell me how to live my life. So what do you think you've been doing? You tell me what rights I've got or haven't got, and what I owe to you for what you've done for me. Let me tell you something. I owe you nothing!

If you carried that bag a million miles, you did what you're supposed to do! Because you brought me into this world. And from that day you owed me everything you could ever do for me like I will owe my son if I ever have another one.

But you don't own me! You can't tell me when or where I'm out of line or try to get me to live my life according to your rules. You don't even know what I am.

Dad, you don't know who I am. You don't know how I feel, what I think. And if I tried to explain it the rest of your life you will never understand. You are 30 years older than I am. You and your whole lousy generation believes the way it was for you is the way it's got to be. And not until your whole generation has lain down and died will the dead weight be off our backs!

You understand, you've got to get off my back!

Dad ... Dad, you're my father. I'm your son. I love you. I always have and I always will.

But you think of yourself as a colored man. I think of myself as a man.[58]

When Prentice declares himself a "man," he differentiates generational perspectives of race and silences the senior Prentice. Interestingly, John and his father have no further interactions in the film, suggesting that the younger generation has had the last word.

In *Guess Who's Coming to Dinner,* the acceptance of Joanna and John's marriage is representative of civility conceptualized as diversity rooted in union, not difference.[59] Confirmation of the marriage first occurs by the mothers, who truly believe that the strength of John and Joanna's love will carry the couple through any difficulties they will encounter.[60] As the parents struggle with their own thoughts, an authentic conversation occurs between Mrs. Prentice and Matt. She is distressed because neither of the fathers is supportive of the couple or willing to change his position. She asks Matt "when it was that he and her husband turned into old men who no longer remembered what it was like to be in love." Wattenberg writes that Mrs. Prentice's challenge to remember love is what moves Matt to change his position.[61] In his speech giving approval to the marriage, Matt notes he had not thought about love. Although thoughts of love certainly were blocked by race, he nonetheless affirms the couple's relationship, stating that the only thing that would be worse, given the nature of their love, would be if they did not marry. Thus, Matt is able to redeem himself and white liberalism.[62] However, as the film concludes, John Prentice Sr. is silenced as his son informs him that he would marry Joanna regardless of what his father thought. In his soliloquy, Matt tells John Sr. that, in time, he will come to see the marriage as a good thing. It is important to note that in order for the final conclusion to be truly civil, all voices should have been included, not just that of Matt Drayton. However, despite its shortcomings, *Guess Who's Coming to Dinner* attempts to open a civil dialogue on difference, diversity, compassion, and love.

Bonnie and Clyde

While *The Graduate* and *Guess Who's Coming to Dinner* take place in the '60s, *Bonnie and Clyde* is the story of an outlaw couple during the Depression. This film combines large doses of sex and violence to appeal to an antiestablishment audience.[63] Bonnie and Clyde's "cross country spree captures the spirit and energy for the youth movement and epitomizes the revolt against institutional authority that found support in young moviegoers of the mid-1960's."[64] The violence depicted in *Bonnie and Clyde* crossed the line of what previously had been shown on Hollywood's screens, perhaps reflecting the increase in violence in the American culture and the new ratings system. Unlikely icons, Bonnie and Clyde were revered by audiences not only for their acts of violence against the establishment but also for their persistence of such acts even when they knew that these acts would result in their deaths.

The film is not about the Depression but rather is about the '60s in that by acting aberrantly, Bonnie and Clyde were considered contemporaries by their audiences as each group struggled against the moral codes and social institutions of its times.[65] The Barrow gang, consisting of Bonnie, Clyde, Buck (Clyde's brother), Blanche (Buck's wife), and C. W. Moss (a mechanic), may also have provided anther point of identification as they resembled the ad hoc extended families that were emerging during the '60s.

Because *Bonnie and Clyde* takes place outside of the educated, upper-middle-class context of the '60s, examples of politeness and courtesy are less explicit; however, a few examples can be identified. For example, when Clyde introduces them he politely states: "This here's Miss Bonnie Parker. I'm Clyde Barrow.... We rob banks."[66] Unfortunately, this introduction is often followed by a violent robbery. Another example of politeness masking a true feeling is the action of C. W. Moss' father, Malcolm, who offers the gang a hideout. In front of Bonnie and Clyde he tells C. W. that it's a good thing his name is not in the newspapers and that "Mr. Barrow has been looking out for your interest." He then declares with pride that "ain't it something" that he has a "coupla big deals" staying in his house. However, when he and C. W. are alone, he expresses anger with his son for getting a tattoo and reveals his true feelings about Bonnie and Clyde:

MALCOLM: You look like trash all marked up like that.

C. W.: Bonnie says it looks good.

MALCOLM: What does Bonnie know? She ain't nothing but cheap trash herself. Look what they do to you. You don't ever get your name in the paper. You just get them pictures printed on your skin, by Bonnie and Clyde. Shoot, they ain't nothing but a couple of kids.[67]

Malcolm Moss, their host, ultimately sets up the couple for their final encounter with law enforcement. In this instance, politeness masks betrayal.

Of the three films, *Bonnie and Clyde* provides the most extensive and violent enactments of uncivil behavior. Arthur Penn, the director, believed that Bonnie and Clyde were "paradigmatic figures of their time and that the violence in the film did not begin to compare with the scenes from the Vietnam War found on television or the images of domestic strife found in the streets of America's cities."[68] The first explicitly violent scene takes place when a bank employee chases Bonnie and Clyde following a robbery. The clerk hops onto the running board, and Clyde shoots him point-blank in the face. Clyde laments that he did not want to murder the man and attributes the killing to the man's own actions. In this case, audiences are asked to sympathize with Clyde and to understand that his violence is prompted by external circumstances and not by his own disposition.

Violence and incivility of a different nature are enacted when the Barrow gang encounters a Texas Ranger who has been tracking them. They capture, torment, taunt, and even take their picture with the lawman. When the ranger spits in Bonnie's face after she kisses him, Clyde beats and almost drowns him. Buck convinces Clyde to handcuff the lawman and set him afloat in a boat, depicting irreverence toward authority not unlike that of the antiwar protestors who were challenging the norms of civil disobedience.

The most graphic violence of the film takes place in the two final gun battles between the Barrow gang and the police. In the first fight, the gang is ambushed at its hotel in Iowa, and Buck is murdered and Blanche injured in the shoot-out. The explicit portrayal of violence in the scene exceeded the sterilized shootings the American movie-going public was accustomed to viewing. However, no scene gained more attention than the final scene of the film, in which Bonnie and Clyde are shot. Penn sought to achieve a "balletic and spastic" quality to depict the scene by using a multicamera shoot, montage editing, and slow motion.[69] From the point at which the flock of birds abruptly flies off, signaling the start of the ambush, to the final image in *Bonnie and Clyde,* after the shooting has ceased, the sequence contains fifty-one shots and runs fifty-four seconds.[70]

Penn's technical construction of the scene provided an unprecedented view of violence presenting multiple perspectives over a time frame much longer than any in which audiences had ever viewed a murder. The legacy for violence in American film had been established as the audience witnesses Bonnie' and Clyde's bodies being riddled with bullets at different speeds and from different vantage points. Unfortunately, the "epochal, radical bloodletting in Bonnie and Clyde has been overwhelmed and overtaken by mechanized spectacles of violence that it helped to inaugurate."[71] Penn was not interested in violence for its own sake but believed that it could dramatize the rebellion against intolerable social conditions and establish martyrdom for the outlaws.[72]

In *Bonnie and Clyde,* the demonstration of civility as respect and a caring for a person's humanity emerged primarily in interactions between the outlaws and the disenfranchised who had suffered great losses in the Depression, usually at the hands of the banks. When Bonnie and Clyde are at their first hideout, a farmer approaches and informs them that this used to be his property before the bank took it away. They empathize with the farmer as Clyde turns and fires three shots into the foreclosure sign. Clyde offers his gun to the farmer, who takes a shot at the sign. A black man approaches, and the farmer tells Clyde that the two of them worked the property together. He asks if it would okay to let his friend take a shot Both men take pleasure in this small act of revenge, orchestrated by Clyde, against the bank, a symbol of the establishment that has taken their livelihood.

In the next instance, in the midst of a robbery, Clyde notices one of the customers, who is a farmer, clutching a handful of money. Clyde asks the farmer if the money belongs to him or the bank. When Clyde discovers that the money belongs to the farmer, he tells him to keep it. In a subsequent scene, the farmer is seen telling the media that "Clyde Barrow did right by me." The connection between the Barrow gang and the disenfranchised is also enacted in a scene in which Bonnie and Clyde have been shot and are on the run. They encounter a group of homeless people camping in a field, and the group offers the outlaws a cup of soup and drinking water, acts of generosity and sacrifice.

Although Bonnie and Clyde do not share a deep romantic love, their relationship provides them with a fundamental human connection. Friedman writes that they are basically individuals who are seeking a communal relationship and it is this need that remains central to the film's continuing appeal.[73] A display of this connection is manifested when Bonnie prints her poems about their exploits in the paper. Clyde turns to Bonnie and says, "You have really made me something." Thus, while the film shows that violence shapes our daily life, it demonstrates that it is the desire for connection that permeates our daily existence.[74]

Discussion

The analyses of *The Graduate*, *Guess Who's Coming to Dinner*, and *Bonnie and Clyde* have provided a framework from which to examine the intersection of civility, film, and the social context of 1967. To restate my goal, I argue that from this investigation an understanding of how we now live in a culture that is dominated by incivilities can be determined. In each film, politeness emerges as the normative discourse; however, the norms of politeness are rejected as they function as inadequate covers for uncivil acts and barriers to authentic communication. As an alternative, the characters often employ uncivil actions (note: with the exception of the racist acts identified in *Guess Who's Coming to Dinner)* to challenge the status quo, paralleling the social and political context of 1967. I contend that the current trends of incivility are a result of uncivil acts becoming normative often without the social and political underpinnings that initiated such actions in the late '60s. Certainly, political and social situations may exist that require challenges to the status quo; however, the pervasiveness of incivility today routinely occurs in everyday encounters between citizens. The films that have been analyzed each provide explanations of and alternatives to the incivilities of the postmodern age suggesting that uncivil acts are no longer our only option.

In *The Graduate,* politeness barred authentic communication about important personal and social issues. Ben never clearly articulates his feelings of alienation and his perceptions of the status quo because his only alternative immobilized him. Similarly, the courteous relationship between Ben and Mrs. Robinson never allows the lovers to share intimate thoughts and feelings. Thus, politeness provides a veneer for social interactions but masks the underlying currents of change that are occurring. The lack of genuine deliberation provides an explanation for Ben, who resorts to an uncivil act to resolve his feelings of love for Elaine. The uncivil act positions Ben as a hero many audiences cheered upon viewing this scene. However, the ending of the film implies that Ben and Elaine may not have resolved their feelings of alienation, reflecting the confusion of the postindustrial world. I suggest that the development of communication models that privilege authentic conversation can provide an antidote to the resultant conditions of *The Graduate.*

In *Guess Who's Coming to Dinner,* politeness also exemplifies the discourse and in this case provides a cover for racism. This film's link to civility is through its rejection of racism and acceptance of the interracial marriage of John and Joanna. The deliberation about this relationship suggests that an alternative worldview can change the nature of discourse about race. The worldview that is suggested in *Guess Who's Coming to Dinner* is the acceptance of diversity, grounded in respect and honesty. Although defined in a limited fashion, this perspective foreshadows contemporary constructions of civility regarding issues of diversity, difference, division, and union.

In *Bonnie and Clyde,* the path to the current state of incivility in society is more clearly defined. Bonnie and Clyde represent a youthful challenge to the status quo via their lifestyle, which is portrayed as illegal, dangerous, exciting, nonconformist, and seductive. The violence and rebellion of the film parallel the occurrences of 1967. As stated earlier, the uncivil behaviors in the film, including the violence, have often been retained as normative without consideration of the context. However, the empathy that Bonnie and Clyde demonstrate to the homeless people of the Depression is an enactment of civility that bears consideration in the face of homelessness today. Further, the importance of community is underscored in the film and bears consideration outside of the context of violence.

In summary, although each of the films provides options for civil behavior, the question arises as to why the audiences of 1967 often supported the uncivil behaviors of the characters, cheering when Ben and Elaine run from the church and applauding the escapades of Bonnie and Clyde. Further, what does that approval bode for civil communication today? I believe that the audiences identified the politeness as ineffective and the status quo as oppressive and viewed the uncivil acts as necessary to bring about change in the late '60s. The connection to current discussions about civility is that by understanding these actions, alternatives to incivilities can be developed. Thus, the challenge facing society is to construct more civil models of communication that can continue to challenge social norms in a manner that is respectful, collaborative, and civil in nature. Clearly, we do not want to return to the shams of politeness of the early '60s but we do not want to continue to exist in a culture dominated by argument and disrespect.

NOTES

1. Stephen L. Carter, *Civility: Manners, Morals, and the Etiquette of Democracy* (New York: Basic, 1998), 9.

2. *Ibid.*, 49.

3. See P. M. Forni, *Choosing Civility* (New York: St. Martin's, 2002); Adam McClelland, "Beyond Courtesy: Redefining Civility," in *Civility*, ed. Leroy S. Rouner (Notre Dame: University of Notre Dame Press, 2000): 78–93.

4. Richard L. Bushman and James A. Morris, "The Rise and Fall of Civility in America," *The Wilson Quarterly* 20(4) (1996): 13–22.

5. See Carter, *Civility: Manners, Morals, and the Etiquette of Democracy*; Deborah Tannen, *The Argument Culture* (New York: Random, 1997); Robert Putnam, *Bowling Alone: The Collapse and Revival of American Community* (New York: Simon & Schuster, 2000).

6. C. Arnett Ronald, Pat Arneson, and Julia Wood, *Dialogic Civility in a Cynical Age: Community, Hope, and Interpersonal Relationships* (Albany: State University of New York Press, 1999), 281.

7. Carter, 38.

8. The four top-grossing films of 1967 were *The Graduate, The Jungle Book, Guess Who's Coming to Dinner,* and *Bonnie and Clyde*. The *Jungle Book* was not selected for the analysis because it is an animated children's film and as such differs significantly from the other films in the analysis.

9. For example, M. Scott Peck writes that the "community building process teaches its participants civility by increasing their consciousness." M. Scott Peck, *A*

World Waiting to Be Reborn: Civility Rediscovered (New York: Bantam, 1997), 293; P. M. Forni writes that "civility means being constantly aware of others and weaving restraint, respect, and consideration into the very fabric of this awareness" in *Choosing Civility*, 9.

10. See Peter McClelland, "Beyond Courtesy: Redefining Civility" and Virginia Strauss, "Making Peace: International Civility and the Question of Culture," in *Civility*, 168–84.

11. McClelland, 88.

12. Arnett et. al., 282.

13. Carter, 15.

14. Peck, 29.

15. Carter, 38.

16. McClelland, 79.

17. Carter, 11.

18. Thomas Benson, "Rhetoric, Civility, and Community: Political Debate on Computer Bulletin Boards," *Communication Quarterly* 44 (Summer 1996): 359–78.

19. Arnett et. al, 282.

20. Carter, 44.

21. Todd Gitlin, *The Sixties: Years of Hope, Days of Rage* (New York: Bantam, 1987), 244.

22. Margot A. Henriksen, *Dr. Strangelove's America* (Berkeley: University of California Press, 1997), 363.

23. Steven Alan Carr, "From 'Fucking Cops!' to 'Fucking Media!': *Bonnie and Clyde* for a Sixties America," in *Arthur Penn's Bonnie and Clyde*, ed. Lester D. Friedman (New York: Cambridge University Press: 2000), 75.

24. Gitlin, 242.

25. The Vietnam War" (database online), available at http://www.historyplace.com.

26. Carr, 75.

27. "World Events 1963–1969" (database online); available at http://www.encarta.msn.com.

28. "The Cold War Years" (database online); available from http://www.cnn.com.

29. Gitlin, 215.

30. *Ibid.*

31. Hendrickson, 359.

32. For example, see Hendrickson, *Dr. Strangelove's America* and Gitlin, *The Sixties: Years of Hope, Days of Rage* for extended discussions of the events that took place in 1967.

33. Hendrickson, 309.

34. Carter, 44.

35. John Belton, *American Cinema/American Culture* (New York: McGraw-Hill, 1994), xxi.

36. Lester D. Friedman, "Introduction: Arthur Penn's Enduring Gangsters" in *Arthur Penn's Bonnie and Clyde* (New York: Cambridge University Press, 2000), 1.

37. Hendrickson, *Dr. Strangelove's America*, 229, quoting Lawrence Suid, "The Pentagon and Hollywood: *Dr. Strangelove or: How I Learned to Stop Worrying and Love the Bomb*, in John E. O'Connor and Martin A. Jackson, eds., *American History/American Film* (New York: Frederick Ungar 1977), 231.

38. Friedman, 2.

39. *Ibid.*, 40.

40. Transcribed by the author from the DVD of *The Graduate*.

41. *Ibid.*
42. Ann Lloyd, *Movies of the Sixties* (London: Orbis, 1983).
43. *Ibid.*
44. *Ibid.*
45. Transcribed by the author from the DVD of *The Graduate.*
46. Douglas Brode, *The Films of the Sixties* (New Jersey: Citadel, 1980), 190.
47. *Ibid.*, 192.
48. Belton, 284.
49. Elizabeth Lasch-Quinn, "How to Behave Sensitively: Prescriptions for Interracial Conduct from the 1960s to the 1990s." *Journal of Social History* 33 (1999): 409–27.
50. Thomas E. Wartenberg, *Unlikely Couples: Movie Romance as Social Criticism* (Boulder: Westview, 1999), 114.
51. *Ibid.*, 112.
52. *Ibid.*
53. *Ibid.*, 112. Kramer's quote is also included on the sleeve of the DVD of the film.
54. *Ibid.*, 113.
55. Lasch-Quinn, "How to Behave Sensitively: Prescriptions for Interracial Conduct from the 1960s to the 1990s."
56. *Ibid.*
57. *Ibid.*
58. Transcribed by the author from the DVD *Guess Who's Coming to Dinner.*
59. Armado Rodriguez, *Diversity as Liberation (II): Introducing a New Understanding of Diversity* (New Jersey: Hampton, 2000).
60. Wartenberg, 117.
61. *Ibid.*, 118.
62. *Ibid.*, 120.
63. Belton, 286.
64. *Ibid.*
65. Friedman, 3.
66. Sandra Wake and Nicole Hayden, eds., *The Bonnie and Clyde Book* (New York: Simon & Shuster, 1972), 56.
67. *Ibid.*
68. Friedman, 130.
69. Prince, 137.
70. Stephen Prince, "The Hemorrhaging of American Cinema: *Bonnie and Clyde's* Legacy of Cinematic Violence. In *Arthur Penn's Bonnie and Clyde,* Lester D. Friedman, ed. (New York: Cambridge University Press, 2000), 130.
71. *Ibid.*, 135.
72. *Ibid.*, 144.
73. Friedman, 5.
74. *Ibid.*

7

Top Guns in Vietnam: The Pilot as Protected Warrior Hero

SHARON D. DOWNEY

Our nation's capital is home to the Vietnam Veterans Memorial, a sacred place of public reconciliation for the "longest, saddest, baddest war America ever fought."[1] Dedicated in 1982, the memorial is no doubt a shrine to contested meanings[2] but evokes a collective sense of loss and, as such, is a wrenching symbol of the Vietnam experience. The same sentiments enveloping the Vietnam Veterans Memorial have been echoed repeatedly in mass media depictions of the war and its combatants for over three decades. Indeed, if Brummett is correct in his observation that much "of the important business of our society is ... done from moment to moment in people's experiences of popular culture,"[3] then the "public dreams"[4] of films and television shows about Vietnam enact a shattering of our "national mythology"[5] and leave a legacy of ideological, "psychological, cultural, [and] spiritual" conflict.[6] Long after the war's end, Vietnam continues to be "refought daily in popular culture," serving as "an evolving ethical battleground" for "America's ... examination of its own conscience."[7]

At first glance, this mass-mediated struggle over the meaning of Vietnam seems remarkably unified — almost a generic Vietnam War narrative. Such tales tend to chronicle the soldier's "gradual deterioration, ... the disintegration of idealism, the breakdown of character, the alienation from those at home, and finally, the loss of all sensibility save the will to survive."[8] Whether Vietnam's warriors are viewed as victims of war (*Coming*

Home, Born on the Fourth of July), more malevolently predisposed because of their traumas (*Taxi Driver, Rolling Thunder, Rambo: First Blood*), inevitably succumbing to an amoral landscape (*The Deer Hunter, Apocalypse Now, Full Metal Jacket, Platoon*), superheroes or noble "grunts" who overcome debilitation and alienation to triumph (*Uncommon Valor, Rambo: First Blood, Part II, Missing in Action*), or social saviors eventually strengthened by war (*Lethal Weapon, Magnum, P.I., Air Wolf, The A-Team*), the Vietnam grunt is at odds with traditional mythic images of American combatants. Linenthal notes that

> the portrayal of Vietnam warriors ... [depicts] warriors concerned and disillusioned about their mission, ... [producing] war narratives which reflect the clash between a *memory* of classical American warrior models and the reality of a war which frustrated all attempts made to symbolize it in traditional patterns.[9]

For all representational purposes, the Vietnam warrior was a would-be but fallen hero whose quest for honor in a failed war was not to be realized.

Yet, rupturing this dominant narrative is a competing image of the Vietnam warrior in fiction and film: the American fighter pilot. Cut to June 1988, a time marked by a growing revisionist history about Vietnam in politics[10] and a developing tension between the prevailing "Vietnam-as-profane" theme in mass media and the "back-to-Nam-to-win-this-time" motif that transformed Rambo and Chuck Norris into cultural icons. It is fifteen years after the return of American POWs (almost all Air Force and Navy aviators), thirteen years after the fall of Saigon, and five years before U.S. air superiority would reign in the Gulf War. In a convention hall in Washington, D.C., not far from the Vietnam Veterans Memorial, a select group of the war's veterans gather for a joint reunion of POWs and River Rats (U.S. Air Force and Navy pilots who flew over the Red River Valley in North Vietnam from 1963 to 1975). The keynote speaker is retired General William C. Westmoreland, former commander of the U.S. forces in Vietnam. The theme of his address is familiar though no less powerful because of it: Had the war been waged by the military instead of politicians and dissenters, he asserts, the United States would have achieved quick, decisive, honorable victory in Vietnam. Those words earn the general an unequivocal and sustained standing ovation.

The story of the "other" Vietnam warriors—sky soldiers—is largely one of absence and invisibility. In most popular or critically acclaimed films about the war, the aviator—if seen at all—is a background figure, either the visage of metal streaking over the jungle to intercede on behalf of trapped combatants, leaving vapor trails and napalm fireballs in its wake, or as nameless, faceless POWs awaiting liberation by the superhero soldiers'

return trip to Vietnam to recover some semblance of victory. The experience of the Vietnam war has been the province of warriors on the ground,
not in the air. This foregrounding of ground troops is somewhat surprising—notwithstanding its dramatic possibilities—if for no other reason
than that Vietnam was principally an air war. In fact, the cornerstone of
U.S. military policy in Vietnam was its air war capabilities; with over "eight
million tons of munitions from aircraft [dropped] onto Southeast Asia,
the air war … was … the largest air war in world history."[11]

However, beginning in the mid–1980s, Vietnam's military pilots made
their appearance on the silver screen in a big way. Although the aviator
formed the backdrop for television series such as *Call to Glory* and *Baa
Baa Black Sheep*, as well as television movies like *Red Flag*, it took the Tom
Cruise-starring megahit *Top Gun* (1986) to reinstate the fighter jock as the
cocky but principled warrior of World War II film stature with enough
right techno-cowboy hero stuff to make him a suitable model for any war
any time. On its heels came three films featuring aviators' experiences in
Vietnam: *Hanoi Hilton* (1987), an account of the capture, incarceration,
and release of American POWs, featuring the experiences of fighter pilot
Lieutenant Commander Patrick Williamson (Michael Moriarty); *Bat 21*
(1989), the chronicle of downed navigator and military strategist Colonel
Iceal Hambleton (Gene Hackman) behind enemy lines and his efforts, as
well as those of EVAC pilot *Bird Dog* (Danny Glover), who rescued him;
and *Flight of the Intruder* (1991), the story of a frustrated navy fighter pilot,
Lieutenant "Cool Hand" Jake Grafton (Brad Johnson), along with his
buddy Virgil Cole (William Dafoe), who, barred by government edict from
direct engagement in the war, secretly fly their stealth A-6 aircraft, the
Intruder, to Hanoi to destroy surface-to-air missile depots, thereby protecting American lives.

This essay analyzes film representations of the U.S. fighter pilot in
Vietnam. I argue that the aviator undergoes and successfully completes
the archetypal hero's quest, a journey made possible rhetorically by situating him within the context of Vietnam, but removing him from the
morally uncertain scene of war. This displacement protects the aviator
from the same physical and ethical fate as his ground-pounding counterparts, thus preserving the honorable image of the warrior. To support
this claim, the essay chronicles the narrative pattern requisite to the hero's
quest fulfillment, comparing and contrasting the films' symbolic elements
with conventional film representations of American ground troops who
failed to emerge heroically. The essay concludes with the implications of
the analysis for the preservation of the warrior's image in post–Vietnam
America.

The Quest and Sequestering of the Aviator

The warrior as hero is a "monomyth" in virtually all cultures, according to Joseph Campbell, and the hero's quest is the "most important archetype underlying American cultural mythology."[12] The quest story involves the journey (act) of a hero-victim (agent) who departs the common day world (scene) in search of a precious object that can be found only by descending to and seeking the power of the gods in the underworld (agency). The hero must overpower the guardians (counteragents), a feat usually requiring helpers who are knowledgeable or magical (co-agents), and then ascend back to the everyday world to use that discovery in beneficial service to his people (purpose). The quest is a familiar narrative structure, its dramatic conventions defining the five elements of the war film genre: the mission, the justification for involvement in the war, the development of the symbiotic relationships within the unit to survive, the stark and open landscape, and the elevation of characters above the madness and violence of the war.[13] It is important to reiterate that numerous scholars argue that mass-mediated depictions of the American soldier in Vietnam are the antithesis of the hero's quest because they portray war as profane and the warrior unable to overcome the insanity of war to emerge as heroic — even when veterans eventually return to the site of war to enact a symbolic mediated victory and resolution of conflict.[14] Films featuring the pilot, however, depart significantly from conventional Vietnam warrior narratives by chronicling the transformation of the aviator into mythical hero and, like other mythic trajectories of the mid–1980s, Vietnam movies "attempt to restore the fictional World War II *master narrative* to Vietnam reinterpretations."[15]

All three films lend an aura of authenticity to their stories by announcing that they are based on real events occurring during the Vietnam conflict. *Hanoi Hilton*, the film with the moniker given by American POWs to the prison on the outskirts of Hanoi, promises to be an account of the POWs' experience at the hands of the North Vietnamese. Indeed, it ends with the note that while 725 American POWs eventually were repatriated, 2,471 soldiers remain MIAs. *Bat 21* opens with the statement that Colonel Hambleton was an Air Force missile intelligence expert whose "access to highly classified information" made him invaluable and heightened the urgency to rescue him from behind enemy lines when his plane was shot down. *Flight of the Intruder* provides an enigmatic message informing the audience that by 1973 the United States Navy had perfected a medium-range aircraft called the A-6, or Intruder, that had no defensive weapons but was capable of infiltrating enemy territory undetected. It apparently was available for use during the Vietnam War.

Unlike the metaphorical surrealism permeating the ground soldiers' combat nightmare in *Platoon* or *Apocalypse Now*[16] or the implausible fantasy of the one-man fighting machine in the back-to-Nam films[17]—both symbolic interpretations of war and warriors—pilot movies lay claim to a verisimilitude which implies both fact and truth and, thus, character accuracy and credibility. In addition, the stories span the totality of the war: While *Hanoi Hilton* covered the period from 1964 to 1973, *Bat 21* chronicled the early escalation of the air war in 1966 and 1967, and *Flight of the Intruder* occurred in 1972 during the march toward the war's end. This sense of realism, then, ostensibly captures the whole rather than a slice of the Vietnam saga, and the essential sameness of characters across the three films provides continuity and stability to warriors' qualities. Buffeted by realism, warrior-pilots undergo a descent-holding-ascent pattern in their journeys toward survival with meaning and honor.

THE FREE FALL: ACT AND SCENE

A potential hero must be deemed worthy to warrant ascension to cultural honor. In the context of war, this means that warriors cannot merely perform their duties with competence but must also possess more intangible inner strengths that set them apart from others of their military ilk. War becomes a testing ground for its participants. The three main characters of the films are career officers, seasoned pilots, and military advisors stationed in Vietnam, engaged in diverse duties in support of the war effort. In the films' first sequences, they embark on routine missions (acts) that end as anything routine but when they are catapulted from their aircraft to the underworld site (scene) of their quest.

In *Hanoi Hilton*, for example, Williamson is part of a two-sortie mission when he and his navigator are forced to eject from their crippled aircraft. Arrested by local villagers, the injured navigator is summarily murdered, and the sojourn of lonely captivity begins for Williamson. Similarly, Hambleton, an aging pilot in *Bat 21*, volunteers to ride as navigator on a mission to observe the site for a U.S. troop deployment designed to thwart an anticipated North Vietnamese offensive. Not far from the target site, the plane is hit, and all perish save Hambleton, who parachutes to the illusory safety of the jungle in enemy territory. In *Flight of the Intruder*, Grafton's troubles begin when the daredevil and his copilot are sent off on what Grafton thinks is a bogus mission to destroy a truck park. On their return, a lone shooter strikes and kills the copilot. Grafton's ensuing rage provokes his need to lead a "real" mission "up North" to destroy the missile-producing manufacturing plants that house the weapons that are killing his friend and other Americans. He discovers, though, that he is constrained by the president of the United States from enacting such a plan.

Their missions aborted, these aviators are dropped literally and figuratively into the zone of war, a scene for enacting a war-within-a-war that the characters must navigate to survive. This scene is strikingly different from — even though it bears some resemblance to— the urban and rural jungles populating other mediated versions of Vietnam. In the grunt's experience, his off-combat time tends to be marked by the decadent underbelly of urban South Vietnam or in the Doors-dominated, hashish-filled tents on military or makeshift bases. In combat, soldiers are enveloped within a terror-ridden, chaotic, jungle "inferno" that strips them of the means and will to act except for the purpose of sheer survival.[18] In the back-to-Nam films, the warrior has to overcome the scenic destructiveness of a corrupt bureaucracy to return to the jungles of Vietnam alone, where he is once again at home with the terrain and where he effectively appropriates the land in pursuit of his goal.[19] For pilots, however, Vietnam's combat site represents uncharted territory for crucible and self-discovery.

These films' characters are forced to trade a relatively privileged, detached, and infinite comfort zone for confrontation in a place that is at once close up and threatening but also curiously stark and not insurmountable. Early on, the Vietnam air films variously establish the credentials of aviators and the stature of their machinery, both depicted as at least somewhat disconnected from the battlefield. *Hanoi Hilton* opens to the inspired strains of military music and the fleeting beauty of an F-4 Phantom soaring through the clouds as it gives way to a press conference featuring Williamson. Telling reporters that his tour in Vietnam is lawfully authorized by government officials and that the citizens of South Vietnam only want "freedom, to think for themselves, and faith," the film merges patriotism, technological power, and the aviator's clarity of purpose in one fell swoop.

This definition of the pilot as worthy defender of nation is similarly portrayed in *Flight of the Intruder.* Jake and his copilot, Murg, first appear on screen during a mission to destroy a parking lot of enemy trucks. It feels like simulated combat for Jake because at the time of his tour of duty encouraging signs at the Paris peace talks had led President Nixon to halt bombing and any fly-overs in North Vietnamese territory. Hot-dogging it anyway, he maneuvers his plane very close to the ground —"wreaking havoc on the jungle"— and Murg is hit by a stray bullet. The innocuous-turned-serious mission makes the film's next scenes of good-natured jousting and jock talk about the superiority of the fighter pilot over all other aviators rather hollow. Yet, the film presents the pilots as "hungry tigers," a select and elite group of fighters with the requisite aggressive, can-do attitude, who have no doubts that they're the "best in the business."[20] Given the constraints on pilots' abilities to act, the opportunity to demonstrate their mettle will occur only by subverting the rules—operating behind the scenes as it were.

Bat 21 offers a glimpse of the value and privilege accorded ranking military officers. The audience is introduced to Hambleton with an array of icons of Vietnam: the helicopter that rises slowly above the hilltops, the serenity and order of the rice paddies, the anticipatory but foreboding music as the camera pans thick jungles and rivers. The conventional symbolic importance of these images is incongruously juxtaposed against the colonel, intelligence expert and golf aficionado, because he is practicing his golf swing and the helicopter interrupts his concentration. Later, back at Operations, the colonel displays the same kind of single-minded passion as he whips a military offensive into shape. In this film, the pilot emerges as a sharp, controlled, problem-solving commander.

The scenes into which the three aviators' free-fall bear none of the accoutrements of other mediated versions of the Vietnam experience. Their initial descent is as quiet as it is banal. Perhaps this is because these pilots have little understanding of what they might encounter; to be sure, typically in war, pilots exist within different kinds of scenes altogether. The archetypal contexts for fliers include the vast openness of the sky and cloistering within the cockpit of a powerful aircraft, both of which are under the self-assured control of the aviator. Indeed, the sky is a benign space of unrestrained nothingness, an uncontaminated independence which pilots utilize to accomplish mission and ego fulfillment. Shoos and George argue that the combat plane is a "mythic beast" which resides as a "central fetish" in a mythic place, a container at one with the pilot as contained machine.[21] Pilot and plane are intricately fused, the latter an extension of the ego of the former. Similarly, Conlon observes that the male psyche is obsessed with machinery, such that

> the soldierly ego works to surround itself with armor, … [and] by rigorous ascetic discipline and military drill, he can recreate himself as a "man of steel." … The fragile ego hopes that a mechanistically armored encasement can keep it together as a unified whole.[22]

This symbiotic relationship between pilot and jet sits in sharp contrast to the other ubiquitous flying machine of Vietnam: the helicopter. But, whereas the helicopter has emerged as the archetypal symbol of the Vietnam War by rhythmically representing the twin themes of tension and abandonment that constitute the ground soldier's narrative, the helicopter also has the power to both insert soldiers into and extract them from the war.[23] As such, this separation of grunt from machine negates an ego function for soldiers dependent upon the chopper because it is not a space they can symbolically claim as their own. For combat pilots, though, planes are safe havens physically and psychologically. To surrender one's aircraft by downing or grounding, then, means more than losing security, weaponry, or one's way; rather, it means losing part of oneself.

As they descend into the nether world, aviators are stripped of their safety net — their "exterior" selves — and, hence, are fragmented. Williamson's and Hambleton's planes are destroyed, leaving only these warriors' interior resources intact. While Hambleton ends up in the enemy jungle, a place he has observed only dispassionately from afar, Williamson finds himself a POW, alone and incarcerated in a claustrophobic cell. For Grafton to contemplate a forbidden mission "up country" to "SAM City" means that his plane must remain invisible and undetected, thus incapable of genuine empowerment. In all three cases, foiled missions yield to larger imperatives to survive, reintegrate into wholeness, and perform their duties. Because these pilots have been robbed of the vestiges of their professional and technical training, the potentials residing in their inner cores must be activated.

THE HOLDING PATTERN: AGENT AND AGENCY

The image of the warrior as hero is chronicled in myth and lore the world over, thus providing soldiers with idealized cultural models for behavior in the military and under combat conditions. In American mythology of war, underscored by the goal of "regeneration through violence" for nation and combatants,[24] the warrior must be able to balance dialectical tensions indigenous to two competing value orientations that arise in the context of battle: militarism and moralism.[25] Just as militarism demands that warriors be proficient, competent, team-oriented, unified, and devastating killers, so too does moralism demand integrity, ethics, and the preservation of humaneness, particularly for the innocents in war. Only by balancing both dialectical values can the warrior emerge as a hero. Anything less means death or surrender to an unethical code of conduct.

Films featuring the grunt's Vietnam experience usually portray soldiers who are unable to maintain militarism or moralism appropriately. The typical soldier is either a terrified, barely trained draftee ill prepared for the jungles, weather, enemy strategies, or hostile environment, or a hardened zealot surviving his combat tour almost mercilessly, adapting to the moral ambiguities of day-to-day existence. In either case, soldiers without clarity of mission or goal substitute survival for the larger national imperatives of defending country, principles of democracy, and protecting fellow soldiers. Because war is envisioned as purposeless destruction, warriors often succumb to the exigencies of scene in order to survive, and because survival is predicated on enacting militarism to the extreme without moralism to curb its impulses, the grunt's status as warrior hero is all but negated.

By contrast, the back-to-Nam films feature a Rambo-like veteran alienated from and incapable of reintegrating into society upon his return from the war. When he is offered the chance to return to the jungle to find and recover American POWs—a clear purpose this time—he accepts the challenge, in part to bring a mission to resolution and also to salvage the spirit he apparently left behind. But this returning warrior is a consummate superhero, an individualist who sheds technology, government, and guides to go it alone.[26] In essence, then, he upsets the dialectical balance of militarism and moralism because, in this version, the warrior experiences no tension at all. Rather, his absolute moral conviction never gets tested, and he is so militaristically superior that he has no worthy adversaries to defeat. Although the superhero succeeds in recovering the moral worth of the soldier, he fails to fulfill the mythical warrior's role.

The American pilot, however, enjoys a special kind of legacy that distinguishes him from the grunt in three significant ways relevant to Vietnam, and simultaneously elevates his real and mass-mediated image to transcend time and be equally valuable in past, present, and future. First, while the warrior has always been revered in myth and lore, the warrior-pilot has the added advantage of triggering the universal human dream to fly. "An impulse rooted deep in our collective unconscious," says Hallion, "the desire to fly has always been one of humanity's strongest aspirations," constituting for Sigmund Freud "a definable human characteristic."[27] Furthermore, that psychic impulse is actualized in religion, for all of the world's major religions include "greater and lesser deities—both 'good' and 'bad'—that could fly."[28] The lure of the flier, then, is irresistible for the pilot, who personifies and gives vent to this mythic delight. Not surprisingly, this impulse has been transferred into contemporary mass media where the pilot and reverence to flight form a dominant film genre, framing thousands of movies.[29]

Second, in the larger social and political milieu framing Vietnam in the 1960s and early 1970s, the war and, by extension, the soldier participating in it may have been unpopular, but the image of the aviator remained appealing. In accounting for this dynamic, Gruener argues that the enduring mystique of the pilot stems from the interrelationships among Vietnam aviator, astronaut, and American POW:

> In the 1960s there was probably no hero more pervasive than the American astronaut. The astronaut was first a pilot, most often a combat pilot, the ultimate American: physically perfect, mentally tough, intellectually gifted, morally pure, and spiritually wild.... The POWs, most of whom were military pilots, were potential astronauts robbed of their destiny by the North Vietnamese.... POW pilots were attractive heroes, could-be astronauts, military men bound to but at the same time separated from the political motivations that started and sustained the war.... Thus, the pilots embodied not only the strength and perfection of the astronaut but also the innocence and complacence of the female victim.[30]

Pilot charisma had the sustaining power to extend all the way from cultural place and outer space to Southeast Asia and serve as an antidote for disillusionment with the war and the sometimes disconcerting actions of American ground soldiers.

Third, the military pilot is a professional, an officer, and typically a career "lifer." Unlike many of the naive recruits or draftees populating films about the grunt's Vietnam experience, pilots were an exceptionally select group who had to pass psychological muster and undergo extensive training before they were let loose on multimillion dollar jets. In addition, flying is popularly conceived as a calling, an instinct that drives both the love of the endeavor and the commitment to make it one's life work. More importantly, however, the career pilot is a "war manager," positioned within the defense system as a legitimate site of knowledge. Gibson uses Foucault's conception of "knowledges" to contrast the roles of soldiers, aviators, and the bureaucracy to develop a thesis about the mechanical power of "technowar" in Vietnam. Whereas the grunt exists close to the bottom of the military stratification system, having but "subjugated" knowledge, the political and military bureaucracies hold the high ground, knowing more and making as well as justifying decisions. The pilot, "because of his professionalism, experience, and management role, fits somewhere between these two poles,"[31] spread throughout the hierarchy to produce knowledge, make command decisions, and enjoy access to information. What this does is establish the aviator as a mediator between the soldier and the upper echelons of military policy making. Yet, the pilot's role is not simply one of divergent knowledges, including control of technology, but also of experiences, for the flier fights *in* war and sets policy *about* war at the same time. That is the aviator's unique province and one source of his enduring appeal in the enactment of war.

The Vietnam air films feature three warriors (agents), each representing facets of the pilot persona. The youngest and lowest ranking is Grafton, in *Flight of the Intruder*. He is all derring-do and cavalier, with the inexperience and innocence it takes to boldly violate orders and surreptitiously plan a dangerous mission. His power consists of knowledge and possession of cutting-edge military hardware to give him the edge to cripple the enemy, provided that he can devise a way to unleash that force. Williamson and Hambleton are older and more experienced, accustomed to leadership positions. While Williamson commands briefings and missions over North Vietnam and fully engages in air combat, his power stems from a conviction about the noble rightness of his duty and his acquiescence to military authority as the twin paths to accomplish military goals. Hambleton, the veteran and highest ranking of the three, is the paradigm war-manager. An operations officer, he has access to a wide array of intelligence information and uses that knowledge to execute the strategic planning of the war.

Still, similarities among the three aviators transcend their differences. They sport the flight suits marking their distinction and a confidence culled from training, officer privileges, and positioning in the military system that gives them heightened awareness and access to classified weapons information. Yet, these knowledges are the first to go when the aviators are downed. Williamson's convictions are transformed from abstract to sorely tested; Hambleton's strategic authority moves from detachment to direct encounter; and Grafton supplants bystanding with subversive engagement. The novel situations in which these fliers find themselves thus are tension ridden, triggering the warriors' impulse to survive.

A tension-ridden context necessitating survival instincts also is clearly an intrinsic component of the Vietnam grunt's experience. In films featuring the ground-pounder, the agency through which to ensure survival is usually unchecked violence stemming from anger or the deployment of war's weaponry to the extreme.[32] In *Platoon*, for example, soldiers seek revenge for the killing of one of their unit by a Viet Cong hiding in a village. The soldiers gather the villagers in the town square, psychologically terrorizing them, and then torture and beat to death a retarded teenager and rape numerous women before razing the village. They use all of the tools in their arsenal less to carry off a mission that advances the cause of war than to vent uncontrollable rage. That rage, and the fear accompanying it, also leads soldiers to disunity and the eventual betrayal of one another. No sacred code of ethics drives soldiers' actions in these works; rather, a combination of crowd mentality, intimidating weapons, and always the overarching vulnerability arising from the need to survive at all costs precipitates the carnage.

In back-to-Nam films, violence remains the principle agency of choice, but it is glorified instead of uncontrolled.[33] In *Rambo: First Blood, Part II,* Rambo appropriates knives, guns, grenades, bazookas, armed helicopters, and bombs in addition to his own hands to remove obstacles to his mission. The pyrotechnics are spectacular as a jungle goes up in flames, and the destruction is so awesome and absolute that it overshadows even the supernatural feats of the Vietnam veteran. The net effect is a tensionless context because a morally superior superhero armed with imposing weapons and technology is indestructible.

The means through which pilots enact their quests, however, are much different from those of grunts. Their principal task, of course, is to extricate themselves from dire circumstances; failure to do so may well result in death or capture. Equally important, a military officer's sworn duty places the nation's needs above self-interest, so failure could undermine the mission's success. Since they are stripped of normal agencies to carry out their duties, these pilots rely on gut instinct, turning relationally to a network of co-agents and internally to intuitions and intelligence honed from professional training.

CO-AGENTS

Combat efficiency and proficiency are contingent on coordinated teamwork. Each aviator realizes from the moment he touches ground — both intuitively and by training — that his survival is predicated on help from others. As he seeks those contacts immediately, he also discovers that his quest is not so alien as to prevent him from implementing some of his learned skills. In *Hanoi Hilton,* it takes Williamson over a year to meet up with another American POW because he has been in an isolation cell for that long to "correct his attitude" about cooperating with his jailers. He is eventually recognized as the senior ranking officer at the prison camp (until a more SRO is captured later), and his first decision is to order mandatory contact among fellow captives, for "contact is everything." For more than eight years of captivity, Williamson embraces the credo that "sticking together" is the key to unity, security, victory, and survival. And, while he serves as the guide for other POWs undergoing their own crucibles in captivity, his fellow POWs collectively become the tutelary figures enabling him to endure.

In *Bat 21,* Hambleton's guide is evacuation pilot Bird Dog, whose job is to fly reconnaissance and pinpoint the location of downed soldiers, make and retain visual contact, and coordinate rescue efforts. Like many mentors of the hero's quest, Bird Dog is the warrior's lifeline. After completing his descent, Hambleton follows military protocol to radio his location to command, whereupon Bird Dog is dispatched to the site. Unbeknownst to Hambleton, the enemy is close by, so Bird Dog becomes the warrior's eyes as he moves Hambleton out of harm's way. Later, Hambleton reciprocates by postponing Bird Dog's rescue attempt when it is unsafe to land. Throughout the film, the fliers continually shift roles, each guiding the other through their joint mission. Eventually the rescue site becomes too dangerous even for Bird Dog to reconnoiter, and he is ordered to sever contact with Hambleton. But Bird Dog merely shifts aircraft, commandeering a helicopter the next morning, and sets out to rescue the colonel himself. He too is shot down, and both officers become co-agents in the rescue and survival quest.

Flight of the Intruder is related less to survivability, at least initially, than it is to combat viability. Grafton realizes he cannot undertake any mission without prior surveillance, but such surveillance is officially prohibited. He learns of a legendary bombardier, Virgil Cole, who has seen Hanoi up close during his three tours of combat duty and knows the location of surface-to-air missile factories and supply depots. Although Cole reveres battle, he is leery of Grafton's far-fetched plan to steal the Intruder, make it to Hanoi undetected, release bombs, and return unobserved to the aircraft carrier. More importantly, Grafton has never seen combat, so Cole is unsure of his credentials as a flier and challenges the aviator to prove himself first. Of course, Grafton passes the test with flying colors, and mission plans proceed. Warrior and guide become one in the invisible plane, and they enact the rest of the quest together. Like the other aviator films, part of the warrior's journey involves discovering the trust and cooperation requisite to placing one's life in the hands of another, thus sealing bonds between fellow warriors.

INTERNAL RESOURCES

The hero's quest is not just about surviving, even within battle, but also about being tested and discovering truths along the way. While aviator films revel in the pilot's persona and his relationship to helpers, the would-be hero's internal resources and the way he uses them to fulfill his destiny frame the intrigue of each work. All three warriors use a combination of instinct, intuition, and intelligence, born of professional training and their military code of conduct, to traverse the minefields in their hostile environments. In effect, they recast these scenes into sites where their skills are useable and influential.

From the moment Williamson steps into the camp in *Hanoi Hilton*, he realizes the irrelevance of any of his prior expectations about the treatment of POWs in wartime. He is told by camp commandant Major No Duc that the Geneva Convention doesn't count because war between the United States and North Vietnam has not been declared. When Williamson refuses to divulge classified information, the major sets the conditions of his existence as a contest of wills and places Willlamson in an isolation cell for the next year. The pattern of the aviator's life from that point on is segregation, followed by integration with other POWs, physical and psychological torture, and isolation once again. Throughout his ordeals, particularly the long stretches of seclusion, he gradually comes to the understanding that resistance is critical for his sanity and for coping with an immobilizing scene.

Active resistance takes three forms in the movie. First and foremost, Williamson must keep his mind and, therefore, hope alive. He accomplishes this feat through faith, in a religious sense with constant prayer vigils, and in a patriotic sense by clinging to the belief that his country will repatriate him. When finally freed from his year-long stretch in isolation, the commandant defines that release as "humane and lenient"; Williamson's response is telling: "lenient, hell, I just outlasted you." Second, he nurtures unity among POWs, because only by presenting a unified front can the captives generate some sense of control over their circumstances. In one of the more inventive sections of the film, the POWs create a communication system to sabotage an order of silence. It combined finger tapping, Morse code, hand and eye signals, the passing of written notes when possible, and discovering weaknesses in stone walls so sound could carry from cell to cell. The initial task of all entering POWs was to learn this code so human contact would boost the new captives' morale.

By far, however, the third tool of resistance for the POW was the U.S. military code of conduct, a set of behavioral standards that simultaneously could undermine the enemy's control and provide order, discipline, and comfort to captives. In imposing the code, Williamson sets up a hierarchy of command, a system for issuing orders, and a series of rules to govern the POW collective. As the POWs' treatment deteriorates—through torture, attempts to pit POWs against one another, threats of isolation and death, and even historically chronicled events like the POWs' march through Hanoi and actress Jane Fonda's visit to the camps—the rules are improvised but remain salient. For example, early on Williamson's edicts call for "manipulat[ing] the enemy, but not antagoniz[ing] them" and "resist[ing] any attempt to act contrite." But when unspeakably brutal torture leads one POW after another to the humiliation of "breaking down," the order switches to "resist as long as possible, then do the best you can."

The veracity of the rules is severely tested when the North Vietnamese hold out the carrot of early release for some POWs. But the order from the POW command authority stands tight that there will be no early release of captives unless they are all freed because, as Williamson states, "the minute you play their game, you've lost control."

The POWs' use of intelligence, inventiveness, improvisation, and internalization of a code of conduct transforms an impossibly constraining scene removed from actual combat into one that remains warlike. In so doing, they carry on the war through active resistance that allows captives to perform as warriors and fulfill their military duties.

Whereas resistance is the only viable strategy open to POW aviators in *Hanoi Hilton*, Hambleton of *Bat 21* has relatively more freedom to maneuver in his jungle environment. He confronts what appears to be a double bind: He knows capture is out of the question, for he possesses too much valuable intelligence information, yet he is uncertain he can endure until rescued. And time is short, for the assault *he* had planned will commence in the area in which he is downed within 24 hours. Consequently, Hambleton must empower himself with whatever resources he possesses to act upon the scene of his struggle.

Because Hambleton cannot be picked up until the next morning, he must spend the night alone in the jungle. He fashions a hiding place from palm leaves and spends a good portion of the evening fearful about his plight and frantic for dialogue with Bird Dog. Gradually, it occurs to him that their conversations and rescue plans may be intercepted by the enemy. Faced with that possibility, he takes out paper and pencil and begins to rationally examine his options. What emerges from this analysis is what Command later calls "brilliant" and "clever." He converts the scene into an imaginary nine holes of golf. His passion for golf stems from his view that it is the only sport genuinely challenging, necessitating skill, deliberation, and tactical choices. Hence, he is obsessed with the game and knows every hole on every air force base in the world, including the length and angle of each. Given that he designed the forthcoming air strike, he calculates how far he needs to move away from the bombing site to be safe for a rescue effort and the distance he can reasonably walk with an injured leg. He then selects golf holes that meet the required distances, draws them on his map, and relays the plan in code to Bird Dog (who has to learn the lingo of golf quickly in order to interpret). The inventiveness of this plan thwarts potential enemy interception, provides Command with his whereabouts at all times, and protects him from the path of the air strike. In effect, he transforms analytical skills into militarism, a move which enables him to appropriate a sport and reconfigure a scene that places him on safe ground once again.

Hambleton is not tested just on survival skills, but also on moral fiber. During the journey to the pick-up zone, the colonel chances upon a farm hut where hunger leads him to steal rice to eat. When he is caught by the owner, Hambleton tries to apologize and signal that he is a friend, but the old man pulls out a knife and attacks him. In self-defense Hambleton kills the farmer, only to find out that the man's family has witnessed the tragedy. After apologizing profusely, he runs to a river, makes a futile attempt to clean his hands, and bursts into tears. Later, he discloses to Bird Dog: "I killed a man today. He wasn't a soldier. I couldn't stop him. I never had to do anything like this before in my life. I'm used to sitting at 30,000 feet with a cup of coffee."

His anguish is heightened when two choppers sent to rescue him are shot down not far from where he is waiting. When villagers begin to shoot the captives, Hambleton is so distraught he comes out of hiding to give himself up. But the commander radios him to vacate the location immediately. These two events lead Hambleton to tell Bird Dog that "people keep dying around me. I'm through killing. I'm through." That conviction is soon tested when he encounters a boy on a rope bridge during a monsoon. They acknowledge each other in passing, their silence creating an unspoken bond. Forced into confronting his militaristic and moralistic impulses, the colonel applies a set of ethical criteria and professional training to cope with the threatening scene in which he finds himself. The resulting empowerment enables him to transform an unfamiliar scene in one more manageable and potentially survivable.

Grafton's dilemma in *Flight of the Intruder* is that he has no war scene in which to fight. Yet, his instincts tell him he is morally obligated to at least attempt to halt threats against American troops even if he cannot overtly pursue a course of engagement. Sustained by a perceived moral righteousness greater than military protocol, he rationalizes that being a warrior in these circumstances means violating the commander's orders. Thus, he initiates a campaign of camouflage and deception as the means to overcome the paralysis of nonaction.

Grafton has one clear advantage that neither Williamson nor Hambleton possessed: an airplane, one that could fight a "one-plane war." But this airplane is not supposed to exist any more than Hanoi is supposed to exist in the warrior's dreams. Nevertheless, throwing all caution to the wind, the lieutenant and Virgil take off under the cloak of darkness and head the stealth aircraft toward Hanoi. Successfully completing the secret mission, they are discovered by the aircraft carrier commander, who orders an immediate court-martial tribunal.

Although the warriors assume responsibility for breaking the faith, they feel no remorse for having handicapped the enemy, for militarism tempered by moral integrity is better than being sitting ducks any day. The two aviators are vindicated, however, when the president rescinds the bombing restrictions; after all, they cannot be punished for doing what the president has just ordered. Their instincts, then, were right on the mark. Virgil later dies when the ship's entire squadron, led by Grafton, head to North Vietnam to resume air strikes. Grafton takes comfort in the knowledge that their deception was worth the sacrifice because, by transforming an inert scene into a controllable one, Grafton set the conditions to do his job in war.

THE HIGH FLIGHT: PURPOSE

If warriors meet the challenges facing them on their journeys in the underworld, they have learned something valuable. This discovery consummates the quest, and warriors can then return to the everyday world to a hero's welcome. Such a welcome was denied grunts in mass-mediated experiences of Vietnam. They learned the difficult lessons that war is hell, and the enemy may well be in us because our penchant for glorifying war masks its essential profanity and destructiveness. The back-to-Nam veteran already knew this by the time he returned to Southeast Asia, but his venture teaches him that the enemy in Vietnam was not the soldier but a corrupt, indifferent military and political bureaucracy that hung soldiers out to dry by endlessly interfering with the scene of war from afar. In the former group of films, the soldier emerges as flawed and often morally wanting; in the latter group, the soldier's core honor and morality are reinstated. But, as these works intimate, rehabilitating Vietnam veterans is too late because their descent into hell was accompanied by no viable avenues of escape.

Vietnam aviator films don't just supply warriors with scenic options but arm them with tools that can redefine the context altogether. A scene that can be rendered vulnerable is one potentially mediated by a warrior possessing qualities culled from military training and higher-order principles. Williamson is eventually released from prison, his resistance having symbolically defeated the enemy. Hambleton's successful extraction is made possible by his own active and strategic intervention. Grafton's mission is productive because it affects the outcome of the war. However, their experiences also leave these officers with more lasting, transcendent truths: Williamson finds faith in comrades and country to be the only foundations that matter; Hambleton understands that war is no game, but a personal, reprehensible tragedy; and Grafton learns the harsh realities that attend participating in war. In acting upon instead of succumbing to the scene of war, they are strengthened and emerge from the crucible of the quest acknowledged heroes, meeting war with honor and achieving "peace with honor."

Conclusions and Implications

This chapter claims that pilots are the protected heroes of the Vietnam War. They existed quietly as professionals performing their jobs before the start of conflict and continued to do the same jobs under combat conditions (and, for the most part, after the war ended). Because of their normal positioning above or behind the scenes of battle, they were influential but relatively invisible as warriors until placed into the scene of war. Even then, though, they remained concealed: alone in the jungle, under radar detection in a cutting-edge weapon, locked in a cage. Removed from the landscape of war, they also escaped association with it as a controlling site of nonredemption for warriors lacking purpose and understanding in a war that apparently made little sense. So, when these films displace aviators from their comfort zones and drop them directly into war, they become visible as individuals, without the baggage accompanying the Vietnam grunt and with a clear mission to pursue. Knowledge, training, and experience provided them with the resources they required to alter the scene and prevent their destruction by it; these skills, in turn, allowed them to emerge as warrior heroes.

As such, Vietnam aviator films challenge the dominant narratives of grunts' experiences in Vietnam because they present a competing narrative of tribulation and triumph, stories about a group of warriors who fulfill a life-altering quest that strengthens them as individuals, integrates them within the larger culture as worthy participants in war, and saves them from the debacle commonly understood as the Vietnam tragedy. Ideologically the discourses tow a promilitary line and feature disciplined, unified, and ethical warriors. While the works do not naturalize war, they carry the message that if war is to be fought, it should be fought by professionals who possess an intractable code of conduct and who are supported unconditionally by their nation.

Aviator films never achieved the same critical or popular success as their grunt counterparts. This certainly suggests that the symbolic experience of the Vietnam War on the ground indelibly captures the crucible of Vietnam, hence providing audiences with the only warranted interpretive framework to understand loss and the reality of war. In this sense, no

alternate narrative about Vietnam warrior heroes can dislodge that meaning. Still, by the time pilot films worked their way into American popular
culture, the difficult process of reconciling the war had begun to recede in
memory. Through the ingrained appeal of the warrior pilot image, then,
these films serve as a reminder of the invisible power of the professional
soldier and the endurance of that image in myth and reality. The aviator
is portrayed as heroic and useable; the persona fuses mythic images of the
cowboy, the adventurer, the rugged individualist, the community savior,
and the technological hero, all of which ideologically control past, present, and future on the ground, in the sky, and over the seas. Most Vietnam pilots made the transition right back into their prewar jobs after their
combat tours ended, later becoming the principal players of the Gulf War
and the generals and policymakers in military and government. Retaining their status and image in post–Vietnam, they continue to be the managers of culture in peace and war.

NOTES

1. Tom Morganthau, "We're Still Prisoners of War." *Newsweek* (April 15, 1985): 94.
2. See Harry W. Haines, "'What Kind of War?': An Analysis of the Vietnam Veterans Memorial." *Critical Studies in Mass Communication* 3 (1986): 1–20.
3. Barry Brummett, *Rhetoric in Popular Culture* (New York: St. Martin's, 1994),
62.
4. Janice Hocker Rushing and Thomas S. Frentz, "The Rhetoric of *Rocky*: A
Social Value Model of Criticism." *Western Journal of Speech Communication* 42 (1978):
64.
5. Harry W. Haines, "The Pride Is Back: *Rambo, Magnum P.I.*, and the Return
Trip to Vietnam," in *Cultural Legacies of Vietnam: Uses of the Past in the Present*, Richard
Morris and Peter Ehrenhaus, eds. (Norwood, N.J.: Ablex, 1990), 120.
6. John Hellmann, *American Myth and the Legacy of Vietnam* (New York:
Columbia University Press, 1986), 222.
7. Jeffrey Walsh and James Aulich, "Introduction," *Vietnam Images: War and
Representation* (New York: St. Martin's, 1989), 7.
8. C. D. B. Bryan, "Barely Suppressed Screams: Getting a Bead on Vietnam Literature." *Harper's Magazine* (June 1984): 69.
9. Edward Tabor Linenthal, *Changing Images of the Warrior Hero in America: A
History of Popular Symbolism* (New York: Edwin Mellen, 1982), 159, 152.
10. See George N. Dionisopoulos and Steven R. Goldzwig, "'The Meaning of
Vietnam': Political Rhetoric as Revisionist Cultural History." *Quarterly Journal of Speech*
78 (1992): 61–79.
11. James William Gibson, *The Perfect War: Technowar in Vietnam* (Boston:
Atlantic Monthly, 1986), 319.
12. Richard Slotkin, *Regeneration through Violence: The Mythology of the American Frontier, 1600–1860* (Middletown, Conn.: Wesleyan University Press, 1973).
13. Stuart Kaminsky, *American Film Genres: Approaches to a Critical Theory of
Popular Film* (New York: Dell, 1974).

14. See David E. Whillock, "Defining the Fictive American Vietnam War Film: In Search of a Genre." *Literature/Film Quarterly* 45 (1988): 244–50.

15. Tony Williams, "Narrative Patterns and Mythic Trajectories in Mid-1980s Vietnam Movies," in *Inventing Vietnam: The War in Film and Television*, Michael Anderegg, ed. (Philadelphia: Temple University Press, 1991), 115.

16. Karen Rasmussen and Sharon D. Downey, "Dialectical Disorientation in Vietnam War Films: Subversion of the Mythology of War." *Quarterly Journal of Speech* 77 (1991): 176–95.

17. *Ibid.*

18. *Ibid.*

19. *Ibid.*

20. Frank J. O'Brien, *The Hungry Tigers: The Fighter Pilot's Role in Modern Warfare* (Blue Ridge Summit, Penn.: Aero/Tab, 1986), 2.

21. James Conlon, "Making Love, Not War: The Soldier Male in *Top Gun* and *Coming Home*," *Journal of Popular Film and Television* 18 (1990):22.

22. O'Brien, 22.

23. Alastair Spark, "Flight Controls: The Social History of the Helicopter as a Symbol of Vietnam," in *Vietnam Images: War and Representation*, Jeffrey Walsh and James Aulich, eds. (New York: St. Martin's, 1989), 92.

24. Richard Slotkin, *Regeneration through Violence: The Mythology of the American Frontier, 1600–1860.*

25. Rasmussen and Downey, "Dialectical Disorientation in Vietnam War Films: Subversion of the Mythology of War."

26. *Ibid.*

27. Richard P. Hallion, *Test Pilots: The Frontiersmen of Flight* (Washington, D.C.: Smithsonian, 1988), 1.

28. *Ibid.*

29. Stephen Pendo, *Aviation in the Cinema* (Metuchen, N.J.: Scarecrow, 1985).

30. E. G. Greuner, *Prisoners of Culture: Representing the Vietnam POW* (New Brunswick, N.J.: Rutgers University Press, 1993), 30.

31. Gibson, 464.

32. Rasmussen and Downey.

33. *Ibid.*

8

Trauma, Treatment, and Transformation: The Evolution of the Vietnam Warrior in Film

KAREN RASMUSSEN,
SHARON D. DOWNEY AND
JENNIFER ASENAS

The primordial grounding of all war narratives, observes Joseph Campbell, rests with the "cruel fact ... that killing is the precondition of all living whatsoever." Thus, nations imbued with a rich legacy of war myths likely are those who have experienced war's triumphs, for they "have survived to communicate their life-supporting mythic lore to descendants."[1] For better or worse, the United States is such a nation, one linked indelibly to a tradition of sacrosanct narratives framed by the principle of regeneration through violence,[2] warranted by a venerated noble purpose, and embodying what it means to be a hero. With the possible exception of World War I, America's experiences in war generally reaffirmed this mythic identity—until Vietnam.

The Vietnam War was America's only military defeat. It also was our longest war, our most protracted undeclared war, our first "living room" war, and our only war marked by the conspicuous absence of heroes.[3] Its legacy, often called the Vietnam Syndrome, created anxiety about our nation's ideology, identity, national mission, foreign policy, and images of what constitutes a warrior and a hero. Even after thirty years, Vietnam apparently still "clings to us hauntingly as unfinished business."[4]

This business of Vietnam has also pervaded the media industry for more than three decades. Because film's dramatic form is particularly well suited to enact significant social conflicts and anxieties,[5] it is not surprising that Hollywood's treatments of the war would downplay politics in favor of symbolic portrayals of warriors' experiences, both in combat and upon returning home. What is surprising, though, is the sheer magnitude, diversity, and disparity of those images. The same exigency that spawned a demented Colonel Kurtz in *Apocalypse Now* produced superman-avenger Rambo and troubled antiwar activist Ron Kovic of *Born on the Fourth of July.* The drug-induced self-destruction of Nick in *The Deer Hunter* stands in precipitous contrast to the quirky rage of Travis Bickle of *Taxi Driver,* the guilt-wracked suffering of Luke and Bob in *Coming Home,* and the antics of various crime fighters extraordinaire such as the denizens of the *Lethal Weapon* saga, *Magnum P.I.,* and *The A-Team.* To explain these incongruities, one could argue that each artifact simply depicts warriors coping differently with the consequences of combat or perhaps that warriors' experiences on the screen continue to mirror widespread cultural confusion about how to interpret the Vietnam era.

We argue, however, that if viewed collectively, narratives about Vietnam combatants reflect a rhetorical movement to define, attend to, and reconcile the cultural trauma precipitated by the Vietnam War. To achieve this end, Vietnam films cast war and the resulting Vietnam Syndrome as a catastrophic illness befalling the warrior. The resulting discourse of healing the warrior is a therapeutic rhetoric that functions symbolically to reinstate the honorable image of the Vietnam warrior, thereby reconciling the Vietnam experience socially. To support this claim, we employ Arthur Frank's narrative schema drawn from research on stories people tell about trauma in general and serious illnesses in particular. We then analyze three illness patterns emerging from films about Vietnam combatants and veterans: chaos, restitution, and quest narratives. We conclude by detailing the social import of the hero's evolution and of the rhetoric producing that hero.

Narratives of Illness

Narratives are stories that "have sequence and meaning for those who live, create, or interpret them" and thus are central to interpretation, decision making, and judgment in general.[6] As a method of sense making, they help people cope with traumatic events. The Vietnam War and subsequent Vietnam Syndrome constitute cultural afflictions resulting in social infirmity. Thus, our examination of the changing image of the Vietnam warrior draws on the work of Arthur Frank, who analyzes stories typically told about illness. Such sagas have to do with repairing a person's interpretation of traumatic disease and its aftermath. Whether they address individual or cultural pathology, people typically adapt and combine three narrative types.[7]

The *chaos* narrative is one of complete wreckage. It is a virtual antinarrative because the "and then" tenor of its story line depicts progressive degeneration, deterioration, and hopelessness. Such discourse lacks traditional narrative order, for it depicts life experiences without discernible sequence or causality.[8] Frank includes a description by a person with chronic illness who is caring for a mother with Alzheimer's:

> And if I'm trying to get dinner ready and I'm already feeling bad, she's in front of the refrigerator. Then she goes to put her hand on the stove and I got the fire on. And then she's in front of the microwave and then she's in front of the silverware drawer. And....[9]

The preceding illustrates the endless turmoil of the chaos experience. It also points to its central exigence: Because the person is living a life out of control, the storyteller's "consciousness has given up the struggle for sovereignty over its own experience." Unable to affect the course of events, she or he is battered and often mute or voiceless because the trauma defies the sense making of articulate expression. Without words and a coherent story, the chaos narrator's tale is "contingent, monadic, lacking desire, and dissociated."[10] Given this lack of pattern and voice, chaos narratives must have structure imposed on them from outside. Hence, persons who narrate the chaos do so only retrospectively when they have distance from the actual experiences.

The storyline of the *restitution* narrative is cyclical; its end is a return to the beginning, for it moves from health to a sickness whose cure leads back to wellness. Reflecting a natural desire to get well and stay that way, it is a structure favored by the medical establishment since it embodies the principle of cure, thereby casting health care personnel in the role of hero. This pattern rests on the assumption that any breakdown is temporary and therefore remediable. Agents do not heal themselves, although often they must exhibit courage and perseverance. The cure for the ailment, however, does not reside within the self. Through the wonders of medical science, wellness seemingly is only a trip to the pharmacy or doctor or therapist away. Television commercials continually reinforce this belief.[11] Central to the restitution narrative, then, is the afflicted person's need to seek outside help and to turn to others who have the insight, skill, and wisdom to effect a cure.

Quests differ from chaos and restitution narratives most importantly in their construction of the narrator's agency. While restitution tales involve outside intervention, chaos stories retain the sufferer's own voice, a voice which often is inarticulate. Quests, however, are about a person's taking charge of recovery. Thus, illness becomes a challenge to be transcended. In these stories people confront their afflictions so as to use the illness constructively; hence, the quest often becomes a spiritual journey. Its narrators search for alternative ways of coping grounded in a sense of purpose, a purpose that allows them to see the experience as a journey having a valuable end.[12]

The quest narrative described by Frank mirrors Joseph Campbell's description of the hero's journey. Its passage begins with departure, when a reluctant hero heeds the call of "destiny" to experience "the darkness, the unknown, and danger." The second phase is the initiation, or the road of trials the hero traverses inward into the "crooked lanes of [the person's] own spiritual labyrinth" to meet external challenges. The barriers encountered often seem insurmountable, yet true heroes succeed by drawing first on internal resources and then on helpers encountered along the way. Experiencing these trials, then, enables the person to emerge transformed, a superior being who has talents and gifts, or in the case of illness, some insight to offer others. The final stage is the return, during which heroes rejoin their community armed with a "life-transmuting trophy" that offers the possibility of collective healing or renewal.[13] But the aftermath of the quest is not always easy because communities sometimes receive the hero's message reluctantly.[14]

Restitution, chaos, and quest narratives are different ways of making sense of experience. In the case of trauma, especially, the three often work in concert with each other. The following analysis of films depicting the experience of Vietnam soldiers and veterans uses illness narratives as a lens to illuminate how the films collectively define warriors' trauma and treatment. Chaos narratives define the problems stemming from Vietnam while restitution and quest stories embody healing treatment and life-renewing recovery.

The Long Road to Recovery

The potpourri of films depicting images of the Vietnam warrior range from those highlighting the war itself (*Apocalypse Now, Full Metal Jacket,*

Casualties of War, Platoon, The Deer Hunter) to those featuring return trips to Vietnam (*Rambo: First Blood, Part II, Uncommon Valor*, the *Missing in Action* series) to works that chronicle veterans' return from the war (*Coming Home, Born on the Fourth of July, In Country, Jacob's Ladder*). They present the illness of the war by detailing its trauma, treatment, and recovery.

CHAOS NARRATIVES AND THE TRAUMA OF SICKNESS

Embedded in a wide range of films are vignettes and extended sequences that portray the debilitating experience of chaos in Southeast Asia and as warriors returned to the United States, thus defining the nature of the illness linked to our nation's experience with Vietnam. Such episodes— both during the war and at home — portray humans out of control in a series of never-ending negative incidents that spiral downward into the depths of degradation, desolation, and destruction.

The chaos of combat is a recurrent feature of many films focusing on the American soldier. Oliver Stone's semiautobiographical *Platoon*, for example, enacts the trauma of ground troops as it traces the experiences of Chris Taylor, who finds his platoon enmeshed in an internal conflict. Its initial scenes plunge warriors and audience into a deadening, fragmented world. The film's opening features a massive air transport disgorging new recruits into a dusty, yellow-brown wasteland to be greeted by the sight of body bags. The camera cuts immediately to an aerial shot of a green jungle and then to exhausted and disoriented men on night patrol as they hack their way through dense foliage, fighting treacherous terrain, insects, snakes, and the sight and smell of rotting corpses.

Although *Platoon* spans four separate battles, those encounters give it little structure. Rather, it is a collage of events: Patrol sequences punctuated by firefights give way to scenes in camp fraught with tension born of the platoon's internal discord, which give way in turn to the brutalization of a native village, all followed by more of the same. Combs captures the work's "and then" quality. He describes it as "an extreme patrol movie" featuring combat footage that is "a sequence of events with no sequence, skirmishes and fire-fights that might all be the same bloody, confused encounter with a cast of characters who ... are all reduced to the same function, to survive or die."[15] Similarly, Cardullo observes that the audience "gets a sense of the chaos, claustrophobia, nearsightedness, anxiety, and swiftness of battle, ... all adding up to the powerlessness felt by the man with a gun amidst a sea of guns."[16]

Apocalypse Now journeys progressively deeper into the madness that is Francis Ford Coppola's vision of the war. It traces the trials of Captain Willard, an intelligence officer directed by his superiors to locate and execute Colonel Walter Kurtz, a West Point graduate whose renegade army mirrors his own insanity. Coppola appropriates the metaphor of Joseph Conrad's *Heart of Darkness* as he depicts Willard's passage into the jungle aboard a patrol boat.[17] As credits roll, ghostlike images of helicopters traverse the screen, the sound of their blades becoming progressively more distinct. The film immediately envelops its main character in war's insanity, for it dissolves to the inverted image of a man's expressionless face as he lies inert on a bed in a hotel room while chopper images morph into a ceiling fan. Thus begins Willard's surrealistic odyssey into a world of macabre images and events. Augmenting this chaos is a cacophony marked by driving music, the percussive din of helicopters and bombs, the wail of victims, and eerie jungle noises, an aural assault that saps the audience's energy.[18] Coppola's work thus layers image upon image, blending the horrible and the hauntingly beautiful to create a vision of a war with neither rules nor purpose.[19]

Born on the Fourth of July is Oliver Stone's rendering of Vietnam veteran Ron Kovic's autobiography. The film dramatizes Kovic's roots, his choice to go to war, his experience of that conflict, and the trauma he transcends after his return. Stone's characterization of the chaos of combat includes two especially frenzied sequences. In the first, Ron and his men overrun a village they find populated mostly by defenseless women and children but then face a surprise attack by the Viet Cong. In the ensuing melee, Ron, blinded by the sun, shoots a soldier from Georgia, a young man he had promised to keep safe only hours earlier. The film shifts quickly to January 1968, when Ron, now on his second tour, refuses to stay down after initially being hurt in a frantic firefight and thus suffers the near-fatal wound that results in his paralysis. The juxtaposition of the two scenes reinforces the film's vision of the inexorable chaos of battle.

This tendency to present the experience of war as a relentless descent into a world void of reason, pattern, and rules also is characteristic of the way various films depict situations faced by returning veterans. In *Born on the Fourth of July* and *Rambo: First Blood*, the main character careens from obstacle to obstacle, his life marked by progressively greater disarray. Kovic survives Vietnam to face despicable conditions in the VA hospital where he and other veterans face inadequate medical care in a hellish, filthy hospital peopled by callous, uncaring personnel. Ron returns home to be met with the disease of friends and family, most notably his uptight Catholic mother. He drowns his sorrows in booze, only to be asked to leave because his actions cause others too much pain. His subsequent experience in a veterans' colony in Mexico is a hollow life built on alcohol, sex, and male bonding. His life takes one bad turn, and then another, and another.

Similarly, *Rambo: First Blood,* based on Charles Morrell's 1972 novel, is the tale of John Rambo's reaction to the "rejection, scorn, and prejudice" he faces when he returns from Vietnam.[20] The movie opens with a solitary male figure striding toward a farmhouse framed by the majestic mountains of the Northwest who discovers that his veteran buddy has died of cancer due to exposure to Agent Orange. Rambo's subsequent life reels downward as he encounters a redneck sheriff who doesn't like his looks and therefore escorts him out of town. Rambo stubbornly returns to face arrest and brutalization. His escape and subsequent capture is a frantic experience during which he eludes temporarily an ever-expanding array of sheriff's deputies, dogs, and national guard forces. He finally vents his rage on the town itself but stops when his former Green Beret commander, Colonel Samuel Trautman, talks him into surrendering, thus sparing the town from complete annihilation. Rambo tells Trautman:

> I came back to the world, and I see all those maggots at the airport, protesting me, spitting, calling me a baby killer and all kinds of vile crap.... [W]ho are they unless they've been there and know what the hell they're yelling about.... Back here there's nothing.... Back there I could fly a gunship. I was in charge of million-dollar equipment. Back here I can't even hold a job.

Rambo, like Kovic, reels from disaster to disaster.

A third example of the chaos faced by warriors in domestic life is the enigmatic *Jacob's Ladder.* The film, a confusing and disturbing work that marches toward death, perhaps is the ultimate chaos narrative. Only its beginning and ending — American soldier Jacob Singer's wounding and death — exist in real time. The rest consists of dreams that merge his past life with an imagined future that never will happen. The work is a surrealistic opus replete with scenes marked by the "and then" quality of chaos narratives.

For instance, a series of fragmented, seemingly inexplicable events depicting Singer's wounding in Vietnam gives way to his awakening in New York on a Brooklyn subway to see a sign which reads, "New York may be a crazy town, but you'll never die of boredom. Enjoy!" Jacob and his partner Jezzie attend a frenetic party at which Jacob becomes dizzy, people turn into demons, and a reptilian appendage wraps itself around Jezzie. The turmoil escalates as he grows increasingly confused. Hallucinations motivate him to contact men with whom he served in Vietnam, only to discover that they too have been encountering demons. Later, Jacob is attacked by one of the apparitions and taken to a hospital, a place filled with long halls where legs and arms litter the floor. He is the ultimate victim, "trapped in ... Vietnam," ignored and betrayed by everyone and "manipulated by his country's military and defense establishments."[21] Jacob is in figurative "Hell"—his life truly is like his first experience in the subway, for every turn leads to a dead end mired in madness.

These and similar narratives define two vivid images: the warrior as victim and as victimizer. Jacob Singer and Ron Kovic are obvious victims, the former of a military that experimented with drugs on its soldiers, the latter of callous military and medical bureaucracies and of a family and society loath to face either his disability or their responsibility for conditions linked to the war. Similarly, the soldiers in *Platoon* and *Apocalypse Now* suffer and die in a war they don't understand.

Overt victimizers populate films like *Rolling Thunder, Heroes,* and *The Ninth Configuration.* The paradigmatic presentation of this figure, however, is Martin Scorsese's *Taxi Driver,* a work that echoes the early 1970s' image of veterans as "violent antisocial individuals who rebelled against an uncaring and accusing society."[22] Robert DiNiro plays Travis Bickle, an ex–Marine who fights insomnia by driving a Checker cab at night. He lives in squalor, alienated in a city he sees as the epitome of corruption. His fragmented identity collapses the Western hero, psycho-vet, political assassin, and urban outsider into one persona.[23] After a beautiful, blonde campaign worker rejects him, he retaliates by attempting to kill the political figure for whom she works. Frustrated in his attempt at assassination, Travis rescues Iris, a child prostitute whom he met when she tried to escape her pimp by jumping into his taxi. The film's tour de force is Travis's victimizing. After he shoots Iris's pimp in the stomach, the camera follows him through the dreary corridors of the young girl's apartment building. En route he shoots an old man in the hand, an event the camera records slo-mo in loving detail; then he and the pimp shoot each other in a scene replete with especially graphic violence and accompanied by the sounds of dripping blood. Ironically, Travis's revenge on a city where (he says) "all the animals come out at night" ironically makes him a tabloid hero because his victims were in the drug trade.[24]

Many films blur the line between warriors as victims and victimizers, thus complicating the portrait of the Vietnam warrior. In *Apocalypse Now,* for example, ordinary, decent soldiers on a patrol boat panic and open fire on a Vietnamese family after they stop to search the family's sampan. After the melee subsides, Willard elects to shoot the one woman who survives the onslaught rather than cope with the inconvenience of taking her to a medical unit. In *Platoon,* the troops chance upon a Vietnamese village shortly after Taylor's company discovers two of their members murdered. Their response is to take revenge by terrorizing a young boy, making him "dance" to a spray of bullets, and then ravaging the village, stopping just short of a complete massacre.

One of the more disturbing examples of this merging of victim and victimizer is Brian DePalma's *Casualties of War*, the story of the brutal abduction, rape and eventual murder of an innocent Vietnamese girl by a group of American soldiers. The film is as much about the prelude to the rape and murder as it is about the outrage itself.[25] "DePalma gives us," Hinson explains, "the anatomy of an atrocity" by chronicling "the unraveling of the moral fabric" which culminates into a "descent into barbarism." The architect of the rape is Meserve, a short-timer whose main interest is surviving the last few weeks of his tour. Two incidents precipitate his rage: the canceling of a leave because "Charlie" is in the town where they take R & R, and the death of the squad's radio man, a devastating sequence DePalma films in excruciating detail, which becomes an event that "seeps into the atmosphere like a poison."[26] These episodes spur talk among the men about hating the Vietnamese, a hatred grounded in frustration and feelings of being betrayed by those they have tried to help. Three of the four soldiers on the patrol join in the rape and murder, two with seemingly little hesitation, one because of peer pressure. And, although the fourth rebels and eventually testifies against them, the film's implication is that in such situations moral compunction is ineffectual because brutality breeds brutalization.

Chaos sequences, then, provide a context and means for understanding the onset of illness plaguing Americans' experiences of Vietnam, thus framing as well as articulating the images of the warrior as victim and victimizer. They allocate blame and responsibility in a complex way, shedding light on aberrant behavior while at the same time intimating that culpability is shared by all: by warriors, leaders, and society at large. The cinematic story of Vietnam does not, however, end with the illness. Hollywood's vision of redress comes in the forms of restitution narratives and quest sagas.

Restitution Narratives and the Treating of Sickness

The core of the chaos narrative has an "and-then" quality that leads to progressively deeper levels of desolation and despair. Restitution stories follow a descent and ascent pattern moving from health to a descent into illness followed by an ascent back to health. The pivotal factor in turning descent to ascent is the intervention of an outside agent. In the cinematic world of Vietnam, restitution narratives are less common than other forms. A number of films, however, treat the malady attendant on Vietnam by intimating that external intervention, which creates understanding, forgiveness, or the feeling of community, can heal personal and cultural wounds.

Early in *Jacob's Ladder*, Jacob Singer finds himself in a subway where a sign on the wall confirms that he indeed is in hell, foreshadowing his future torment. Mired in a psychotic dream and chased by images of "horns peeping though people's heads or reptilian members protruding from garments,"[27] he turns to others who fought in Vietnam, only to find them helpless in the face of the same torture. Respite comes from two sources: visits to his cherubic-faced chiropractor, the miracle worker Louis, and periodic dreams of his family, his wife Sara and their children.

Chiropractor Louis appears at various junctures to literally and figuratively set Jacob straight. After the apparitions he thought were hallucinations attack him in an alley, Jacob ends up in a hospital in traction. As he works on Jacob a surgeon snickers, "there's no way out." Louis, however, finds a way and rescues him. Bathed in light, the chiropractor wheels Jacob through surreal corridors to safety. Once in his office, he quotes Meister Keckhart:

> The thing that burns in hell is the part of you that won't let go of your memories, your attachments.... Devils ... are not punishing you.... They're freeing your soul. If you're ... holding on, you'll see devils tearing your life away. But if you've made your peace, then the devils are really angels, freeing you from the earth.

In other words, by letting go Jacob can, as the sign on the subway intimates, find a way out.[28]

For Singer, deliverance comes from his second and most potent form of respite, his family. Various scenes in their apartment radiate visually the warmth and love that bind them together even though Jacob and Sara lost their son Gabe in a tragic traffic accident.[29] In a final dream Jacob returns, weary and worn and perplexed, to that apartment to be met by Gabe. The young boy comforts him, extending his hand to his father and leading him up a gently lit staircase that travels upward into the light. And so, Jacob ascends to find redemption and peace.[30] In walking into the light with his son, Jacob leaves the nightmare forever behind him. Immediately after his ascent, the film returns to real time, to medical staff in a field hospital in Vietnam who pronounce Jacob Singer dead, remarking that he fought hard to live. Jacob's rehabilitation, in this case his admission to heaven, is impossible on his own or through other veterans. Reconciliation is possible through connection with his family and Louis. Drawing on Louis's wisdom, Jacob accepts his fate and allows the healing touch of his son to restore his soul. His ascent to heaven and health is possible because of the care of others.

Coming Home presents a more complex cure for the victimized veteran, one in which he is an active participant. It is the tale of a love triangle that features a wife who, while waiting for her marine husband to return from war, falls in love with a paralyzed veteran of that war. Bob Hyde is a commissioned officer for whom Vietnam is the key to promotion. While he is away his wife Sally volunteers at a VA hospital where she meets Luke Martin, an angry, paralyzed veteran. Initially Luke is hostile toward her, for he assumes that her volunteerism is a hollow attempt to make herself feel good by helping the "gimps." Soon, however, they forge a relationship. Luke gives Sally comfort, understanding, and love. Sally's affection is the catalyst for Luke to find the courage to become independent, reach out to the community of veterans, and become part of the larger society.

Bob, who has found the war horrific and therefore intolerable, returns from suffering a gunshot wound that we later learn was self-inflicted. After being informed by government agents, who have been keeping tabs on Luke because of his antiwar activities, about Sally's affair, Bob confronts her in their living room holding a gun. Sally tries desperately to explain what happened while he was gone, telling him that she still loves him, but to no avail. Setting aside self-interest, Luke shows up in the middle of the crisis. Because their experiences in Vietnam make them brothers, Luke can reach Bob in ways that others cannot.[31] Compelled to help a fellow solider, Luke tells Bob that he's "not the enemy. The enemy's the fucking war.... You don't want to kill anybody here. You have enough ghosts to carry around." Even though Bob is "not confined to a wheel chair, ... his situation is more desperate.... Bob's mental trauma goes deeper, created by the failure of the institutions and values he had trusted."[32] Unable to withstand the betrayal of his wife, his community, and his ideology, he commits suicide.

A comparison of the life patterns of Bob and Luke marks Coming Home as a restitution narrative that speaks to the necessity of an outside agent's aid if the warrior is to recover. Early in the film Bob is fit, although arguably already deluded by military hype and therefore already into his descent into sickness. His background and training ill prepare him for the reality of Vietnam and thus he takes the "coward's" way out by shooting himself in the foot. On his return home, however, his bruised and guilt-ridden psyche is too shattered to cope with his own failure and his wife's betrayal; he also cannot accept the help of anyone else, be that person Sally or fellow veteran Luke. Thus, left with inadequate internal resources and unable to grasp the hands offered to him, he chooses to die, thereby enacting only the descent trajectory of the restitution narrative.

In contrast, Luke enters the film wracked with sickness. He listens to the conversations of other disabled veterans who try to make sense of their experience but remains bruised, hostile, angry. In a rage, he screams at the hospital staff and at Sally. As they spar, she manages to get his attention, chastising him for his self-centeredness and cruelty. Eventually he agrees to go to her house for dinner, an event that sparks a love affair. Unlike Bob, Luke can accept outside help. Thus he is able to ascend toward health. He moves out of the VA hospital into an apartment and modifies his car so that he can be independent. As he becomes increasingly self-sufficient, he is able to sustain his relationship with Sally and aid others. Realizing that he cannot keep quiet about the atrocities of the war, he revolts. He rejects the hackneyed masculinity that draws young men into the service and becomes a spokesperson for disabled veterans. Luke's commitment changes him from "a confused, volatile cynic to a thoughtful antiwar activist."[33] He continues to break free of the constraint and alienation from which he suffered early in the film. At the end of *Coming Home*, the audience sees Luke speaking to a group of high school students, telling them

> I have killed for my country.... I don't feel good about it. Because there's not enough reason, man. To see your best buddy get blown away. I don't see any reason for it. And there's a lot of shit I did over there that I find hard to live with.... I don't feel sorry for myself.... I'm just telling you, there's a choice to be made.

His testimony serves as a counterpoint to the spiel of a pair of recruiters.

His ascent to health, then, demands two things. First, he has to have the personal strength and insight to realize that unmitigated frustration and rage beget themselves. Second, he has to avail himself of the healing that comes through bonding with others, through communal connection. Sally represents civilian culture, a community from which the Vietnam veteran is excluded. Hence, her help is the catalyst for his recovery.[34] Thus, Luke's relationship with Sally and with other veterans garners him the empathy and sensibility necessary for one who has a voice to which others will listen. He is a survivor of trauma who, because of courage, insight and interconnection, contributes to his own healing.

In Country, Canadian director Norman Jewison's movie about reconciliation, is the story of a daughter who didn't know her father, a mother who didn't get to say good-bye, and a veteran who couldn't let go. The film begins with soldiers boarding a military aircraft on their way to Vietnam to the accompaniment of a voice-over which says that they are the leaders in a fight that "will never be forgotten. The Viet Cong is never going to forget you. America is never going to forget you…. America loves you." In the next scene they are walking down a river, lit by dozens of flares descending to the earth. Suddenly, the scene shifts because those events were the memory of Emmett Smith, a veteran who lives with his niece Sam in a town named Hopeville (Kentucky). After Sam comes across a shoe box with letters and a picture of her father, Dwayne Hughes, who died in the war when Sam was a month old, she becomes curious and begins to ask Emmett and his veteran buddies about the war, an experience about which they remain resolutely reticent. She eventually turns to her grandparents for information about her father and in the process learns of the depth of the pain they still feel. The Hugheses give Sam her father's diaries. She camps out one night to read them in private, awakening the next morning startled by Emmett's presence. He finally tells her about his experiences in Vietnam, about the emptiness in his heart, about feeling as if he is half dead. Sam, Emmett, and Dwayne's mother visit the Vietnam Veterans Memorial, where each finds a measure of closure. The film ends with the three walking away from the memorial, arms around each other.

In Country is about healing the malaise of a community marked indelibly by Vietnam. At its center is teenaged Samantha, who worries about Emmett, her uncle, but mostly searches for information about and understanding of the father who was killed in the war, believing that such knowledge somehow will make her whole. Filmed mainly from her point of view, it also reveals the plight of Emmett and other veterans, as well as of those linked to them. Unlike Sam's father, Emmett and buddies Pete, Earl, and Tom did return. But they came back marred to a community that, like Sam's now remarried mother, wants to ignore memories of the anguish of Vietnam. The veterans, of course, do not have that luxury. Emmett, for example, suffers the physical effects of Agent Orange and bears the psychological scars of combat. He lives a passive, aimless life. During thunderstorms, which terrify him, he yells at God or perhaps at just the sky, "Show me your face!" Emmett and the other veterans are a group apart, united by a shared pain.

Thus, the film details the results of Vietnam's descent, its illness. As in *Jacob's Ladder* and *Coming Home,* bonding among veterans is not enough, for the sickness is pervasive, not confined to them. Thus, when Emmett journeys with Sam and Mrs. Hughes to visit the Vietnam Veterans Memorial, his and their experiences at the wall constitute a formal rite in which warrior and family support each other as they join with the larger community, with the nation, in commemorating the dead by acknowledging rather than ignoring the pain of Vietnam. *In Country* posits complex conditions for recovery in which the injured give each other support so that each can find her or his own health.

Although *Coming Home, Jacob's Ladder,* and *In Country* differ from each other significantly, they share important characteristics. Each places the blame for the illness associated with Vietnam outside the veteran: Jacob is the victim of army experiments; Luke fell prey to a misguided, narrow patriotism as well as to injury in war and a hostile society; Emmett's community deceived him by pledging to honor his sacrifice. Each also suggests that the warrior must have help if he is to heal: Jacob needs Louis's wisdom and the love of his family; Luke must accept the help Sally offers so he can bond with other veterans and become their spokesperson; Emmett must journey to the wall with Sam and Mrs. Hughes so that each of them can find solace through that collective action. Thus all intimate that community is the key to healing. However, for healing to take place members of the community must accept responsibility for their part in the warrior's pain, must fulfill their duty to effect healing, and must acknowledge that their own sickness can dissipate only if they accept those responsibilities. These restitution narratives, then, proffer a complex portrait of a victimized warrior and culture acting reciprocally to return to health.

Quest Narratives and the Transformation of the Warrior Hero

While chaos narratives graphically portray the trauma and moral uncertainty attendant on warriors fragmented by war, restitution narratives depict the sharing of grief and culpability, thus uniting veterans and society. Uneasiness born of a lack of closure permeates both narrative trajectories, however, for neither trauma nor treatment alone can ground recovery of the kind of warrior-hero so important in an individualistic culture. Victimizers, even if multidimensional and understood, are not good candidates for hero status, and victims do not become heroes simply by being saved through their union with others, even if they contribute actively to their own recovery.

Nor surprisingly, then, many post–Vietnam war films highlight the individual warrior's search to heal self. Such a struggle becomes intrinsically personal, obliging the veteran to go it alone on his voyage of recovery. Narratives following the pattern of the quest feature persons who undergo transformations into unconventional heroes who can then return to the community as saviors valued because of what they can give their society.

The Deer Hunter, Oscar-winning best film in 1978, ostensibly chronicles the differing effects of the war on three best friends from a small Pennsylvania town — Michael, Nick, and Steven. But Michael is the film's protagonist because he is the sole member of the trio psychically prepared to endure the trials of war and thus answers his country's call.[35] His preparation comes in the metaphoric form of the deer hunt, a ritual which Michael, who understands the sacred relationship between hunter and hunted, enacts by embracing a "one shot" credo. His quiet discipline and consummate skill serve him when, having answered their country's call, he and his two friends endure trials in Vietnam that mark them forever. Michael, Nick and Stevie are captured and incarcerated in rat-infested cages in a river. Forced to play Russian roulette by the enemy, Michael talks the Viet Cong leader into tripling the number of bullets in the gun, thereby transforming the game into a contest where his skills are useable. The inventiveness of this plan affirms his credentials as a warrior and enables the men to avert certain death.

Michael's initiation does not end after returning home. He joins in the community's grief over the fates of Nick, allegedly missing in action in Saigon, and of Stevie, now a paraplegic living in a VA hospital with others irreparably damaged by the war. He cannot assimilate easily into life in his hometown of Clairton because his experiences set him apart from the rest. When he begins to suspect that Nick is responsible for sending money for Stevie's rehabilitation, he travels back to Saigon to find his best friend. This is a solitary journey and a personal crusade: For all intents and purposes, Stevie and Nick no longer exist, and his community can neither comprehend nor does it deserve to be contaminated by the damage war has inflicted on their own. Michael becomes ready to truly return to his community prepared to assume his role as leader through two culminating experiences.

In the first, he ventures once again into the mountains to participate in the ritual of the hunt. Alone this time, he stalks a magnificent buck. Finally getting the animal in his sights, he pulls the gun away, firing instead into the sky and then saluting the deer by yelling an "O.K." that rings out through the mountains. He sheds the warrior's yoke of violence because he no longer needs a kill to consummate the hunt. In the second, he goes back to Saigon to find Nick after bringing a reluctant Stevie home. In the dark and seedy decadence of Saigon's gambling dens, he finds a drug-dependent, disconnected Nick playing Russian roulette for profit, a game which Nick finally loses after Michael succeeds momentarily in penetrating his self-induced stupor. The tragedy comes to an end when Michael consummates the quest by bringing his friend back home.

The film's final scenes have symbolic social significance because the ritual of grieving for Nick merges with an act of commemoration for the warrior, thus restoring a reborn Michael to the community. Having fulfilled the goodness requirement of the hero by returning Nick and Stevie to their home and having shed the mantle of violence that contaminates warriors out of war, he clearly is at the center of the group of mourners who, as they gather in John's bar to honor Nick, begin to sing "God Bless America." Set against the senselessness of Nick's death and Stevie's disability, the song's themes of national pride and unity are particularly disquieting.[36] Yet, implicit in this scene is its affirmation of Michael's status coupled with the nostalgic pull of remembrance, for America's war legacy and for war's fallen. This symbolic unity may not erase the pain or confusion about the Vietnam experience, but it does connect remembrance and reintegration within a context of healing. In the comfort of ritual and the spirit of recovery, the community honors Michael's return, for it needs his presence.

In contrast, a spate of veterans in mid-1980s films return to Vietnam to repatriate American POWs left behind. These warriors sported no less than superhero status. Such back-to-Nam trips include works like *Uncommon Valor*, *Missing in Action, Parts 1, 2, and 3*, TV series like *Magnum P.I.*, *Simon and Simon*, and of course the watershed work of them all, *Rambo: First Blood, Part II*.

Rambo II portrays the veteran who goes back to Southeast Asia to enact a spiritual rebirth, accomplish at least a surrogate victory, and mediate the trauma of failure in Vietnam. The opening scenes find Rambo slaving in a quarry, his penalty for the mayhem inflicted in the first Rambo flick. Trautman appears once again to rescue him, this time promising a presidential pardon if he heeds the call to return to Vietnam in search of POWs possibly imprisoned there. Rambo agrees somewhat reluctantly given his distrust of military hierarchy, the government, and society in general, mainly because he is the capable and committed veteran who seeks the legitimation of triumph.

His road of trials is spectacular. Traveling to Thailand, he meets the film's real villain, CIA agent Murdock, a shifty, sleazy technocrat who orders Rambo to photograph any POWs he might find but otherwise leave their rescue to a better-equipped force. A dubious Rambo embarks, laden with all manner of equipment. Airlifted to a drop point near the suspected POW camp, as he attempts to jump from the plane he becomes entangled

in his gear and has to cut loose his equipment to free himself. Thus shedding the trappings of technology, he begins his mission armed with his wits,
a buffed-out body, a knife, and not much else.[37]

Once on the ground, he meets his local guide, the Vietnamese guer-
rilla fighter, Co Bao, who becomes his love interest and helps him escape
when he is captured by Russians and North Vietnamese. A Russian sniper,
however, kills Co Bao, leaving an enraged Rambo to continue the fight
alone.[38] Rambo and a lone POW he has rescued make their way to the
pickup point only to be abandoned by Murdock, whose real agenda was
to prove, for some devious political reasons, the nonexistence of American POWs. Betrayed in Vietnam once again, Rambo sets out to free the
rest of the imprisoned Americans. In the process, he leaves a trail of death
and destruction, eventually returning with his grateful charges to demonstrate to his nation and the world the indomitability of the lone American warrior and to lay bare the sources of that warrior's betrayal. In doing
so, he "affirms the long-cherished American cult of the individual who
goes outside the law to get the job done."[39]

Rambo II locates responsibility for the veteran's plight with a venal
bureaucracy and a "technologically obsessed, mercenary American military establishment."[40] Simultaneously, the work presents an invincible warrior who, thwarted by powerful, manipulative forces, has "no alternative
but to function as a mutated World War II hero in an utterly hostile ...
environment."[41] The havoc he wreaks, then, is both necessary and laud-
able; it alone can free Rambo and cleanse the society to which he returns.

When he gets back, Rambo confronts the villainous Murdock and
wipes out a bank of computers with an M-60. Telling Trautman he and
other veterans merely want the society for which they fought to love them
as much as they love it, he strides off into the Thai sunset, realizing he can
never fully be a part of that society. Rambo's boon to his culture, thus, is
fairly complex. In one sense, this warrior affirms a willingness to sacrifice
himself for the very society he blames for his suffering and alienation. To
reconcile that contradiction, Rambo must defeat the enemy both abroad
and at home. He accomplishes both feats with a ritualistic purification
through water and fire, an action that at least vicariously exorcizes the
demons of Vietnam plaguing society. At the same time, he demonstrates
militaristic efficiency, effectiveness, and an absolute moral conviction that
grounds a renewal of faith in warriors. In another sense, however, he is
marked forever by experiences that separate him from the society he serves,
perhaps confirming that neither he nor other warriors can erase Vietnam's
traumatic legacy but can only reinstate their image as honorable and valuable.

The boon implicit in *Born on the Fourth of July* is an antiwar message resulting from the veterans' excruciating experience of war. Oliver Stone drew on the authority of his status as a Vietnam veteran in two of his highest-profile films: the academy-award-winning *Platoon* and his "extended wail of sorrow for the wounded veteran," [42] *Born on the Fourth of July.* The former presents the experiences of the ordinary soldier enmeshed in the horror of Vietnam. The latter, a work Doherty describes as moving from "innocence (induction) through experience (combat) to knowledge (disillusionment),"[43] adapts Kovic's autobiography to the big screen, dramatizing his transformation from victim into confrontive cultural hero.

The film begins with an array of images of Americana: Kovic as a child playing soldier and baseball, celebrating his birthday on July 4 and experiencing a childhood kiss, competing in sports and coping with his dogmatic Catholic mother, and falling in love — with both a girl and the idea of becoming a marine. Stone's portrait of Kovic's youth in Massupequa, New York, depicts an array of forces responsible for his fateful choice to go to Vietnam: the church, the state, the movies, and a mother who stands for "blind Americanism and matriarchal repression at all costs."[44]

Kovic's call comes at the hands of marine recruiters visiting his high school who talk like John Wayne and tell an enthralled Ron that those who dare to join the marines will find out whether they've "got what it takes," whether they "really are men." Ron protests when his father attempts to dissuade him: "Don't you know what it means to me to be a Marine? ... I wanna go to Vietnam, and I'll die there if I have to." His mother, of course, thinks he's doing the right thing. The film thus establishes Ron as a clean American kid, an unspoiled, red-blooded virgin victimized by jingoistic patriotism. His departure takes place shrouded in omens of doom.

Most of the film chronicles Ron's initiation, which defines the forces central to the veteran's subversion. In Vietnam he participates in actions that inculcate a guilt he cannot purge. For example, when he tries to take responsibility for a friendly fire incident described earlier, his commanding officer tells him: "I don't need anybody to come in and tell me this shit." His own wounding and subsequent paralysis is a foolish attempt at bravery, an action seemingly motivated by the need to punish himself.

He comes home to a VA hospital in the Bronx, where he and other men endure horrific conditions. After breaking and nearly losing a leg in his determined but vain attempts to walk again, he returns to a town and family uncomfortable with his presence and all he represents. Confused by a society that shuns him, frustrated with a mother who rejects him, humiliated at his aimlessness and impotence, Ron's life becomes destructive. After a fight with his mother over his drunkenness, he finally leaves to join other veterans in self-imposed exile in Mexico. His experiments there with sex and male bonding, however, prove inadequate; as Burgoyne observes, "the illusion of fraternity, of an integral male world that the paralyzed veterans in Mexico try to sustain ... soon collapses into the naked expression of guilt and self hatred."[45] However, Ron's descent into complete disarray and despair eventually triggers an ensuing move toward recovery.

His trip back involves making amends and facing responsibility for what happened in Vietnam, even though the film clearly implies that those actions surely were understandable. He journeys to Georgia to see the family whose son he shot. Ron describes his role in Billy Wilson's death and is granted understanding if not absolution. When he leaves, the strains of *When Johnny Comes Marching Home* play in the background. The camera fades to a flag and then focuses on a group of veterans marching, protesting against the war.

Ron's atonement readies him to become the "castrated Vietnam vet" who is a "powerful anti-warrior."[46] During the film's closing scenes he shares the knowledge gained on his quest by becoming a public spokesperson for war protesters, carrying out his mother's vision early in the film that some day he would speak to a large group of people who need to hear his words. Denied a hearing by the Republicans, he triumphantly enters the hall of the Democratic National Convention in 1972 preparing to address the delegates and the nation. Surrounded by protesters and other veterans, he finally is home, for now his country can hear him. At film's end its protagonist can play the role of hero to a misguided nation, for he is now in the "symbolic position of fathering the nation anew."[47]

Films which enact the trajectory of the quest foreground an individualistic hero. Michael's success is a product of his innate nature. He fights external conditions and his personal demons to emerge transformed into a person who, the film strongly implies, will be a valued community leader. Superhero Rambo also saves himself to return to confront a society that has rejected him. The film's ending intimates that he will remain forever on the cultural fringe, available when called as he always has been. Ron Kovic emerges from his quest transformed, now able to speak cultural truths to a society at long last able to listen. Collectively, these and other films reclaim a transformed warrior who is of his society but also set apart from it, for such is the status of heroes.

The Recovery and Its Import

The images of the warrior as victim, victimizer, and transformed hero are the product of distinct but interrelated narrative patterns. Chaos narratives present the victim and victimizer along with the conditions creating those two images, images often merged in the same figure. Restitution narratives proffer a complex portrait of warrior and community engaged in a reciprocal process of healing. Quest sagas follow the beleaguered warrior through trials experienced during and after Vietnam to his triumphant transformation into leader and hero. This last, elevated image appears to have played out in subsequent versions of the Vietnam warrior. Although sagas addressing the experience of the war and the veteran's plight upon returning home disappeared fairly quickly from U.S. popular culture, the figure of the warrior-veteran persisted, albeit in altered form.

"[S]urvivors of traumatic historical events," explains Sturken, "are often awarded moral authority ... [which many times results in their being represented] as figures of wisdom in popular culture."[48] Such surely is the case with the Vietnam veteran. By the mid-1980s he permeated film and television in many forms, acting always, however, as the somehow superior individual who could take action others could not or possessed a moral judgment they did not have. He starred in *Magnum, P.I., Air Wolf, The A-Team*, and *Simon and Simon*; in countless cop or P.I. supermarket novels; and in films such as the *Lethal Weapon* series, not to mention being the U.S. President in *Air Force One*. Audiences generally knew little if anything about the characters' warrior credentials, but just having experienced Vietnam seemed enough.

The narrative formula for these works is a form of the restitution narrative, although considerably less complex than that employed in works like *Coming Home* and *In Country*. *Lethal Weapon*, for example, follows the fortunes of two police officers, Martin Riggs and his older, wiser, more stable partner, Roger Murtaugh, both Special Forces veterans. Riggs, whom Kehr describes as "a sociopath with powerful suicidal tendencies,"[49] bears the marks of Vietnam. Yet he and Murtaugh team up to function like the medical personnel described by Frank: Their special skills enable them to rip disease in the form of shenanigans by corrupt veterans running a drug ring from the fabric of society, thus saving their community. This and similar stories are tales of a patient and a society made ill through some form of social evil and then returned to health via the intervention of hero-saviors who often break laws and other social rules to effect a cure. Such a hero's charge is to intercede, to fix things; rarely do they emerge transformed, armed with cultural truth to communicate to others. Like Magnum and similar figures, their function is to remain, like the typical Western hero, fundamentally on the margins of society, ready to intervene when needed, as inevitably and frequently they will be.[50]

The image of the Vietnam warrior, then, presents a marked contrast to the gentleman soldier of World War II films made famous by John Wayne and others. He has been by turns dangerous psychovet, tragic but often sympathetic and courageous victim or victimizer, triumphant hero, and a savior who is the panacea for social ills. Uniting this array of images is a rhetoric of therapeutic individualism.

The impetus toward healing, especially on an individual and ultimately private level, bespeaks an orientation similar to what Dana Cloud labels "therapeutic discourse," a rhetoric characterized by words like "'personal responsibility,' 'recovery,' and 'adapting.'" Such talk, which has permeated American popular culture for three decades, began as the dominant culture's response to the conflict and fragmentation of the 1960s. It is a discourse that domesticates dissent by depicting issues in the public sphere in private terms, focusing "on the personal life of the individual as locus of both problem and responsibility for change."[51] As such, it has three characteristics that point toward its fit with cinematic discourses presenting the evolving image of the warrior-veteran since Vietnam.

First, it acknowledges social problems as well as structural factors producing such dis-ease yet simultaneously defines the solutions of those problems as being a private matter, a question of personal initiative. Second, it consequently embodies a philosophy of liberalism that privileges "individual autonomy and responsibility over and above collective identification and action." And, third, the rhetorical strategies used to advocate that autonomy and responsibility employ the "conservative language of healing, coping, adaptation, and restoration of a previously existing order."[52] In essence, its therapeutic terminology produces a logic that can acknowledge sociopolitical — i.e., structural — reasons for cultural ills but simultaneously place the responsibility for dealing with those problems — for effecting a cure — squarely in the hands of the autonomous individual.

The sociopolitical factors acknowledged by the films analyzed here are legion. *Casualties of War*, *Platoon*, and *The Deer Hunter* all foreground the brutality of combat and the horror of war in general. Many other films indict the military as represented by effete players of games in *Apocalypse Now*, insensitive officers in *Born on the Fourth of July*, and cruel faceless forces who experiment on American soldiers in *Jacob's Ladder*. At other times the forces contributing to the dis-ease of Vietnam are closer to home: families, social institutions, and women like Ron Kovic's mother, who touts a brand of false patriotism and then fails to accept the results that patriotism created. Regardless of the pointedness of such criticism, however, the responsibility for discovering a way out of the morass lies with the individual warrior. Kovic finds his way by himself as he confronts the guilt he carries from the war and rises above it; Rambo breaks free from technology and bureaucracy to liberate POWs; Riggs, Murtaugh, Magnum and the rest work autonomously to fight evil, often breaking rules that hobble the rest of us. The message, then, clearly is that redress for Vietnam comes when the warrior changes himself, not the system that demanded his sacrifice. Such discourses call for individual, not collective, action.

Thus, the evolving image of the warrior is a clear affirmation of the principle of individualism. As enacted in films like *In Country* and *Coming Home*, restitution as a mode of warrior and cultural healing is relatively complex because those and other works imply a mutual causal approach to healing the veteran's wounds and those of his culture. Quest sagas, by contrast, may point to societal pain and culpability, but the solution they proffer confers responsibility on the individual warrior. He must heed the call, endure the trials, and emerge strengthened by them, armed with insights, skills, and truths that benefit the community at large. The successors to heroes such as Michael, Ron Kovic, and Rambo are the heroes and saviors like Riggs, Murgaugh, and Magnum, as well as denizens of *The A-Team*, who have the skill to intervene, to act outside normal social boundaries, to remedy social ills.

If such figures—whether heroes or saviors—affirm the efficacy of action, if their stories are mandates for all to acknowledge responsibility, and if those stories promote cultural cohesion, then their appeal certainly is understandable. Yet, they also warrant a cautionary note. As appealing and entertaining as both heroes and their successors are, cavalier enjoyment of them and what they represent probably is not a good idea. If the experience of war becomes "a voyage of self-discovery," then the result is that war surely must be "reintegrated and rendered tolerable to the American conscience," perhaps unthinkingly so.[53] If violent skills are seen as necessary for social safety and if the "hero acting alone" apparently must use them to achieve "independence and freedom from oppression,"[54] then the result is not only "the passive acceptance of heroic violence ... but its very institutionalization as a way of life. We end up," Taplin explains, "in a society where the redemption of earthly paradise is the task of lone, asocial crusaders and *only them.*"[55]

NOTES

1. Joseph Campbell, *The Hero with a Thousand Faces* (New York: Meridian, 1969), 169.

2. Richard Slotkin, *Regeneration through Violence: The Mythology of the American Frontier, 1600–1800* (Middletown, Conn.: Wesleyan University Press, 1973), 5.

3. Sharon D. Downey and Karen Rasmussen, "Vietnam: Press, Protest, and the Presidency," in *Silencing the Opposition: Government Strategies of Suppression of Free-*

dom of Expression, Craig R. Smith, ed. (Albany: State University of New York Press, 1996), 179.

4. Sidney H. Schanberg, "Soldiers Still Missing in Action Enduring Scar of Vietnam War." *The Oregonian* (November 11, 1987), C5.

5. Janice H. Rushing and Thomas S. Frentz, "The Rhetoric of *Rocky*: A Social Value Model of Criticism." *Western Journal of Speech Communication* 48 (1978): 64–75.

6. Walter R. Fisher, "Narration as a Human Communication Paradigm: The Case of Public Moral Argument." *Communication Monographs* 51 (1984): 2–3, 9.

7. Arthur W. Frank, *The Wounded Storyteller: Body, Illness, and Ethics* (Chicago: University of Chicago Press, 1995), 53, 75.

8. *Ibid.,* 97.

9. *Ibid.,* 99.

10. *Ibid.,* 104, 98, 104.

11. *Ibid.,* 77, 79, 90, 87, 86.

12. *Ibid.,* 115, 117.

13. Campbell, 58, 77, 101, 137, 166, 193; Frank, 118.

14. Frank, 119.

15. Richard Combs, "Beating God to the Draw: *Salvador* and *Platoon*," *Sight and Sound* (Spring 1987): 137.

16. Bert Cardullo, "Viet Nam Revisited." *The Hudson Review* (Autumn 1987): 464.

17. For discussions of the relationship between *Apocalypse Now* and Coppola's film, see E. N. Dorall, "Conrad and Coppola: Different Centres of Darkness." *Southeast Asian Review of English* 1 (1980): 19–27; William M. Hagen, "Heart of Darkness and the Process of *Apocalypse Now*," *Conradiana* 13 (1981): 45–43; Robert LaBrasca, "Two Visions of 'The Horror!'" in *Heart of Darkness: An Authoritative Text*, Robert Kimbrough, ed. (New York: W. W. Norton, 1988), 288–93.

18. Nora Sayre, "At War in the Movies." *The Progressive* (February 1980): 52.

19. Karen Rasmussen and Sharon D. Downey, "Dialectical Disorientation in Vietnam War Films: Subversion of the Mythology of War." *Quarterly Journal of Speech* 77 (1991): 185.

20. Susan Jeffords, *The Remasculinization of America: Gender and the Vietnam War* (Bloomington: Indiana University Press, 1989), 127.

21. Ken Jurkiewicz, *Jacob's Ladder*: Viewer Response, Selective Remembrance, and Collective Amnesia in Post-Political America." *Literature/Film Quarterly* 26 (1998): 230.

22. David Everett Whillock, "The Fictive American Vietnam War Film: A Filmography," in *America Rediscovered: Critical Essays on Literature and Film of the Vietnam War*, Owen W. Gilman, Jr., and Lorrie Smith, eds. (New York: Garland, 1990), 305.

23. Barbara Mortimer, "Portraits of the Postmodern Person in *Taxi Driver, Raging Bull,* and *The King of Comedy*." *Journal of Film and Video* 49(1–2) (1997): 30.

24. Rasmussen and Moss argue that *Taxi Driver* creates an irony that challenges the viability of the principle of regeneration through violence. It does so through an integration of the pattern of the classic Western with formal properties drawn from conventions linked to film noir. See Karen Rasmussen and Kirran Moss, "The Western Meets *Film Noir*: The Argumentative Terrain of Martin Scorsese's *Taxi Driver*," *Arguing Communication and Culture*, G. Thomas Goodnight, ed. (Washington, D.C.: National Communication Association, 2002), 613–20.

25. Roger Ebert, review. *Casualties of War. Chicago Sun Times* (Columbia Pictures) August 18, 1989 (database online); available from http://www.suntimes.com/ebert/ebert_reviews/1989/08/368527.html.

26. Hal Hinson, review. *Casualties of War. Washington Post* (Columbia Pictures) August 18, 1989 (database online); available from http://www.rottentomatoes.com/ click/author-50/reviews.php?cats=&letter=c&sortby=default&page=3&rid=3446 .
27. Carol Fry, "The Viewer and The Film." *Literature/Film Quarterly* 26 (1998): 224.
28. *Ibid.*, 223.
29. *Ibid.*, 225.
30. Ken Jurkiewicz, "*Jacob's Ladder*: Viewer Response, Selective Remembrance, and Collective Amnesia in Post-Political America," *Literature/Film Quarterly* 26 (1998): 230.
31. James Conlon, "Making Love, Not War: The Soldier Male in *Top Gun* and *Coming Home.*" *Journal of Popular Film and Television* 18 (1990): 25.
32. Eben J. Muse, "Romance, Power, and the Vietnam War: Romantic Triangle in Three Vietnam War Films." *The Durham University Journal* 86 (1994): 312.
33. Martin F. Norden, "The Disabled Vietnam Veteran in Hollywood Films." *Journal of Popular Film and Television* 13 (1985): 17.
34. Muse, 311.
35. Janice Hocker Rushing and Thomas S. Frentz, "*The Deer Hunter*: Rhetoric of the Warrior." *Quarterly Journal of Speech* 66 (1980): 401.
36. Rasmussen and Downey, 188.
37. McGregor argues that Rambo cannot be dependent on technology because of its link to a science dependent on corporate support, i.e., on bureaucracy. See G. McGregor, "The Technomyth in Transition: Reading American Popular Culture." *American Studies* 21 (1987): 403.
38. Wimmer contends that Co's death is necessary because to be a hero Rambo must fight alone, not be dependent on a female or the feminine. See Adi Wimmer, "Rambo: American Adam, Anarchist and Archetypal Frontier Hero," in *Vietnam Images: War and Representation*, Jeffrey Walsh and James Aulich, eds. (New York: St. Martin's), 188.
39. Gaylyn Studlar and David Desser, "Never Having to Say You're Sorry: Rambo's Rewriting of the Vietnam War." *Film Quarterly* (Fall 1988): 13.
40. *Ibid.* See also Stephen C. LeSeur and Dean Rehberger, "*Rocky IV Rambo II*, and the Place of the Individual in Modern American Society." *Journal of American Culture* 11 (1988): 26.
41. Harry W. Haines, "The Pride is Back: *Rambo, Magnum, P.I.*, and the Return Trip to Vietnam," in *Cultural Legacies of Vietnam: Uses of the Past in the Present*, Richard Morris and Peter Ehrenhaus, eds. (Norwood, N.J.: Ablex, 1990), 111.
42. Marita Sturken, "Reenactment, Fantasy, and the Paranoia of History: Oliver Stone's Docudramas." *History and Theory* 36 (1997): 69.
43. Thomas Doherty, "Witness to War: Oliver Stone, Ron Kovic, and *Born on the Fourth of July*," in *Inventing Vietnam: The War in Film and Television*. Michael Anderegg, ed. (Philadelphia: Temple University Press, 1991), 255.
44. Devin McKinney, "Review of *Born on the Fourth of July* (Universal Studios)." *Film Quarterly* (Fall 1990): 46.
45. Robert Burgoyne, "National Identity, Gender Identity, and the 'Rescue Fantasy' in *Born on the Fourth of July.*" *Screen* 35 (1994): 225.
46. Doherty, 263.
47. Burgoyne, 232.
48. Sturken, 68.
49. Dave Kehr, "Winning the War 20 Years after Tet, Hollywood Triumphs in Vietnam." *Chicago Tribune* (February 11, 1988): Arts 16.

50. Janice Hocker Rushing, "The Rhetoric of the Western American Myth. *Communication Monographs* 50 (1983): 16.

51. Dana L. Cloud, *Control and Consolation in American Culture and Politics: Rhetorics of Therapy* (Thousand Oaks, Calif.: Sage, 1998), xiii, 1.

52. *Ibid.*, xiii, 88, xiii, 3.

53. Michael Comber and Margaret O'Brien, "Evading the War: The Politics of the Hollywood Vietnam Film." *History* 73 (1988): 251.

54. Stephen C. LeSeur and Dean Rehberger, *Rocky IV, Rambo II,* and the Place of the Individual in Modern American Society." *Journal of American Culture* 11 (1988): 31–32.

55. Ian M. Taplin, "Why We Need Heroes to Be Heroic." *Journal of Popular Culture* 22 (1988): 138.

9

American Hero Meets Terrorist: *True Lies* and *Patriot Games* After September 11, 2001

SUZANNE MCCORKLE

The illusion of America's invulnerability to significant terrorist attack was merely shaken by Ramzi Yousef's 1993 attack on the World Trade Center, which killed 6, and Terry McNichols's homemade fertilizer bomb, which killed 168 in the Oklahoma City federal building in April 1995. After thousands were killed by followers of Osama bin Laden's Al Qaeda network on September 11, 2001, illusions of U.S. invulnerability to terrorism disintegrated. The physical attack on the World Trade Center and the Pentagon symbolically assaulted U.S. and first-world culture. Those who watched the two airliners crash into and take down the World Trade Center in New York grew afraid to walk down an airplane jet way. They experienced a transformed frame of reference from serene confidence to feelings of uncertainty and insecurity.

While many profound instances of life transformation can be documented after what became known as "the events of 9/11," the shift in reference regarding the individual citizen's perception of cultural vulnerability and personal mortality is of particular interest to this study. President Bush was quoted on *CNN Headline News* on December 28, 2001, saying: "American's culture turned to one of alertness." In particular, this chapter examines the probable shift in how Americans view films with terrorist themes.

Two films with terrorist plots are especially noteworthy within this context: *True Lies* and *Patriot Games*. Each film is first critiqued for its general plot features and portrayal of the American hero's battle against terrorism. Next, the psychological theory of terror management is presented. Finally, a terror management perspective is applied to a pre–and post–9/11 viewing of the films.

True Lies *and* Patriot Games

The 1994 film *True Lies,* directed by David Cameron and starring Arnold Schwarzenegger and Jamie Lee Curtis, is an "R" rated action-romance adaptation of the French *La Totale!* Its domestic gross was around $146 million, with an additional $219 million garnered overseas.[1] The film's dramatic special effects are by Digital Domain.

Schwarzenegger plays secret agent Harry Tasker, who has concealed his occupation from his wife (Jamie Lee Curtis) through fifteen years of marriage and raising a child. Cameron describes the scenario as "what would happen if James Bond had to go home and answer to his family. So, what this becomes is a kind of marital fable cloaked in a candy coating of action and adventure."[2] Harry's lies rob his family of commitment and intimacy. He misses birthday parties while "working late." The family unit is unraveling.

The film unfolds two intertwining plots. In the "A" story (the world of the secret agent), Harry Tasker clandestinely works for the Omega Sector — a watchdog for nuclear terrorism — while posing as a computer salesperson. Harry jokes with his sidekick co-spy, Gib (Tom Arnold), and toys with femme fatale, Juno. Charlton Heston makes a cameo as the head of the Omega Sector. Meanwhile, in the "B" story, Harry's wife, Helen, is bored with her (she thinks) Willy Loman husband who travels too much. She is subsequently lured into near infidelity by Simon (Bill Paxton), who pretends to be a secret agent. Harry illegally uses Omega Sector's resources to teach Helen and pseudo-spy Simon a lesson, blackmailing Helen into thinking she is working for a secret spy agency when she really is going to a hotel for a surprise meeting with Harry. Meanwhile, terrorists sneak Soviet era nuclear weapons into the United States, kidnap Harry and Helen (both try protect their partner from their own secret-agent activities), take them to the Florida Keys, and leave Harry to die in a nuclear explosion.

Through a series of action-packed sequences, Harry and Helen escape their captors and with the help of the U.S. marines, arrange for all Americans to be safe from the nuclear explosion on one of the Florida Keys. The terrorists, however, have kidnapped Harry and Helen's daughter, Dana, and are holding her captive in Miami. Harry appropriates a Harrier jet and flies to Miami, where he rescues his daughter, who has already foiled the terrorist plot by stealing the only key to the nuclear weapon. The head terrorist, Akim Abu Aziz (Art Malik), is killed when father and daughter (she is clinging perilously to the outside of the Harrier) shoot off the missile Aziz is clutching. The missile flies through the wreckage of a building, blowing up Aziz and a helicopter full of his followers.

Throughout the film, Helen transforms from a repressed and mousy wife to a sexy and smart secret-agent partner for Harry. The family unit is reinvigorated. The film's ending scene shows the reunited family thumb wrestling when Harry and Helen receive a phone call for an assignment.

The terrorists in *True Lies* are motivated politically in opposition to U.S. policy in the Middle East. Aziz says, "You have killed our women and children, bombed our cities from afar like cowards and dare to call us terrorists." He demands the U.S. pull its military out of the Persian Gulf or he will set off the nuclear weapons in U.S. cities. He calls the nuclear explosion "a pillar of holy fire."

In many aspects, *True Lies* is a cartoon version of terrorism — a standard hero-villain plot that is strung together with special effects and chase scenes. David Wilcock's Internet review calls the film fun, but stupid: "[S]ome of the scenes would just not happen in real life."[3] We may be fortunate that the helicopter chase scene from the screenplay did not make the opening of the film. "Fun" is a common description of the film. Director Cameron says

> I was intrigued by the idea of this secret agent who is perfect in a way. He speaks all these languages, he's got a degree in nuclear physics, he can fly a helicopter and a jet and he never loses a fight. Both Arnold and I thought we could have a lot of fun with it and that's how we got started on the screenplay for *True Lies.*[4]

In contrast, the 1992 release of *Patriot Games* follows the political and action genre of the reluctant hero. *Patriot Games*, directed by Phillip Noyce, grossed around $83 million in the United States.[5] (The video is also available, subtitled in Spanish, Greek, French, Croatian, Italian, and Portuguese.) Taken from one of author Tom Clancy's best-selling technological thrillers, the plot is both complex and terrifying.

While in London, Jack Ryan (Harrison Ford) foils a terrorist attempt to kidnap the Minister of State for Northern Ireland, Lord Holmes (James Fox), and his family, killing the 16-year-old brother of IRA-offshoot mem-

ber Sean Miller (Sean Bean). Ryan says, "I just couldn't stand by and watch
those people get killed."

Sean is tried and convicted but escapes with his terrorist buddies
while being transferred to prison. The group dashes off to Africa to a terrorist training camp, where Sean convinces them to let him have revenge
on Jack Ryan. The attempt fails but seriously injures Ryan's wife (Annie
Archer) and daughter (Thora Birch). Ryan rejoins the CIA to try to protect his family from future terrorist attacks. Helped by information from
mainstream IRA fundraiser Paddy O'Neil (Richard Harris), U.S. satellite
technology locates the terrorist camp in Africa. Ryan and others watch via
live satellite as paratroopers attack the terrorist base — killing all who are
there.

The Irish ultraterrorists had, however, already left. An informant had
disclosed that the royals Ryan saved would visit his seaside home in America. The Irish terrorists attack the home, but the Ryan family, guests, and
the royals escape unscathed. Ryan kills Sean Miller in an improbable boat
chase scene. The main plot of the film contrasts Sean's drive for revenge
with Ryan's dedication to protecting his family. James Earl Jones has a
small part as Ryan's CIA boss, Admiral Greer.

In *Patriot Games*, the terrorists are motivated initially by patriotic
zeal for independence for Northern Ireland, a general hatred of the British,
and disdain for those in the IRA who do not share their "no rules"
approach. As the film progresses, Sean Miller, the main antagonist, is
increasingly motivated by a personal desire for revenge on Ryan, who killed
his brother while foiling the attack on the royal family.

Patriot Games is described as "a stolid, reactionary thriller in which
the good old nuclear family becomes the last line of defense against the
favorite action-movie staple, a group of international terrorists."[6] While
the Tom Clancy book of the same name has a more plausible plot, particularly the ending, both book and film rely upon a hero who is drawn
into fighting terrorists because of his own sense of morality and his desire
to defend his family: "Not for honor. Not for country. For his wife and
child."

Terror Management Theory

The psychological theory of terror management is adapted in this
essay to create a framework for critical analysis. Sheldon Solomon, Jeff
Greenberg, and Tom Pyszczynski reviewed the more than thirty years of
empirical research testing cultural anthropologist Ernest Becker's theory

that knowledge of one's own mortality was a significant motivator of human behavior.[7] They created a social psychological construct called *terror management* and established situations to test the theory that mortality is a pervasive motivator of human behavior.

Terror management theory acknowledges that humans are self-reflexive. Humans understand that death is inevitable and out of their control. This knowledge can, and in some cases does, debilitate those who live in constant terror of their inevitable death. At minimum, a constant awareness of death provokes anxiety and a low quality of life. Terror management theory explains how humans cope with this anxiety through self-esteem and cultural worldview:

> Throughout recorded history, observers of humankind have noted two basic tendencies that pervade human behavior and seem to underlie a great deal of what is both noble and contemptible about our species: a desire to maintain a favorable self-image — manifested as egotism or a need for self-esteem; and a desire to promote the beliefs and values of one's culture, often at the expense of others — manifesting as ethnocentrism or prejudice.[8]

Terror management research confirms that high self-esteem and adherence to one's worldview ameliorates the terror of knowledge of mortality. Self-esteem is constructed in the context of a worldview that establishes the standards of right and wrong, good and bad — requiring that the values of one's culture be accepted as a matter of faith, since values are not empirically verifiable. Not all humans, however, accept the *same* worldview or value standards. Psychologically, the mere existence of others with different worldviews can be anxiety producing. Because the order sustained by culture is threatened by the existence of others, they may cause reactions, such as reassessing one's worldview, reaffirming one's worldview, derogating those who are different, or learning to live with ambiguity and diversity.

Terror management theory posits that feelings of significance (self-esteem) are possible only when one is motivated by one's culture to attain worthy characteristics and attributes. A type of symbolic immortality is achieved by sustaining and uplifting a cultural worldview that will live on after the individual is gone.[9] In short, terror management theory posits:

- Knowledge of death causes anxiety and terror.
- Terror is controlled by immersion in a cultural worldview and the belief that one is living up to one's cultural standards.
- The two buffers to terror and anxiety are self-esteem and defense

of one's culture (either through positive affirmation of one's own culture or denigration of others).

Empirical studies lend credence to terror management theory. A series of studies shows that the higher one's self-esteem, the less anxiety is produced when people are exposed to reminders of death. Research further indicates that reminders of death that cause anxiety lead to a variety of cultural defenses, including (1) greater praise for those who are models of the culture; (2) greater ethnocentrism, increased perception that there is a widespread social consensus around values; and (3) aggression, derogation, or blame of those who are different.[10] An exception to the ethnocentric effect occurs when values of tolerance are emphasized prior to the reminder of death. Those who are depressed prior to being reminded of death respond with even stronger investments in their worldview.

Similar to early research on fear appeals in speeches,[11] subtle reminders of mortality create more anxiety than explicit and enduring reminders. Solomon and his colleagues explicitly state that the effects found in empirical studies arise from both laboratory and natural conditions and cite television, novels, and movies as sources of anxiety-producing death reminders.

Terror Management and Terrorist Films

Action-oriented films portraying mayhem and multiple deaths create a mortality stimulus and fear of death. They simultaneously model the self-esteem and culture defense reactions that will buffer fear of death. Movies depict a microcosm of life explainable through terror management theory. This section of the chapter explores the probable functioning of *True Lies* and *Patriot Games* as morality tales to moderate fear of death before and after the true-life terrorist attacks on New York and Washington, D.C., in September 2001.

Three questions derived from the tenets of terror management theory are addressed during this analysis: What are the mortality or death prompts in the films? What cultural values are highlighted in the films? What are the reactions within the films to the mortality prompt? The three questions are answered from the perspective of the lead characters, who are portrayed as mainstream members of the European-American cultural model. I acknowledge that the questions would be answered differently if the perspective were taken of protagonist characters, but that analysis is not the focus of this chapter.

MORTALITY PROMPTS: *TRUE LIES*

In *True Lies*, the mortality or death prompts are examined from the perspective of Harry Tasker, his wife and daughter, and the American film viewers. Harry is, as the screenplay attests at his character introduction, our hero. Harry has been a spy for 15 years. He exudes the nonchalance we expect of film heroes. In the opening scene, Harry swims under ice to secretly crash an oil billionaire's party and steal his computer records, sets explosives in case he needs a distraction later, and speaks French and Arabic to fill out his disguise. When a guard becomes too threatening, Harry sets off the explosives, defeats two Dobermans, and kills numerous guards who chase him on skis and snowmobiles. Harry kills them all.

Our hero's second mortality threat occurs when he lures the terrorists into following him into a mall restroom. Two terrorists, faintly Middle Eastern looking, hide a machine gun and pistol beneath their coats and enter the restroom behind Harry to carry out an assassination. Harry foils the attack by wearing sunglasses that allow him to see what the terrorists are doing behind him through a small camera in a pack of cigarettes he strategically planted on the counter. After a long fight, he kills one terrorist and subdues the other. Now, Harry has the situation under control until the third terrorist, Aziz, enters firing his machine gun. Harry uses the handcuffed terrorist as a shield, and another tense sequence ensues. Our hero eludes the machine gun fire until he can snatch a dropped handgun and fire back at Aziz. Aziz flees at the first sign of resistance.

Harry's third mortality prompt occurs when he chases Aziz through the city, both on stolen transportation — Aziz on a motorcycle and Harry on a horse. Aziz finally jumps from one high-rise building to another on his motorcycle. Harry attempts to follow, but his horse intelligently balks, throwing Harry over the side of the building. He dangles over the edge, saved only by the reins and a well-trained horse that backs up when asked.

Next, Harry and Helen are captured in a hotel after he tricks her into thinking she is working as a spy. They are drugged and taken to the Florida Keys. Surrounded by terrorists, Harry is asked to identify and describe one of their stolen nuclear weapons on videotape. He resists but complies when Helen is threatened. Harry is drugged again and about to be tortured when he picks his handcuffs, kills the torturer, and attacks the terrorists—facilely handling a variety of weapons and cobbling a flame thrower from a gas tank. Meanwhile, Aziz buries an armed nuclear weapon in cement so that his plan to blow up the island as a demonstration of his resolve cannot be foiled. Harry's partner, Gib, arrives in a helicopter in time to save Harry from the nuclear explosion.

Finally, Aziz threatens Harry and the kidnapped Dana. Harry arrives in a Harrier jet to save Dana from being dropped to her death from a crane atop a Miami skyscraper. Aziz jumps onto the jet and tries to stab and shoot Harry. Harry and Dana outsmart Aziz by flipping the plane and then shooting off the missile that Aziz is clinging to—which flies through a building and explodes the final helicopter manned by the remaining terrorists.

Though there are numerous threats to Harry's life, when the film was released viewers probably did not take them seriously. We know Harry is the hero in this genre film and, hence, is unlikely to come to any harm. The film cues that the mortality prompts aren't serious by inserting humor. Harry and Gib joke their way through the action. The sequences also are fantastically overdone. By the time the film is over, Harry has shot and killed 20 to 30 terrorists, who have not managed to wound Harry, even though he is tied, outnumbered, and outgunned.

Helen's mortality issues begin when Simon lures her from her lackluster marriage by pretending to be a spy who needs her help. Harry overhears one of their conversations and bugs her office. Thinking she is having an affair, Harry and the Omega crew follow to where Simon is trying, unsuccessfully, to seduce her. The black-clad and masked Omega crew—wielding heavy arms—burst in on Simon and Helen and whisk them away in unmarked vehicles. Helen is interrogated by the disembodied and altered voices of Harry and Gib, which give her an assignment to help Omega force. She pretends to be a hooker who must plant a bug in a suspect's hotel room—in reality the suspect is her husband, Harry. The terrorists burst in and kidnap them. They are taken to Florida, where Helen faces the same threatening terrorists as Harry. She sees him appear to die in a fire and is almost executed by Juno. She leaves in a stretch limo, guarded by Juno—knowing Harry is either dead or stranded on an island where a nuclear bomb will soon explode. Juno and Helen fight in the limo over control of a handgun after jets blow up the other terrorist vehicles and the bridge. Helen beats Juno unconscious with a wine bottle and pops out of the sunroof of the limo that now is careening down the highway (the driver was shot during their fight). Harry, hanging down from a helicopter, yells to her that the bridge is out. After a few harrowing misses, Helen grabs Harry's arm and is pulled to safety as the car plunges off the bridge. Back on land, they kiss while the nuclear bomb explodes in the background, cueing the viewer that the situation isn't really serious. The couple is reunited and all is well, temporarily. As *Newsweek* noted: "*True Lies* is the sort of movie where lovers kiss against the billowing mushroom cloud of an atomic bomb and no one worries about fallout."[12]

While Helen's mortality threats show her as alternately strong and weak, the viewer also does not take these threats too seriously. Helen tries to save Harry when they are kidnapped, thinking he is an innocent salesperson and she is the spy. As Helen says while on the Florida island when Harry shoots a terrorist who is holding her hostage, "I married Rambo."

Dana's character is very disappointed in a father who is never around and misses her birthday party. We do not see her kidnapping on screen but see her as the captive of Aziz in a Miami high-rise building. Dana bravely steals the arming key from the nuclear bomb while Aziz is pontificating for a news camera. Aziz and the terrorists shoot at Dana, who climbs out onto a crane and threatens to drop the key; Aziz chases her. Just when all seems lost, Harry shows up in a Harrier jet and persuades Dana to jump to daddy. She does, they escape. Dana's helplessness seems more real and terrifying in some respects, but when our hero arrives, the viewer knows things will turn out well.

The mortality threat in the film is the most credible when the family is in danger. As Art Malik (Aziz) says in the video release's introduction, "it's a fun type film, therefore I hope no one takes it too seriously."

MORTALITY PROMPTS: *PATRIOT GAMES*

The mortality or death prompts in *Patriot Games* are analyzed from the perspective of Ryan, his wife and his daughter, and the viewer of the film at the time of its release. The mortality prompts begin with Jack walking to meet Cathy and Sally in a park. As soon as they meet, terrorists blow up and attack a car. Ryan first protects his family and then runs to tackle one snow mask-wearing terrorist and shoots another gunman, who is Sean Miller's younger brother, Patrick. Ryan is wounded in the shoulder. Two other terrorists escape. The police arrive with their own weapons, amidst sirens and chaos.

The general violence of the troubles in Northern Ireland is established in the film through the internecine warfare that erupts among the IRA sects and a music video that chronicles British injustices. At his trial, Sean Miller appears fanatical and dangerous, swearing revenge on Ryan. A sense of danger looms.

Despite Admiral Greer's reassurances and Ryan's belief that "the IRA's not stupid. They're not going to follow me all the way here," they do. Sean and accomplices unsuccessfully try to ambush Ryan outside his Annapolis workplace and, after a dramatic sequence in which desperate Ryan tries to phone Cathy in her car, succeeds in machine gunning his wife's sports car, which careens off the road to a near-fatal crash. Cathy and Sally are severely injured. Sally loses her spleen and is hospitalized for weeks.

The final mortality threat to the Ryan family occurs while the royals are visiting the Ryan home. The terrorists attack, killing all the guards and police, and enter the darkened home with full military gear and night-vision goggles. Ryan, however, has anticipated their attack and hidden the guests in the basement while he sneaks upstairs to rescue his wife and daughter. A female terrorist, Annette, almost traps Cathy, but Cathy hits her over the head with an unloaded shotgun. The Ryans hide in the attic; Sean shoots at them through the ceiling. They escape down the roof to rejoin the rest of the party in the basement.

After shooting the mole-terrorist Watkins (Hugh Fraser) in the knee to get information out of him, the party escapes down the terrorists' ladder onto a stormy beach. Ryan lures the terrorists away from the rest of the group by driving off in one of the terrorists' boats. When they realize Ryan is alone, most of the terrorists want to turn back to finish the plan — to get the royals. Sean's real objective, though, is revenge. He kills the other terrorists and chases Ryan through the stormy sea, shooting Ryan's boat and starting a fire. Ryan ineptly tries to put the fire out. Sean jumps into Ryan's boat. A life-and-death struggle ensues. Ryan inadvertently kills Sean when he pushes him onto a sharp boat anchor. Meanwhile, the boat drives toward a rock outcropping. Ryan notices at the last moment and jumps into the sea just before the boat crashes and explodes. He is alone in the sea — exhausted — without even a life jacket. A rescue helicopter spots the fire and comes to his aid. The audience probably is not surprised by these outcomes. As bank-hostage taker Gabriel (John Travolta) says in the film, *Swordfish*, "The bad guy can't win. It's a morality tale. One way or another, the bad guy has to go down."

The threats to Jack, Cathy, and Sally Ryan are somewhat credible in human terms—a deranged individual seeking revenge. While the threats are real, they are not threats of mass destruction and generally don't involve innocent bystanders. The film is a psychological joust between the terrorists' plans and Ryan's ability to predict their actions. Sean calls Ryan on the phone to taunt and threaten him, saying: "You should look after your family better." From the perspective of the audience at the time of the film's release, the IRA terrorists seem threats mainly to those who travel abroad. The attacks on the Ryan family seem more like individual acts of criminal behavior than a terrorist plot that might affect the viewer personally.

CULTURAL STATEMENTS: *TRUE LIES*

True Lies is as a much morality play as an action-adventure comedy. While the hero competently navigates physical danger, his family and marriage are in peril due to his neglect. It's "nothing but people lying to each other," says Jamie Lee Curtis (Helen Tasker) in the home video release. Harry has lied for 15 years about his job and was frequently absent. His partner, Gib, buys the souvenir gifts for Harry's daughter, Dana, because Harry doesn't think of it. Dana steals money from Gib's wallet. Harry says, "She knows not to steal. I've taught her better than that." Gib replies, "Yeah, but you're not her parents, anymore, you and Helen. Her parents are Axl Rose and Madonna. The five minutes you spend with her a day can't compete with that kind of constant bombardment." Gib suggests she is stealing to buy drugs or get an abortion because she is "boinkin" her boyfriend. Helen lies about her secret meetings with Simon and flirts with infidelity. Harry is most affected emotionally when he thinks Helen is having an affair.

Oddly, when Harry is tempted to commit his own infidelity with Juno, it is the seemingly amoral Gib who reminds Harry through his hidden earphone that he's married. Lies, infidelity, and family disunity are the antivalues in the film, with their opposites as the desired state of cultural harmony and balance.

Juno and the terrorists comprise the "other" that, within terror management theory, threatens the culture of the Tasker family and the viewer. For the anxiety created by the mortality threat to be lessened, "our" culture must be elevated and the "other" culture must be defeated or denigrated.

In *True Lies*, the others are Middle Eastern. Aziz is described in the screenplay as a "defiant-looking Syrian with a full beard." Many of the terrorists have dark hair and beards or are unshaven. They wear military clothes draped with military paraphernalia, carry machine guns, and shoot them into the air. Aziz, in particular, is shown several times in wild-eyed close-ups, looking fanatical. Though the villains are presented stereotypically, one of the agents in Omega Sector also looks Middle Eastern.

Some reviewers noted *True Lies* also has a strong value message of violence toward women and traditional stereotyping.[13] Women commonly are called "bitch" or "pussy." Aziz strikes Juno in a rage. When it seems that Helen has committed adultery, Harry stalks her and Gib says, "Women —can't live with 'em; can't kill em."

Within the world of the film, if the dangers create anxiety and fear of death, only reinforcement of culture and denigration of the other can exorcise the fear and anxiety. In *True Lies*, the wicked woman character, Juno, and virtually all of the terrorists die.

The film ends with a cut to two years after the terrorist episode. The family is together at night around the table thumb wrestling. The phone rings with an assignment for agents Boris and Doris—Harry and Helen are spies together now. On assignment, they spot Simon, now a waiter, doing his spy routine on an attractive female guest. "Doris" pretends she is going to shoot him — with her lipstick. He pees in his pants, gaining victory for marriage and fidelity over scheming philanderers. The film happily ends with Boris and Doris dancing a tango while Gib pleads in their earphones for them to get back to business.

CULTURAL STATEMENTS: *PATRIOT GAMES*

Patriot Games is also a morality play about the family. Ryan's entire motivation in the film is encapsulated in its subtitle, "Not for honor. Not for country. For his wife and child." Ryan's conscious motivation is personal — to save his family. Unconsciously, his initial actions against the terrorists are based on value — what the terrorists are trying to do enrages his sense of civilized morality.

Family is the thread that unites the film's plot. In the opening scene, the Ryan family is playing monopoly in their London hotel. Ryan calls a friend to see if Sally's goldfish are well back in the States; he doesn't want Sally to be disappointed when they return home. His first thought after a bomb explodes in London is to see if his family is safe. Ryan's first act after being attacked on the street in Annapolis is to find his wife. He goes back to work at the CIA, which he detests, to protect his family. After the boat chase scene, the film shows Cathy and Sally resting on Ryan's protective shoulders. The film ends with the entire family making breakfast and talking about names for Cathy's unborn child. Ryan is portrayed as a peaceful man driven to violence to protect his family.

Ryan's sense of helplessness in being able to protect his family is shown in one scene where he reads to Sally in her hospital bed: "The sun did not shine, it was too wet to play.... I wish we had something to do.... All we could do was sit, sit, sit, sit, and we did not like it, not one bit. And then, something went bump...." Ryan's storytelling is contrasted with a shot of him sitting forlornly in the cafeteria when IRA fund-raiser Paddy O'Neil (Richard Harris) walks in and puts a wrapped present on the table. It contains an Irish doll and a manila envelope of photographs, including the hint Ryan needs to find the terrorists in North Africa.

The Ryans are an idealized nuclear family. After they return home from London, Ryan lights the fireplace and Cathy becomes ill with morning sickness. Their London hotel tryst has resulted in conception, and there is hope of a baby Ryan at some future time. She is a noted eye doctor; he is a professor and author. Cathy picks up Sally from school. The family cooks and plays games together. Producer Noyce calls their Chesapeake Bay home "The temple of patriarchy.... It's the house of a family because the movie is about family."[14]

Sean represents the counterfamily. He is described as shooting a priest in Derry during confession and a "bad boy." He loves his family as much as Ryan, but his wrong values and actions lead to his brother's death. Sean is consumed by a desire for revenge, leading to the doom of all around him. Sean's terrorist group is shown as immoral. A rival leader commits adultery. Sean and his leader, Kevin O'Donnell, kill unarmed British guards and their own compatriots, bookshop owner Dennis Cooley and Buckingham Palace mole Watkins. Critic David Denby calls the plot the same old terrorist villain stuff, asking: "What do [the terrorists] stand for apart from violence? What do they think they will accomplish? Are you surprised to hear that the filmmakers aren't interested in any of that? The IRA members are *terrorists*, i. e., vicious, and they must be destroyed. That's all you need to know."[15]

Symbolically, the viewer is instructed to alleviate any mortality anxiety created by the film by reaffirming and protecting the nuclear family. Not supporting Irish liberation efforts at fund-raising in the United States (money to buy guns) is offered as a strategy for reducing Irish terrorism.

After September 11, 2001

Did the public viewing of these films change after a real terrorist attack on New York and the Pentagon? Video rental giant Blockbuster thinks so. A message was taped to *True Lies* and several other films saying: "In light of the acts of terrorism in September 11, 2001, please be advised this product contains scenes that may be considered disturbing to some viewers." *True Lies,* in particular, contains terrorism themes that resemble reality — Middle Eastern terrorists motivated by political aims plot to destroy U.S. cities. Ironically, many video storeowners actually found that after 9/11, viewers were, in fact, attracted to films like *Die Hard* and *True Lies* because of the terrorism theme and plots where the hero wins.[16] Supposedly, watching a hero win helps reinforce cultural messages.

In *True Lies,* Aziz is described as hardcore, ultrafundamentalist, and fanatical. He is linked to car bombings and airplane crashes. The group's name is Crimson Jihad, and they smuggle four nuclear weapons into the United States. The name "Crimson Jihad" is chillingly evocative after September 11. Aziz's speeches remind the viewer of Osama bin Laden's tapes from Afghanistan — both film and real terrorists call for a withdrawal of

U.S. troops from the Persian Gulf and threaten destruction. The film spies are urged by Trilby (Charleton Heston) to find the terrorists before "somebody parks a car in front of the White House with a nuclear weapon in the trunk." Terrorists explode a nuclear bomb in the Florida Keys and threaten to explode another in Miami if the United States doesn't pull its military from the Persian Gulf.

The general plot seems familiar and reminds the viewer of the deadly terrorist attack on New York City's twin towers. The threat of nuclear bombs in the United States seems more probable. The mortality salience for the viewer is enhanced. Terror management research indicates that depression, which was widespread after the events of September 11, exacerbate the impulse for cultural reinforcement. If terror management theory is correct, the film also instructs viewers on how to reduce their anxiety and regain balance — reenergize the nuclear family and debase those who are "other" (Middle Eastern terrorists). While the film is careful to show the terrorists as generally Middle Eastern and does not paint them directly as religiously motivated, viewers are likely to perceive the film terrorists within the familiar framework of an Al Qaeda follower.

Patriot Games contains threats that are more personal, but less salient after the events of 9/11. No threats of mass destruction exist in the film, and civilians are not targeted at random. The actions on American soil are either motivated by personal revenge or attempts to kidnap foreign royalty for political gain. Symbolically, the terrorists are a threat to the family, but the threat is targeted at one particular family. No message of tolerance is present in either film.

Summary

Terror management theory provides a framework for critical analysis of films. In particular, terror management theory provides a mechanism to analyze and highlight the values and cultural messages films convey after scaring the audience and reminding viewers of their own mortality. Just as Kenneth Burke[17] suggested that Western culture plays out a spiritual cycle of guilt, then victimage, and then redemption, terror management theory empirically identifies a cognitive and behavioral cycle in human behavior of fear of death, then anxiety, then cultural reinforcement or denigration of others, and then anxiety reduction. *True Lies* and *Patriot Games* are films utilizing terrorist attacks in the United States as a primary plot vehicle. The mortality prompt in both films is followed by cultural enhancement of traditional family values and reinforcement of the otherness of Irish and Middle Eastern terrorists. These films offer both mortality prompts and cultural enhancement or denigration messages— wrapped up with music, special effects, and popcorn. Any films with terrorist plots involving airplanes and weapons of mass destruction (the 1996 Kirk Russell film, *Executive Decisions,* is an additional example) may elicit strong mortality effects and anxiety.

If watching the violence in these films creates anxiety in portions of the audience, viewers could look to one of the two offered means of anxiety reduction. The United States Census shows only 69 percent of households are families of any type and only 24 percent fit the film model of two-parent households with children.[18] An exact imitation of the family bonding in the films is an unlikely source of reaffirmation for most viewers. We can only speculate, at this juncture, how viewers with their myriad cultural values and family composition might interpret the imperative to reinforce culture through family values.

Continued analysis of terrorism films and their cognitive impact seems necessary, in light of the sustained international popularity of the terrorism plot in films such as Schwarzenegger's *Collateral Damage,* India's *Bharat Bhagya Vidhata,* and the BBC's film *Smallpox 2002 — Silent Weapon.* While violent films were temporarily postponed after the events of September 11, 2001, Hollywood soon returned to business as usual. As Patrick Goldstein observed in a November 2001 *Los Angeles Times* article, "If you drove past 20th Century Fox in October, you might have seen the giant billboard at the entrance to the studio that showed two firemen raising the American flag over the rubble of the World Trade Center. But the billboard's been painted over — it now touts the Farrelly brothers' comedy, *Shallow Hal.*"[19]

NOTES

1. Box Office Mojo, "Arnold Schwarzenegger" (database online); available from http://www.boxofficemojo.com/Arnold.htm.

2. 90s' Highlighted Films," *History of Fox* (database online); available from http://www.tcfhe.com/capsule/true.htm).

3. David Wilcock, "*All-reviews.com Movie/Video Review: 'True Lies'*" (database online); available from http://www.all-reviews.com/videos-2/true-lies.htm.

4. 90s' Highlighted Films."

5. The Numbers, *Patriot Games* (database online); available from http://www.the -numbers.com/movies/1992/OPATR.html.

6. Tom Watt in *Patriot Games.* (database on-line); available from http://www. xceco.on.ca/~walford/abound/lofty1.thm).

7. Jeffrey Greenberg, Sheldon Solomon, and Thomas Pyszczynski, "Terror Management Theory of Self-esteem and Cultural Worldviews: Empirical Assessments and Conceptual Refinements," *Advances in Experimental Social Psychology* 29 (1997): 61–139.

8. Greenberg, Solomon, and Pyszczynski, 61.

9. *Ibid.*, 65.

10. Reviewed in Greenberg, Solomon, and Pyszczynski.

11. Reviewed in Gerald R. Miller, Michael Burgoon, and Judith Burgoon. "The Function of Human Communication in Changing Attitudes and Gaining Compliance," in *Handbook of Rhetorical and Communication Theory,* C. C. Arnold and J. W. Bowers, eds. (Boston: Allyn & Bacon, 1984).

12. "Arnold's Back!" *Newsweek* (July 18, 1994), 58.

13. See R. Corliss, "Lies, True Lies and Ballistics," *Time* (July 18, 1994), 55–56; A. Lane, "The Spy Who Loved Me," *The New Yorker* (July 25, 1994), 77–79; *True Lies* and Sexual Violence," *Rolling Stone* (1994), 96–97.

14. J. Emerson, "Noyce's On," *Film Comment* 28 (July/August 1992), 73.

15. David Denby, "Same Old Stuff" *New York* (June 8, 1992), 58.

16. D. Germain, "*Action Films Easing Back into Theater*" (database online); available from http://www.onlineathens.com/stories/020902)/mov_020902008.shtml).

17. Kenneth Burke, *The Philosophy of Literary Form* (Baton Rouge: Louisiana State University Press, 1941).

18. J. Fields and L. M. Casper, "America's Families and Living Arrangements" (U.S. Census Bureau: Department of Commerce, June 21, 2000).

19. Patrick Goldstein, "The Big Picture: Changed Forever? No, Two Months," *The Lost Angeles Times* (November 13, 2001) (database online); available on Lexis-Nexis.

10

Stanley Kubrick and America's "Strange Love" of War

NANCY LYNCH STREET

On April 4, 1967 — three years after *Dr. Strangelove* appeared in theatres in America, exactly one year before he was assassinated, and eight years before the Vietnam War ended — Dr. Martin Luther King, Jr., spoke at the Riverside Church in New York City. In this speech, he linked his opposition to the Vietnam War with the civil rights movement.[1] King began his speech by saying,

> I come to this magnificent house of worship tonight because my conscience leaves me no other choice.... "A time comes when silence is betrayal." That time has come for us in relation to Vietnam.... Even when pressed by the demands of inner truth, men do not easily assume the task of opposing their government's policy, especially in time of war.... I come to this platform tonight to make a passionate plea to my beloved nation. This speech is not addressed to Hanoi or to the National Liberation Front. It is not addressed to China or to Russia.... Neither is it an attempt to make North Vietnam or the National Liberation Front paragons of virtue, nor to overlook the role they can play in a successful resolution of the problem.... Tonight, however, I wish not to speak with Hanoi and the NLF, but rather to my fellow Americans who, with me, bear the greatest responsibility in ending a conflict that has exacted a heavy price on both continents.[2]

Within the nonviolent spirit of MLK, and within the context that follows, I analyze *Dr. Strangelove* using concepts from Kenneth Burke, René Gerard, and others regarding the human capacity for choice and responsibility, as well as the (apparent) need for blood sacrifice.

In his *Iron Law of History*, Burke says,

Here are the steps
In the Iron Law of History
That welds Order and Sacrifice:
Order leads to Guilt
(for who can keep the commandments:)
Guilt needs Redemption
(for who would not be cleansed!)
Redemption needs a Redeemer
(which is to say, a Victim:)
Order
Through Guilt
To Victimage
(hence: Cult of the Kill)[3]

Among other of Burke's goals, his linguistic objective is "the purification of war." Realizing, along with René Girard,[4] that the time for Stone
Age blood sacrifice and victimage had passed, Burke cites historical
episodes as central to his belief (as in his analysis of *Mein Kampf*).[5] Burke
also hypothesizes that our ancient and modern dilemma is rooted in our
desire for perfection, stating that "we are rotten with perfection." This
declaration binds us to the concept of order. In communication terms,
this means "order from our own perspective." Since no two persons or
two nations may have the same perspective (in space and time), obviously
conflicts will arise out of differences in perspective as to what is perfect —
or in order.

In this chapter, I examine the issues discussed above, while probing
at the concept of war as "insanity," or "madness" as depicted through the
characters in *Dr. Strangelove*. Utilizing Kenneth Burke's concepts of guilt,
victimage and salvation, I also discuss the use of war as sacrifice and as
diversionary strategy, designed to keep a citizenry quiescent, as well as the
impact of distance. Finally, following the lead of Martin Luther King, I urge
thoughtful assessment of the consequences of war and the benefits of non-
violence and dialogue. Kubrick's *Dr. Strangelove* is a message for our time
and is as relevant today, perhaps more so, as it was thirty-five years ago.

Historical Background

A major goal of the Cold War, as waged by the West, was the eradi-
cation of communism from this planet. With the fall of the Berlin Wall in
1989 and the dissolution of the Soviet Union in 1991, the Cold War seemingly ended (although in 2003, China, Cuba and North Korea are still

standing). In truth, while the Soviet Union and the United States played the superpower game from the end of World War II in 1945 to 1991, the "tectonic plates" shifted beneath the game board. Despite our espionage system and ever-increasing military technological superiority, we apparently did not foresee the directions from which new, decisively different threats to national security might emerge. Given the events of the past few years, beginning with (but not limited to) what has come to be known as "9/11," it appears that we have been looking in all the wrong places. According to the Bureau of Public Affairs in *Significant Terrorist Incidents, 1961–2001: A Chronology,* there were more than 125 terrorist incidents during the Cold War era and its aftermath.[6]

In 2003, as the United States promulgated its war on terrorism[7] by gearing up for confrontation (once again) with Iraq, North Korea was also playing its nuclear card, challenging United Nations' inspectors at "its nuclear power plant (i.e., bomb-factory) at Yongbyon."[8] North Korea's position was clear — it wanted both the help with reactor plants promised in the 1994 agreement with the United States, as well as recognition of North Korea by the United States. While the Clinton administration (apparently) willingly signed this agreement, the Bush administration chose to ignore it, even to the point of refusing to keep diplomatic lines open between North Korea and the United States. According to a January 2003 article in the *New Yorker* by Seymour M. Hersh,

> Last June, four months before the current crisis over North Korea became public, the Central Intelligence Agency ... report made the case that North Korea had been violating international law — and agreements with South Korea and the United States — by secretly obtaining the means to produce weapons-grade uranium.... The document's most politically sensitive information, however, was about Pakistan ... [which] had been sharing sophisticated technology, warhead-design information, and weapons-testing data with the Pyongyang regime. Pakistan, one of the Bush Administration's important allies in the war against terrorism, was helping North Korea build the bomb.[9]

Pakistan's actions have been termed the "'worst nightmare' of the international arms-control community: a Third World country becoming an instrument of proliferation."[10] In any event, should the situation with North Korea veer further out of control, or, should George W. Bush and Dick Cheney decide to go for North Korea's Kim Jong Il's "head on a platter," the cost in human life, not to mention quality of life for many in several countries, especially South Korea and the United States would be enormous.[11] According to Hersh, "The Pentagon has estimated that all-out war would result in more than a million military and civilian casualties, including as many as 100,000 Americans."[12]

Thus, two out of three of the countries (Iraq and North Korea) named in President Bush's 2002 "axis of evil" (Iran, Iraq and North Korea) emerged to challenge America's bid for worldwide military, oil and economic hegemony in 2003.[13] The world is once again on tenterhooks, just as it was in 1962 during the standoff between the Soviet Union and the United States over the placement of Soviet missiles in Cuba. In that era, there would have been a mutual nuclear holocaust had diplomacy not intervened. Commentators note that the 2003 situation is reminiscent of the Cuban missile crisis, except that, according to *New York Times* writer Serge Schmemann,

> Lest anyone forget, that was a time when legions of very serious people in the United States and the Soviet Union spent their time devising ways to ensure that whoever shot first would die second. The doctrine was called MAD "mutual assured destruction"—and it came with a package of equally cute ideas like "use 'em or lose 'em" (unleash your nukes if you think they might be destroyed.... The real name of the game, of course, was deterrence.[14]

Since that time, as Schmemann notes, a great deal has changed. Third World countries have acquired nuclear weapons. In 1998, India and Pakistan acquired nuclear weapons. Other states are apparently in process of developing nuclear weapons. But, as Bruce Blair, president of the Center for Defense Information observes,

> They [South Asian planners] are still sorting out virtually all of the key issues, particularly the challenge of ensuring tight central control over nuclear forces that may be placed on launch-ready alert during peacetime or a crisis. The acute dangers of a breakdown of control or faulty intelligence leading to a mistaken or unauthorized launch are far from solved.[15]

One sees, then, that the danger of nuclear weapons may be even greater than during the Cuban missile crisis, due to the wide range (nuclear, chemical, biological and missile) of weapons of mass destruction (WMD) now available or nearly available worldwide.[16] Iraq is not thought to have nuclear weapons but is suspected of retaining weapons of mass destruction. Meanwhile, it is unclear at this time whether the North Koreans have nuclear weapons. In any event, among the world's "states possessing, pursuing or capable of acquiring weapons of mass destruction" (as of 2000) are the following[17]:

Algeria (N), Belarus (N)　　　　　France (NCM), India (NCBM)
Bulgaria (B), Chile (C)　　　　　　Indonesia (C), Iran (N*CBM)
China (NCBM), Cuba (B)　　　　　Iraq (N*CBM), Israel (NCBM)
Ethiopia (C), Egypt (CBM)　　　　Kazakhstan (N*), Laos (N*)

Libya (CBM), Myanmar (C)   Vietnam (CB), United Kingdom
North Korea (NCBM), Sudan (C)   (NCM)
Syria (CBM), Taiwan (CBM)   United States (NCBM)
Thailand (C), Ukraine (N*)

The awakening of the American people in the sixties and our good fortune in having many capable leaders in perilous times brought about significant change in America, though not without a price — the assassinations of John F. Kennedy, Robert F. Kennedy, Malcolm X and Martin Luther King. In film, with the McCarthy era behind them, directors such as Stanley Kubrick (*Dr. Strangelove*), John Frankenheimer (*Black Sunday*) and others sought to illuminate the world we lived in. This included the "containment world," the "superpower world," the "preglobalization world," the "civil rights world," the "antiwar world," the "gender issues world," the "sexist world" and the "bomb world." Recently, another "world" has been added to the list — the "weapons of mass destruction (WMD) World." Some of these latter weapons were already in use in Vietnam. One such weapon was commonly known as Agent Orange, which poisoned not only the Vietnamese — allies and enemies — but also our own soldiers and perhaps their progeny.

Today, following the Persian Gulf War and our persistent bombing of the Iraqi population, it appears that the uranium in the bombs which the United States dropped in 1991 (and afterward) may have caused a significant surge in cancer among children in Iraq. Should this prove to be true, we will have extended our reach with weapons of mass destruction, which, as the chart above indicates, is plausible — the United States has all four categories of weapons of mass destruction in its arsenal, some of which we have apparently used with few qualms. But using these weapons is not a given; we are not somehow forced to use them against other persons. We can choose to use them or not. Or have we already gone past the point of no return? Is there a point of no return?

Kenneth Burke's World

In Burke's view, persons are seen as critical organisms in the environment, coupled with the evolutionary development of language and the introduction of "the negative." Inherent in making and communicating choices (Burke's concept of action) is the possibility of saying "no." This potential is not found in nature, despite the objection (which Burke notes) that "someone might say as in rebuttal, 'Then how about negative electricity? Isn't that as natural as positive electricity?'"[18] He points out that it might just as fittingly have been called cathodic electricity.[19] In this chapter, I am concerned with the linguistic ability to say "yes" or "no," as a choice maker. Choice presages and engages responsibility. Having made a choice, one is responsible.

Burke argues for a difference between action (initiative) and motion (acted upon)—humans act (thus the dramatistic emphasis); all other things in nature are either in motion or put in motion (as are missiles or nuclear warheads). With this distinction, Burke introduces the evolutionary motif of reciprocal adaptation between, in particular, the human organism and the environment. Persons are not, within this perspective, either determined or acted upon. They are both acting and acted upon and thus ambiguously both free and determined, subjective and objective. Within the developing social environment, complete with hierarchy, mystery, command and a host of "thou shalt nots" embodied within religion and law, the person seen as organism with individual and corporate perspective still takes action, implying choice. As Burke points out, the negative "Thou shalt not kill" strikes "the resonant gong: 'Kill!'"[20]

On the international level (for purposes of this chapter) and taking the linear view, Burke's concept of guilt (not sin) arises out of the established order. However, one can just as easily say that guilt arises out of order as out of disorder. Guilt may then be considered, as in the case of Nazi Germany, the dissolution of order and the attempt to regain some sense of person, place and state. I think that it is fair to say that the United States, since Vietnam and its humiliations as well as the Persian Gulf War and the war in 2001 in Afghanistan, suffers, like pre–World War II Germany, from a need to regain "face" in the world. In neither case did we rout the "faces of evil" (either Saddam Hussein or Osama bin Laden). Despite being the world's greatest military and economic power, we still can't win. The shame of this situation goads our male leaders to greater excess, to an endless war on terror. Is it possible that their attention span may be arrested in puberty? In many ways, that is what Kubrick is saying in *Dr. Strangelove.*

Dr. Strangelove—*Synopsis and Script*

The film opens with music. We hear the tune "Try a Little Tenderness." Inside a B-52 bomber, the camera focuses on the plane's complicated control panel and its code book. As the order comes through to activate "Plan R," the crew—the cowboy pilot Major "King" Kong (Slim Pickens) and Lieutenant Lothar Zogg (James Earl Jones) and Goldie cannot believe the order.

KONG: Goldie, did you say wing attack, Plan R?

GOLDIE: Yes, sir, I have.

KONG: Goldie, how many times have I told you guys that I don't want no horsing around on the airplane?

GOLDIE: I'm not horsin' around, sir, that's how it decodes.

KONG: Well, I've been to one world fair, a picnic, and a rodeo and that's the stupidest thing I every heard come over a set of earphones. You sure you got today's code?

BOMBARDIER: Major Kong, is it possible this is some kind of loyalty test? You know, give the "go" code and then recall to see who would actually go?

KONG: Ain't nobody ever got the "go" code yet. And old Ripper wouldn't be giving us Plan R unless them Russkies had already clobbered Washington and a lot of other towns with a sneak attack.

In this scene and in the scenes following, which take place in the B-52 bomber, we hear "Johnny Comes Marching Home" as the plane continues on its doomed path. What one notices here is the assumption that Washington has already been hit, otherwise Ripper would not be asking for Plan R. The idea that a crazed Ripper might want to not only off himself, but also the entire world, never enters the calculation.

Kong ends the scene by saying:

> Look boys, I ain't much of a hand at makin' speeches.... Heck, I reckon you wouldn't even be human beings if you didn't have some pretty strong personal feelings about nuclear combat.[21]

Meanwhile, back at the war room, participants maintain decorum and are well dressed and, except for a few, impassive in the face of a nuclear holocaust. In this scene the viewer meets Peter Sellers as President Muffley, who has just been informed of the looming catastrophe and has requested, much to the horror of General Turgidson, that the Soviet ambassador be brought to the war room. The Russian ambassador, Alexei, is asked to speak to the Russian premier (Dimitri Kissoff), setting up the call from the president. Alexei characterizes his premier as a drunk and a womanizer (apparently this gives no pause). President Muffley explains that an American general (General Jack Ripper) "went and did a silly thing." The phone conversation becomes more and more ludicrous, as the two presidents bicker as though playing marbles, rather than discussing a nuclear holocaust.

MUFFLEY: Hello? Hello, Dimitri? Listen, I can't hear too well, do you suppose you could turn the music down just a little? Oh, that's much better. Yes, fine, I can hear you now, Dimitri. Clear and plain and coming through fine. I'm coming through fine too, eh? Good, then…. Now then, Dimitri. You know how we've always talked about the possibility of something going wrong with the bomb. The bomb, Dimitri. The hydrogen bomb. Well now, what happened is, one of our base commanders, he had a sort of, well, he went a little funny in the head. You know…. Well, I'll tell you what he did, he ordered his planes … to attack your country. Well, let me finish, Dimitri…. Well, listen, how do you think I feel about it? Can you imagine how I feel about it, Dimitri? Why do you think I'm calling you? Just to say hello? Of course I like to speak to you. Of course I like to say hello…. I'm just calling up to tell you something terrible has happened…. I'm sorry, too, Dimitri. I'm very sorry. All right! You're sorrier than I am! But I am sorry as well.[22]

The phone conversation between the presidents ends with the American president asking, "Who should we call?" Dimitri apparently responds, "The People's Central Air Defense Headquarters." Naturally, he does not know the number of the defense headquarters, advising the president to call Omsk information for the number. The scene ends when Alexei speaks to Dimitri in hushed tones and responds to American questioning by saying, "The fools, the mad fools, the doomsday machine." This machine turns out to be scheduled to detonate when attacked by an enemy, thereby ensuring mutual destruction of the major powers, as in the case of the B-52 which is loaded for bear and an hour away from Moscow.

The scene shifts to the base command of General Ripper, now dead, leaving his British adjutant, Lionel Mandrake (Peter Sellers), to attempt to persuade the conquerors that he must make a call to the president of the United States, which initiates a hilarious scene ending with Mandrake finally making the call. This scene ends with Mandrake ordering Colonel Bat Guano (Keenan Wynn) to shoot the soft drink vending machine so that he will have change to make a station-to-station call. In a jab at the American propensity to respect private property over people, Kubrick has Guano say that the machine "is private property. You are going to have to answer to the Coca-Cola company!"

In the next scene, we witness a jubilant war room. General Turgidson delivers a prayer, yet another feature of American warfare. He is interrupted by a call from Premier Kissoff— they have managed to shoot down only three of the four bombers alerted by General Ripper prior to his demise. The fourth plane, that of Major "King" Kong, is coming in under the radar. President Muffley is beside himself and says to Premier Kissoff, "You must give it everything you have — and will this set off the doomsday machine?" The manner in which the two world leaders talk to one another is immature pabulum, revealing the incredible risks the world has been taking in allowing two men and their half-witted, power hungry, sexually and socially retarded underlings to decide who will live and who will die.

Not long after, Dr. Strangelove (Peter Sellers) whirls around in his wheelchair, cigarette in gloved hand, ready to inform his listeners in the war room about the doomsday scenario as it affects, not the millions who will die, but rather those who will, theoretically, live "for 100 years underground" and the advantages these men will have as the ratio of males to females will be ten to one! This grabs the attention of all, including the president.

Confusing the president with Hitler, Strangelove calls him "Mein Führer" and proceeds to regale his listeners with the delights awaiting those who will go underground. These men "won't envy the dead," as they will not see the dead, for "when they go down, all will be alive." Strangelove attempts to keep control of his body, but his clear joy at the thought of a subterranean playground makes this difficult. Meanwhile, General Turgidson, clearly titillated by the ten-to-one prospect (in the national interest and for breeding purposes only, to be ready to replenish the earth when all is clear), brings up the concept of family values. For what is an administration without lip service to family values?

Next, Dr. Strangelove reminds his audience that all must sacrifice. Caught up in the discussion and taking the usual Cold War perspective, General Turgidson asserts that in view of this new information, we must not allow "a mine shaft gap." Again the target is the Cold War slogans of "gaps," which must incite us to further wartime preparations, regardless of whether there is any truth to the claim. Truth may be a casualty of men who want to go to war. The real truth may be that everyday life is boring — a little war adds sparkle to men's lives — those who live through the killing fields, wherever they may be. And, of course, should we overcome the "mine shaft gap" the children of our male leaders will emerge unscathed, primed to inflict devastation on the planet once again.

Real to Reel

Stanley Kubrick's satirical, dark comedy, *Dr. Strangelove,* made its debut on the world stage in 1964. Ironically, the "Strangelove" release was held back due to civil rights disturbances, a war climate and recent polit-

ical assassination — just as films were held back in September 2001 — and
for similar reasons. In 1964, many in the Western world stood drenched
in fear, anger and sorrow following the assassination of President John F.
Kennedy.[23] At that time, *Dr. Strangelove* also played to a bomb-shelter
audience programmed to be terrified of a nuclear holocaust and thus to
support the military's every wish and whim without question. This situation would change significantly in the coming years as civil rights leaders such as Martin Luther King and others from all walks of life also
embraced the ideology of peace (which can be antiwar, but need not be).

Likewise, *Black Hawk Down* and other films were held back following the Al Qaeda attack on New York, Washington, D.C., and Pennsylvania on September 11, 2001. One heard little dissent over the declared war
on terror, which followed as the Bush administration took the UN-backed
Western military forces to Afghanistan seeking revenge and the head of Al
Qaeda leader Osama bin Laden. This war secured the capital city of Kabul
but little else, severely depleting our national resources, not to mention
the resources of the people of Afghanistan. Several years later, the Afghani
people still live in tents amid the rubble of the bombings of two wars in
twenty years. There is virtually no infrastructure, save for military use.
Warring warlords control the areas outside the militarized Kabul zone.

The continual waging of war has been, in part, responsible for the economic distress felt by middle-class Americans and the working poor. While
bombing Afghanistan (once again) to rubble and doing little to rebuild
that country, we moved on to gathering momentum for an attack on Iraq.
This propensity to continually wage war adds immeasurably to the national
debt while subtracting from available funds for social welfare, education
and renewed infrastructure, e.g., roads, health care, social services and
education. Given this setting the words of Martin Luther King in 1967
seem oddly appropriate:

> We are adding cynicism to the process of death, for they [our men in the
> military] must know after a short period there [Vietnam] that none of
> the things we claim to be fighting for are really involved ... [and] that
> we are on the side of the wealthy and the secure while we create a hell
> for the poor.[24]

America's "war against terror" started in Afghanistan, where pilots
bombed the country "back to the Stone Age." In point of fact, there really
wasn't much to destroy, since Kabul had already been bombed to rubble
during the Cold War (when America backed the Taliban against the former Soviet Union).

Soon after, the world faced the threat of returning to Iraq — the scene of the Gulf War in 1991—where we tried to once again eradicate the "face of evil," Saddam Hussein. In March 2003 (as this book goes to press), despite economic embargoes, starving and medically depriving Iraqi children, the United States has not been able to capture or kill Saddam Hussein — or to internationalize his oilfields. In addition, there are worldwide protests regarding the proposal of the United States to take the rest of the world to war with Iraq. I can only think that Martin Luther King, Jr.— were he alive — would have been marching with them.

Meanwhile, the UN is insisting that the weapons inspectors sent to Iraq be allowed to do their job — without pressure from the White House. As I write this, today (January 27, 2003) is the deadline given the weapons inspectors to present their assessment of Iraqi military resources, as well as to evaluate Iraq's resolution to disarm. Speaking before the UN, the inspectors indicated they might need several more months. The Bush administration is not pleased. At this time, the United States has amassed some 80,000 troops on the borders of Iraq, while demanding that the rest of the world let us go to war — now. Even worse, other nations are obliged to go with us. Perhaps this is the typical behavior of Texas cowboys and governors. In an article in the *Economist,* titled *The Future Is Texas,* the author says, in addition to noting that the White House is Texan-occupied territory, that

> The San Antonio region is the living embodiment of the military-industrial complex, with an army base, two air-force bases, a huge army medical centre, dozens of defense-related firms and a big community of military retirees.... The 16,000-acre Pantex plant in west Texas secretly assembled thousands of nuclear warheads during the cold war, and now maintains what remains of America's nuclear arsenal.... Violence is not limited to the military variety.... In 2000, George Bush's last year as governor, the state executed 40 people. Today, 452 people are languishing on Texas's death row, 12% of the country's total.[25]

Obviously, Texas is ready for various preemptive strikes. Perhaps it's something in the water, as General Jack Ripper says in *Dr. Strangelove,* when he prepares to "launch a pre-emptive strike to stop a Communist infiltration which is 'sapping and impurifying all of our precious bodily fluids'"[26] Jack drinks only vodka and denies women his bodily fluids to avoid this contamination.

Strangelove *Revisited*

This is an appropriate time to revisit Kubrick's brilliant portrayal of men playing at war. Rife with sexual innuendo, when not embracing the fascist Aryan ideology or the sexual bennies which will accrue to bomb-sheltered powerful males, "Strangelove" also takes on our reliance on technology to keep safe, communication fallacies in the "fail safe" system, gender imbalance in decision making, as well as women as the enemy — and source of contamination, as in WMD other than nuclear.

Through the characters of General Ripper (Sterling Hayden) and General Turgidson (George C. Scott), we are treated to the mindless madness of the American military male. Meanwhile, the hapless President Muffley further delineates the total lack of comprehension (he is clueless) of what we have wrought in the pursuit of military, oil and economic hegemony.

The film utilizes its story line and characters well. First, we have General Jack Ripper, commandant of a military base and privy to the code necessary to send the B-52 bombers with weapons to end the world. He orders a squadron of B-52 bombers to "Code Red," setting off the process which will lead to a nuclear holocaust.

General Jack Ripper is a severely disturbed man who has lost his ability to have sex. Determining that this event is a "commie" plot, he denies his essence to women, drinks only vodka and eventually totally loses it and blows his own head off, taking the vital return code with him. Unfortunately, in this nuclear scenario, only Jack Ripper has the code and he commits suicide before Mandrake can wrest it from him. Where are the fail safe methods now?

Meanwhile, back at the war room, General Turgidson outlines the difficulty of recalling the B-52 bombers to the pacifist American president (possibly representing the paucity of public knowledge) as events unfold. Despite General Turgidson's objections, President Muffley invites the Soviet ambassador to the war room. The Soviet ambassador puts Muffley in touch with the Soviet premier and amidst many sexist jokes, the three try to work out a strategy to stop the B-52s. Turgidson is not happy about this but from time to time manages to hold his tongue while chewing gum incessantly. What is noticeable about these sequences is that the war room is filled with men, few of whom speak. When, however, voices are raised and mild combat ensues, President Muffley sternly reminds the men that "Gentlemen, you can't fight in here. This is the War Room!"

Women are nowhere to be found in the war room or at the base, making the film a repository for sexual innuendo. Later, this milieu is repeated when Strangelove muses on a world below ground, in the bunkers, where males may copulate with appropriate females as they await their return to the surface of the earth.

Finally, Mandrake is able to extrapolate the code "OPE" from Ripper's scribbling on a pad of paper. The bombers respond to the code and return to base, except one whose radio receiver has been damaged. This bomber is the original bomber, whose captain is Major "King" Kong. Kong, a cowboy, after many problems, goes down riding the bomb in the ultimate macho incarnation. And the world comes to an end in a nuclear cloud, despite the ineffectual efforts of both the Soviet president and the American president.

Chris Sheridan, in his analysis of the film, says,

> The act of war is primarily a male activity that is inextricably lined with the male sex action. Like a sword, the penis penetrates the body, then "fires" semen during ejaculation like bullets from a gun. In the event of procreation, the sperm forces its way into the egg like an army forcing its way into a fortification. And, as in war, may the best sperm win. Thus, killing and reproduction are virtually the same in metaphor. The weapons of modern war, missiles, cannons, and torpedoes, are incredibly similar to the phallus. The bigger the gun, the bigger the penis; the bigger the explosion, the bigger the ejaculation. And what could be bigger than a hydrogen bomb. Yee Haw-ing like a rodeo bull rider Major Kong straddles the long, cylindrical nuclear bomb between his legs and rides it all the way down from the plane to its target below—the largest penis and ejaculation imaginable.[27]

Overall, *Strangelove* also helps one to understand the evolution of modern warfare and its distance from its devastation and "collateral damage" (the dead). In addition to the distance between the perpetrator and the victim created through the new air warfare so popular during the first Gulf War on the "green" screen, America also suffers from myopia due to the distance between America and other countries and our understanding of the havoc, the cruelty, the death and dying experienced by much of the rest of the world in the past one hundred years.

FILM AND WAR

Kubrick's film was one of seven Cold War films produced by Hollywood in 1964. As Joyce A. Evans notes in her book *Celluloid Mushroom Clouds: Hollywood and the Atomic Bomb*, 1964 was also the year in which yet another communist nation, China, detonated an atomic bomb, while the United States escalated its intervention in Vietnam.[28] In 1963, the United States and the USSR agreed "to establish a hotline link to minimize risk of accidental war."[29] This hotline plays a prominent role in *Dr. Strangelove*.

Kubrick's work in *Strangelove* (which parodies many dimensions of the lunatic escapades of the "managers" of the superpowers) is based upon a serious novel by Peter George titled *Red Alert*. As Evans indicates, the "genre of the Hollywood atomic war film, with its narrative style and ideologically tinged conventions, had become so standard and familiar that it could now be successfully parodied."[30] Of course, Kubrick goes further than *Red Alert* and also

> provides a thoughtful criticism of American defense policy and the military establishment. It suggests, as does *Fail Safe*, that the military does not truly control the bomb and that a nuclear accident is inevitable. [31]

As discussed earlier, the same conundrum faces all of us today, as the newly nuclear nations attempt to develop systems to effectively control deployment of nuclear warheads. The problems are not yet solved. Further — I would wager — Americans have the same problems encountered by President Muffley in *Dr. Strangelove*.

Tom Englehardt, in *The End of Victory Culture: Cold War America and the Disillusioning of a Generation,* says that in the seventies, with the disenchantment over Vietnam, "The very word *war* had fallen into disrepute as an attraction for the child audience and the United States had been shorn of a version of its history that was close to a secular religion."[32] As he develops his theme, Englehardt also notes the racist quality of our "moral right to kill" any of "them" (clearly illustrated through the George C. Scott's character, General Turgidson), which sought to prevent the westward expansion and appropriation of land and natural resources, including Indians, Mexicans and later yet another "savage, non-white enemy," the Japanese.[33] The story or myth which we had constructed was built on the righteous knowledge that God was on our side (God, after all, being white, though the American mix is getting more colorful), that we were fighting against savages (not privy to God's word) and, finally, that we were not defeated. Thus, the Victory Culture mythological umbrella entered the American century unscathed and intact. The ringing phrase "godless Communism" became our battle cry.

Myth is not untruth. It is, however, a product of time, space and culture and, once believed, becomes true, serving us for good or ill. A major premise of this chapter is that the Cold War (a quite natural extension of Englehardt's Victory Culture with the advent of atomic and nuclear weapons) has become a kind of security blanket. Without our Cold War superpower status— which we once shared with the Soviet Union — we (Americans) seem lost as the sole superpower. Even though we could not go to war with one another due to the nuclear threat, we could — and did — engage with one another through our proxies, as we did in Vietnam and Afghanistan.

Cold War Dreams and Realities

By the end of World War II, two superpowers emerged — Russia and the United States. These two had been at loggerheads with one another since the Russian Revolution of 1917, when a "new" government, led by Marxists Lenin, Trotsky and other Bolshevik leaders, replaced the tsar's rule over a land inhabited primarily by illiterate serfs and an elite ruling caste.[34] The Cold War actually began with that Communist regime taking control of Russia. In any event, communism was more feared and hated than fascism by some Western democracies, creating something of a conundrum when, during World War II, England and the United States were, given the circumstances of Hitler's provocation, forced to join forces with Russia.

Prior to the end of the war, the Great Powers — Russia, the United States and Great Britain — met at Yalta to divide up Europe once the war was over. These political decisions would have a heavy impact upon the second half of the twentieth century, much of it dubious; they were based upon ideology and assisted in the official birthing of what came to be known as the Cold War, a morality play in black and white acted out upon the world stage. In the American version of the Cold War script, we were instruments of God, saving the world from godless communism. Armageddon was to be the denouement. In Stanley Kubrick's *Dr. Strangelove* we come face to face with the end of the world.

INTERIM CULTURAL NOTES AND ISOLATION

Following World War II, new technologies, including the evolutionary development of the computer and nuclear warheads, proliferated. The United States and Russia (later to be christened the "evil empire"), both on the UN Security Council, engaged in a daily propagandistic media war, much as the United States and China have done until recently. Fiction and fact became indecipherable during the Cold War, creating an enveloping fog of fear, demagoguery and disinformation aimed at stroking "people's bigotry and intolerance to the point of international strife."[35] Yet, the closest that most Americans would come to war during this period was through "print, theater, screen or playtime experience."[36] Some believed that "God had placed this great nation between two seas for a purpose," meaning to save the world at this critical juncture. In fact, the geography of the United States has had the effect of isolating her, not just between two seas, but between lines of communication.

While the United States has the telecommunications infrastructure to import television programming from Europe and Asia, it does not do so. While the United States could easily import foreign films and make them available to the general public, it does not. While we could learn other languages, we do not. While we could read newspapers and magazines from abroad, we do not. Safe in our cocoon, we view primarily our own world — and find it good. This syndrome may also be called isolationism. Being isolated, we become insular; convinced of the goodness of our position, we do not often want to walk in another's shoes (particularly those of the "third world").

Thus, when called upon to act in the world, we can act only from our own myopia. Cold War superpower status was then the perfect vehicle for us when thrust center stage at the end of World War II. In the way of morality plays, there is only the hero and the villain to attend to seriously. All others are bit players and of little consequence.[37]

In the West, and most especially in the United States, the Cold War became the *Weltanschauung* (or worldview), a mythological viewpoint from which the United States attempted to impose its seemingly benign worldview — or hegemony — upon others. This benign worldview meant, of course, that all other nations should adopt American culture and its economic system (our brand of globalization), i.e., take those countries by force which do not follow our directives or accept exploitation in the name of "free trade."

At the end of World War II, the physical and mental world — East and West — was a very different place from what it is today. Having "won" that war, while the United States adopted the Marshall Plan and other agencies for war relief and rebuilding, we also had first dibs on valuable resources in war-torn countries. The countries we chose to help included those of Western Europe. Eastern Europe, long lagging behind Western Europe in modernity, we "gave" to the Russians. We also quite often took the scientists and other educated personnel from all countries, who led the sea change in developing weapons (including weapons of mass destruction), as well as our space program.

During the period of the Cold War, the West changed greatly. In the United States, we forged ahead with new communication systems — television, satellite transmission, computers, telephone connections. The country became "wired." A military-based economy in peace time meant jobs, good salaries. We became the world's primary arms manufacturers and entertainment producers. Americans bought homes, the government built a highway system interconnecting the entire country, and the Tennessee Valley project brought electrification to the countryside. We no longer lacked, outside the cities, the infrastructure (communication, transportation) denied so many third-world countries today.

We developed a national school system; public universities proliferated. By the time the Cold War ended, America was transformed from the lifestyle of the Depression. Indeed, life in America today is significantly different from the way it was in even the fifties and sixties in America. Mentally, the Cold War still grips the imagination. Even so, during that era, Americans were urged to do their part and persuaded that they had some responsibility for survival. Air raid alarms, the building of private and public bomb shelters, directions for how to stand in the doorway or lie in the street in the event of a nuclear attack were made available. Children were taught in schools to "duck and cover" under their desks. Those who obeyed the rules would either be saved or be less likely to die. The big lie. It still boggles the mind that a nation of thinking people bought into such rubbish. And what of a government which could create such a scenario?

Two recent films which illustrate this perspective are *Blast from the Past* and *October Sky*. Viewing these films at the end of the twentieth century was revealing; the distance we have traveled from bomb shelter mentality to today is unremarkable — and sheds light on problems in adaptation for the United States to the "now."

Today, our illusions are somewhat different, though we still maintain distance from the rest of the world and its troubles and devastation, much of it wrought by the United States foreign policy (read military actions) and our lucrative arms and other war materiel industries. We no longer build and stock bomb shelters in the backyard as we see in *Blast from the Past*. Instead, beginning with President Reagan in the eighties, we prefer the mythological world of director Steven Spielberg in *Star Wars*. This film is closer to the American Western genre than it is to science fiction.

Darth Vader wears black, the good guys wear white, representing evil and good. The action takes place in the sky. In short, a morality play, with a canopy. Also, it moves the devastation from the ground to the skies. The war we see is "clean," we are not required to review "collateral damage," i.e., the hair of women and children, eyeglasses and baby shoes, as one sees when one "visits" Auschwitz. We see only the bombs, not the scattered remains of the victims. We do not have to match a hand to an arm or a foot to a leg to make an identification. Our wars are conducted at a distance.

Final Thoughts

Kubrick's film is meant to help us see. Yet much has changed in the intervening years since "Strangelove" was released. If anything, the world is a more fearsome and distraught place. The United States is more powerful than ever. The way in which wars are staged today was unthinkable in World War II. War and film seem to be what we do best in the United States. The United States has not signed the Nuclear Test Ban Treaty for obvious reasons. Kubrick's film (unlike others of this genre) ended with a scene of the entire world blowing up in a huge and beautiful mushroom cloud and, in the background, the music of "We'll Meet Again Some Sunny Day." Perhaps we will.

Truth to tell, the United States, then and now, has often had difficulty finding a suitable enemy to attack, although the domino theory provided enough commies to keep us busy on the land, in the air and on the sea. With the end of the Cold War, the American media seemed to be filled with venom, raising doubts about China, which had just emerged some ten years previously from its Cold War isolation. For a while in the mid-to-late nineties, both North Korea and China were kept under close watch. It was not until the terrorist attack of 9/11 that the United States could fix its sights — literally — on a target. Unfortunately, the many terrorist groups around the world make our newly declared war on terror one with moving targets. With terrorist groups all over the world, the American military and the CIA must be everywhere. Thus, we have a dual-pronged dilemma, the possibility of nuclear terrorism proliferating, as well as terrorists with more smarts than money or weapons. In a high-tech world, we must also stoop to deal with low-tech events or with technology gone wrong — as a consequence of the human factor. We learned this when our own planes were hijacked and slammed into the World Trade Center. "Strangelove" was a harbinger of where we find ourselves today, in the twenty-first century. Strange love indeed.

Near the end of his life and in that same speech at the Riverside Church in New York City, Martin Luther King implored his listeners:

> Somehow this madness must cease. We must stop now. I speak as a child of God and brother to the suffering poor of Vietnam. I speak for those whose land is being laid waste, whose homes are being destroyed, whose culture is being subverted. I speak for the poor of America who are paying the double price of smashed hopes at home and death and corruption in Vietnam. I speak as a citizen of the world, for the world as it stands aghast at the path we have taken. I speak as an American to the leaders of my own nation. The great initiative in this war is ours. The initiative to stop it must be ours.... The image of America will never again be the image of revolution, freedom and democracy, but the image of violence and militarism.[38]

NOTES

1. Martin Luther King, Jr., *I Have a Dream: Writings and Speeches that Changed the World,* James M. Washington, ed. (New York: HarperCollins, 1992), 136.
2. *Ibid.,* 137.
3. Kenneth Burke, *A Rhetoric of Religion* (Berkley: University of California Press, 1970), 4–5.
4. René Gerard, *Violence and the Sacred,* Patrick Gregory, trans. (Baltimore: John Hopkins University Press, 1977).
5. Kenneth Burke, "The Rhetoric of Hitler's 'Battle,'" in *Methods of Rhetorical Criticism: A Twentieth Century Perspective,* Robert L. Scott and Bernard L. Brock, eds. (New York: Harper and Row, 1972), 245–57.
6. U.S. Department of State, Office of the Historian, Bureau of Public Affairs, *Significant Terrorist Incidents, 1961–2001: A Chronology* (January 6, 2003) (database online); available from http://www.fas.org/irp/threat/terror_chron.
7. In the war on terrorism the United States military and its "guns for hire" encircle the globe in response to Osama bin Laden's Al Qaeda attack on the twin towers in New York and the Pentagon in Washington, D.C., and bringing down of a United Airlines flight in Pennsylvania on September 11, 2001. This attack on the United States is commonly known as "9/11."
8. "Closing Pandora's Box," Economist.com (January 6, 2003) (database online); available at http://www.economist.com/world/asia/displaystory.cfm?story_id=1516079.
9. Seymour M. Hersh, "The Cold Test," Annals of National Security, *The New Yorker* (January 27, 2003): 42.
10. *Ibid.,* 43.
11. *Ibid.,* 47. Further, given 9/11, as well as the proliferation of WMD, one can no longer rule out the possibility of not only American soldiers either wounded or dead, but also American civilians.
12. *Ibid.,* 45.
13. Iraq has the second largest number of oilfields in the world, after Saudi Arabia. The Pentagon has drawn up plans for the American military presence to protect these oilfields indefinitely, should there be a second war with Iraq.
14. Serge Schmemann, "Nuclear War Strategists Rethink the Unthinkable," *The New York Times* (January 19, 2003), 14.
15. *Ibid.*
16. For information on which states have weapons of mass destruction, see "States Possessing, Pursuing or Capable of Acquiring Weapons of Mass Destruction," *FAS: Intelligence Resource Program* (database online); available from http://www.fas.org/irp/threat/wmd-state .htm.
17. N = nuclear; C = chemical; B = biological; M = missiles: N* = not completed in 2000.
18. Kenneth Burke, "A Dramatistic View of the Origins of Language," *Quarterly Journal of Speech* 38 (October 1952): 252.
19. *Ibid.*
20. *Ibid.* The work here is also from an unpublished dissertation by Nancy Lynch Street, "Social Justice: An Interpretation of the Rhetoric of Legal Justice and the Rhetoric of Moral Justice," (Ph.D. diss., University of Colorado, 1980): 43–64.
21. All quotes not specifically cited in reviews are from *Dr. Strangelove:* A Continuity Transcript.
22. *Ibid.*
23. Personal recollection reminds me that, in the turbulent sixties in America,

there were some who were pleased at this turn of events, primarily because of the administration's support of the civil rights movement in America. At the time one southern gentleman said to me "It's too bad they didn't get his brother, too." Of course this wish was fulfilled in 1968 when both Robert F. Kennedy and the Rev. Martin Luther King were assassinated for their charismatic leadership and beliefs.

24. Martin Luther King, 145.

25. "The Future is Texas," *The Economist* (December 21, 2002): 29–30.

26. James Berardinelli, review. *Dr. Strangelove, or How I Learned to Stop Worrying and Love the Bomb* (database online); available from http://movie-reviews.colossus.net/movies/d/dr–strangelove.html (January 6, 2003).

27. Chris Sheridan, "All's Fair in War and Sex: *Dr. Strangelove*, Communication and the Primal Male Urges," http://www.youknow.com/chris/essays/film /strangelove. html 1995 (January 6, 2003).

28. The major Cold War films selected by Evans in 1964 include *Dr. Strangelove, Failsafe, The Time Travelers, Monstrosity, the Atomic Brain, Demon from Devil's Lake, The Horror of Party Beach,* and *Seven Days in May.* These films were selected because they met the following requirements: (1) the film text had to make specific reference to atomic war or its aftermath, atomic testing and its effects, radiation, atomic technology, postatomic holocaust societies on earth or imaged planets, or atomic scientists; (2) the film had to be a feature-length fictional drama. This requirement excluded documentaries, short-subject films, and cartoons, but included dramatizations of real events, or docudramas; and (3) the film had to be produced and released by the U.S. commercial motion picture industry between January 1, 1949, and December 31, 1964. It had to be distributed in commercial theatres (15). The author generated data through quantitative and qualitative methods, utilizing content analysis. From this data, Evans "defined three major periods of the development of nuclear images in Hollywood" (15).

29. *Ibid.,* 19.

30. *Ibid.,* 163.

31. *Ibid.*

32. Tom Englehardt, *The End of Victory Culture* (University of Massachusetts Press, 1998), 14.

33. *Ibid.*

34. "The Next Tsar," *New Yorker* (July 6, 1998): 44–53. "Tsar Nikolas II, his wife Alexandra and, we think, all of his children, including Anastasia were murdered by the Bolsheviks at Ekaterinburg on July 17th, 1918. Through DNA testing, the bones have been proven to be those of the Tsar and his family. The bodies have been removed from the first gravesite and were reburied on July 17, 1998 in the Peter and Paul Fortress, near St. Petersburg founded in 1703 by Peter the Great, where generations of Romanovs are buried."

35. David L. Hall and Roger T. Ames, *Anticipating China: Thinking through the Narratives of Chinese and Western Culture* (Albany: SUNY Press, 1995), 375.

36. Englehardt, 5.

37. Parts of this chapter were abstracted from paper by the author titled "Baiting the Dragon: The Lingering Cold War with China," presented at the Popular Culture Convention, San Diego, April 1999.

38. Martin Luther King, 145.

Filmography*

The Alamo (1960) — DIRECTOR: John Wayne; CAST: John Wayne, Richard Widmark, Laurence Harvey, Richard Boone, Frankie Avalon, Chill Wills
Apocalypse Now (1978) — DIRECTOR: Francis Ford Coppola; CAST: Martin Sheen, Marlon Brando, Robert Duvall, Frederic Forrest, Dennis Hopper, Sam Bottoms, Laurence Fishburne, Scott Glenn
Bat 21 (1988) — DIRECTOR: Peter Markle; CAST: Gene Hackman, Danny Glover
Big Jim McLain (1952) — DIRECTOR: Edward Ludwig; CAST: John Wayne, Nancy Olson, James Arness, Alan Napier, Veda Ann Borg, Hans Conried
Bonnie and Clyde (1967) — DIRECTOR: Arthur Penn; CAST: Faye Dunaway, Warren Beatty, Gene Hackman, Estelle Parsons, Michael J. Pollard, Denver Pyle
Born on the Fourth of July (1989) — DIRECTOR: Oliver Stone; CAST: Tom Cruise, Willem Dafoe, Raymond J. Barry, Caroline Kava, Frank Whaley, Jerry Levine, Kyra Sedgwick, Stephen Baldwin, Lili Taylor, Tom Berenger
The Bridge on the River Kwai (1957) — DIRECTOR: David Lean; CAST: Alec Guinness, William Holden, Jack Hawkins, Sussue Hayakawa
Casualties of War (1989) — DIRECTOR: Brian de Palma; CAST: Michael J. Fox, Sean Penn, John C. Reilly, John Leguizamo, Thuy Thu Le
Coming Home (1978) — DIRECTOR: Hal Ashby; CAST: Jane Fonda, Jon Voight, Bruce Dern
Dr. Strangelove (1964) — DIRECTOR: Stanley Kubrick; CAST: Peter Sellers,

Information for this list was gathered from several sources, including TLA Film, Video, DVD Guide: 2002–2003, David Bleiler, ed. (New York: St. Martin's, 2001); Amazon.com (database online) (available at http://www.amazon.com/exec/obidos/subst/home/all-stores.html); Video Universe (database online) (available at http://www.cduniverse.com); and TV Guide Online (database online) (available at http://www.tvguide.com/Movies/database).

George C. Scott, Sterling Hayden Keenan Wynn, Slim Pickens, Peter Bull, James Earl Jones

Flight of the Intruder (1991)—DIRECTOR: John Milium; CAST: Danny Glover, Willem Dafoe, Brad Johnson, Rosanna Arquette, Tom Sizemore

The Fountainhead (1949)—DIRECTOR: King Vidor; CAST: Gary Cooper, Patricial Neal, Raymond Massey

The Graduate (1967)—DIRECTOR: Mike Nichols; CAST: Anne Bancroft, Dustin Hoffman, Katharine Ross, William Daniels, Murray Hamilton

The Green Berets (1968)— Directors: Ray Kellogg, John Wayne; CAST: John Wayne, David Janssen, Jim Hutton, Aldo Ray, Raymond St. Jacques, Bruce Cabot, Jack Soo

Guess Who's Coming to Dinner (1967)—DIRECTOR: Stanley Kramer; CAST: Spencer Tracy, Sidney Poitier, Katharine Hepburn, Katharine Houghton

Hanoi Hilton (1987)—DIRECTOR: Lionel Chetwynd; CAST: Michael Moriarty, Jeffrey Jones, Aki Aleong, George Carlin, Stephen Davies, John Diehl

High Noon (1952)—DIRECTOR: Fred Zinnemann; CAST: Gary Cooper, Grace Kelly, Thomas Mitchell, Lloyd Bridges, Lon Chaney, Jr., Katy Jurado

In Country (1989)—DIRECTOR: Norman Jewison; CAST: Bruce Willis, Emily Lloyd, Joan Allen, Kevin Anderson, Judith Ivey

Jacob's Ladder (1990)—DIRECTOR: Adrian Lyne; CAST: Tim Robbins, Danny Aiello, Elizabeth PeñaJason Alexander, Macaulay Culkin

Let There Be Light (1945)—DIRECTOR: John Huston (documentary)

Lethal Weapon (1987)—DIRECTOR: Richard Donner; CAST: Mel Gibson, Danny Glover, Gary Busey, Mitchell Ryan, Darlene Love

Patriot Games (1992)—DIRECTOR: Philip Noyce; CAST: Harrison Ford, Anne Archer, Patrick Bergen, Sean Bean, Richard Harris, James Earl Jones, Samuel L. Jackson

Platoon (1986)—DIRECTOR: Oliver Stone; CAST: Charlie Sheen, Willem Dafoe, Tom Berenger, Forest Whitaker, John C. McGinley, Kevin Dillon, Johnny Depp

Rambo: First Blood, Part II (1985)—DIRECTOR: George P. Cosmatos; CAST: Sylvester Stallone, Richard Crenna

Seven Days in May (1964)—DIRECTOR: John Frankenheimer; CAST: Burt Lancaster, Fredric March, Kirk Douglas, Edmond O'Brien, Ava Gardner

Taxi Driver (1976)—DIRECTOR: Martin Scorsese; CAST: Robert De Niro, Jodie Foster, Cybill Shepherd, Harvey Keitel, Albert Brooks, Peter Boyle

True Lies (1994)—DIRECTOR: James Cameron; CAST: Arnold Schwarzenegger, Jamie Lee Curtis, Tom Arnold, Bill Paxton, Tia Carrere, Charlton Heston, Art Malik

The War at Home (1996)—DIRECTOR: Emilio Estevez; CAST: Kathy Bates, Martin Sheen, Kimberly Williams, Emilio Estevez

The Way We Were (1973)—DIRECTOR: Sydney Pollack; CAST: Barbra Streisand, Robert Redford, Bradford Dillman, Viveca Lindfors, Murray Hamilton, James Woods

Bibliography

America Rediscovered: Critical Essays on Literature and Film of the Vietnam War. Edited by Owen W. Gilman Jr. and Lorrie Smith. New York: Garland, 1990.
American History/American Film. Edited by John E. O'Connor and Martin A. Jackson. New York: Ungar, 1977.
Arguing Communication and Culture. Edited by G. Thomas Goodnight. Washington, D.C.: National Communication Association, 2002.
Arnett, Ronald C., Pat Arneson, and Julia Wood. *Dialogic Civility in a Cynical Age: Community, Hope, and Interpersonal Relationships.* Albany: State University of New York Press, 1999.
Auster, Al, and Leonard Quart. *American Film and Society since 1945.* New York: Praeger, 1984.
Baker, James Thomas. *Ayn Rand.* Boston: Twayne, 1987.
Belton, John. *American Cinema/American Culture.* New York: McGraw-Hill, 1994.
Biskind, Peter. *Seeing Is Believing: How Hollywood Taught Us to Stop Worrying and Love the Fifties.* New York: Pantheon, 2000.
Boot, Max. *The Savage Wars of Peace: Small Wars and the Rise of American Power.* New York: Basic, 2002.
Brill, Lesley. *John Huston's Filmmaking.* New York: Cambridge University Press, 1997.
Brode, Douglas. *The Films of Dustin Hoffman.* New York: Citadel, 1991.
Brummett, Barry. *The Films of the Sixties.* New York: Citadel, 1980.
_____. *Rhetoric in Popular Culture.* New York: St. Martin's, 1994.
Burke, Kenneth. *Attitudes toward History.* Boston: Beacon, 1959 (reprint).
_____. *A Rhetoric of Religion.* Berkeley: University of California Press, 1970.
_____. *A Grammar of Motives.* Berkeley: University of California Press, 1974 (reprint).
Campbell, Joseph. *The Hero with a Thousand Faces.* 2nd ed. Princeton, N.J.: Princeton University Press, 1968.
Carter, Stephen. *Civility.* New York: Harper Perennial, 1998.
Cloud, Dana L. *Control and Consolation in American Culture and Politics: Rhetorics of Therapy.* Thousand Oaks, Calif.: Sage, 1998.
Cultural Legacies of Vietnam: Uses of the Past in the Present. Edited by Richard Morris and Peter Ehrenhaus. Norwood, N.J.: Ablex, 1990.
Davis, Ronald. *Duke: The Life and Times of John Wayne.* Norman: University of Oklahoma Press, 1998.

Disabled Veterans in History. Edited by David A. Gerber. Ann Arbor: University of Michigan Press, 2000.

Doherty, Thomas. *Projection of War: Hollywood, American Culture and World War II.* New York: Columbia University Press, 1993.

Durgnat, Raymond, and Scott Simmon. *King Vidor, American.* Berkeley: University of California Press, 1990.

Englehardt, Tom. *The End of Victory Culture.* Amherst: University of Massachusetts Press, 1998.

Evans, Joyce A. *Celluloid Mushroom Clouds: Hollywood and the Atomic Bomb.* Boulder: Westview, 1998.

Ferro, Marc. *Cinema and History.* Translated by Naomi Green. Detroit: Wayne State University Press, 1988.

Festinger, Leon. *A Theory of Cognitive Dissonance.* Stanford: Stanford University Press, 1957.

Films of Peace and War, Book 2. Edited by Robert Hughes. New York: Grove, 1962.

Forni, P. M. *Choosing Civility.* New York: St. Martin's, 2002.

Frank, Arthur W. *The Wounded Storyteller: Body, Illness, and Ethics.* Chicago: University of Chicago Press, 1995.

Fried, Richard M. *Nightmare in Red: The McCarthy Era in Perspective.* New York: Oxford University Press, 1990.

Friedman, Lester D., ed. *Arthur Penn's Bonnie and Clyde.* New York: Cambridge University Press: 2000.

Gehring, Wes D. *Handbook of American Film Genres.* New York: Greenwood, 1988.

Gerard, René. *Violence and the Sacred.* Translated by Patrick Gregory. Baltimore: John Hopkins University Press, 1977.

Gianos, Phillip L. *Politics and Politicians in American Film.* Westport, Conn.: Praeger, 1999.

Gibson, James William. *The Perfect War: Technowar in Vietnam.* Boston: Atlantic Monthly Press, 1986.

Girgus, Sam B. *Hollywood Renaissance: The Cinema of Democracy in the Era of Ford, Capra, and Kazan.* New York: Cambridge University Press, 1998.

Gitlin, Todd. *The Sixties: Years of Hope, Days of Rage.* New York: Bantam Books, 1987.

Greuner, E. G. *Prisoners of Culture: Representing the Vietnam POW.* New Brunswick, N.J.: Rutgers University Press, 1993.

Grobel, Lawrence. *The Hustons.* New York: Avon, 1989.

Hallion, Richard P. *Test Pilots: The Frontiersmen of Flight.* Washington, D.C.: Smithsonian, 1988.

Heider, Fritz. *The Psychology of Interpersonal Relations.* New York: John Wiley, 1958.

Hellmann, John. *American Myth and the Legacy of Vietnam.* New York: Columbia University Press, 1986.

Henriksen, Margot A. *Dr. Strangelove's America.* Berkeley: University of California Press, 1997.

Herman, Judith Lewis. *Trauma and Recovery: The Aftermath of Violence — From Domestic Abuse to Political Terror.* New York: Basic/Harper Collins, 1992.

Huston, John. *Open Book.* New York: Alfred A. Knopf, 1980.

I Have a Dream: Writings and Speeches that Changed the World. Edited by James M. Washington. New York: HarperCollins, 1992.

Inventing Vietnam: The War in Film and Television. Edited by Michael Anderegg. Philadelphia: Temple University Press, 1991.

Jeffords, Susan. *The Remasculinization of America: Gender and the Vietnam War.* Bloomington: Indiana University Press, 1989.

John Huston: Interviews. Edited by Robert Emmet Long. Jackson: University Press of Mississippi, 2001.

Kaminsky, Stuart. *American Film Genres: Approaches to a Critical Theory of Popular Film.* New York: Dell, 1974.

Kort, Michael G. *The Cold War.* New York: Columbia University Press, 1998.

Linenthal, Edward Tabor. *Changing Images of the Warrior Hero in America: A History of Popular Symbolism.* New York: Edwin Mellen, 1982.

Lipschutz, Ronnie D. *Cold War Fantasies: Film, Fiction and Foreign Policy.* Lanham, Md.: Rowman & Littlefield, 2001.

Lloyd, Ann. *Movies of the Sixties.* London: Orbis, 1983.

MacCann, Richard Dyer. *The People's Films: A Political History of U.S. Government Motion Pictures.* New York: Hastings House, 1973.

McGilligan, Patrick, and Paul Buhle. *Tender Comrades: A Backstory of the Hollywood Blacklist.* New York: St. Martin's Griffin, 1997.

Methods of Rhetorical Criticism: A Twentieth-Century Perspective. Edited by Robert L. Scott and Bernard L. Brock. New York: Harper and Row, 1972.

O'Brien, Frank J. *The Hungry Tigers: The Fighter Pilot's Role in Modern Warfare.* Blue Ridge Summit, Penn.: Aero/Tab, 1986.

Peck, M. Scott. *A World Waiting to Be Reborn: Civility Rediscovered.* New York: Bantam, 1994.

Pendo, Stephen. *Aviation in the Cinema.* Metuchen, N.J.: Scarecrow, 1985.

Perspectives on John Huston. Edited by Stephen Cooper. New York: G. K. Hall, 1994.

Peterson, H. C., and Gilbert C. Fite. *Opponents of War, 1917–1918.* Westport, Conn.: Greenwood, 1986 (reprint).

Pratley, Gerald. *The Cinema of David Lean.* Cranbury, N.J.: A. S. Barnes, 1974.

Putnam, Robert. *Bowling Alone: The Collapse and Revival of American Community.* New York: Simon & Schuster, 2000.

Reflections in a Male Eye: John Huston and the American Experience. Edited by Gaylyn Studlar and David Desser. Washington, D.C.: Smithsonian, 1993.

Rethinking the Trauma of War. Edited by Patrick J. Bracken and Celia Petty. New York/London: Free Association, 1998.

Roberts, Randy, and James S. Olson. *John Wayne, American.* Lincoln: University of Nebraska Press, 1995.

Rodriguez, Amardo. *Diversity as Liberation (II): Introducing a New Understanding of Diversity.* New Jersey: Hampton, 2000.

Rouner, Leroy S., ed. *Civility.* South Bend: University of Notre Dame Press, 2000.

Sayre, Nora. *Runningtime: Films of the Cold War.* New York: Dial, 1982.

Schatz, Thomas G. *Hollywood Genre: Formulas, Filmmaking, and the Studio System.* Philadelphia: Temple University Press, 1981.

Silencing the Opposition: Government Strategies of Suppression of Freedom of Expression. Edited by Craig R. Smith. Albany: State University of New York Press, 1996.

Slotkin, Richard. *Regeneration through Violence: The Mythology of the American Frontier, 1600–1800.* Middletown, Conn.: Wesleyan University Press, 1973.

Tannen, Deborah. *The Argument Culture*. New York: Random, 1997.
Wake, Sandra, and Nicole Hayden, Eds. *The Bonnie and Clyde Book*. New York: Simon & Shuster, 1972.
Wartenberg, Thomas E. *Unlikely Couples: Movie Romance as Social Criticism*. Boulder: Westview, 1999.
Whitfield, Stephen J. *The Culture of the Cold War*, 2nd ed. Baltimore: The Johns Hopkins University Press, 1996.
Wills, Gary. *John Wayne's America*. New York: Simon & Schuster, 1997.
Wise, David, and Thomas B. Ross. *The Invisible Government*. New York: Random House, 1964.

About the
Contributors

Marilyn J. Matelski is Professor and former Chair of the Department of Communication at Boston College and teaches courses in intercultural communication, mass communication theory, and cultural diversity in the media. She has written eleven books, along with numerous journal articles and reviews concerning media and its uses. Some of her previous titles include *The Soap Opera Evolution, Daytime Broadcast Television Programming,* and *TV News Ethics* (also translated into Turkish), *Vatican Radio: Propagation by the Airwaves,* and *Messages from the Underground: Transnational Radio in Resistance and in Solidarity* (coauthored with Nancy Lynch Street) and *Soap Operas Worldwide: Cultural and Serial Realities.* Her latest book, coauthored with Nancy Lynch Street, focuses on American businesses in China and was published by McFarland in 2003.

Nancy Lynch Street is Professor, past Chair and Graduate Coordinator of the Department of Communication Studies and Theatre Arts at Bridgewater State College (BSC), and is currently serving her fourth year as Co-Coordinator of the college's Center for Academic Research and Teaching. Street teaches courses in intercultural communication, communication theory and Cold War rhetoric and film. In 1985 (and again in 1988), she became BSC's first exchange professor with Shanxi Teacher's University (STU) in Linfen, Shanxi province, PRC. In 1988 and 1990, Street also received Fulbright study grants to research culture and economic development in China, Korea and Taiwan. Her book relating to these experiences and research, *In Search of Red Buddha,* a study of a Chinese educational work unit during escalating economic and social change in China, was published in 1992. Her most recent book, *American Businesses in China: Balancing Culture and Communication,* was published by McFarland in 2003.

Richard A. Kallan is Chair and Professor of Communication at California State Polytechnic University, Pomona. He received his doctorate from Northwestern University. Over the years, he has taught a variety of courses, including classes in media history, ethics, and criticism. His research, which focuses primarily on the rhetorical dimensions of popular artifacts, has been published in *Communication Monographs, Journalism Quarterly, Journalism and Mass Communication Educator, Federal Communications Law Journal,* and *Journal of Popular Culture.*

Bonnie S. Jefferson is an Adjunct Assistant Professor at Boston College. Her areas of research include the rhetoric of the Cold War, specifically American anticommunism, and the rhetorical forms used to teach anticommunist assumptions to the public. She has studied the anticommunist messages found in popular periodicals (such as *The Readers' Digest* and the Hearst newspaper chain) political cartoons, as well as popular films of the Cold War era. Her most recent work is an examination of anticommunist messages found in John Wayne films.

Donald A. Fishman is an Associate Professor of Communication at Boston College. His academic interests are communication law, crisis communication, and Cold War Era persuasion. Fishman is the winner of the 1998 Franklyn S. Haiman Award for Distinguished Scholarship in Freedom of Expression and the 2001 Phifer Award for Outstanding Scholarship in Parliamentary Procedure.

John J. Michalczyk, currently Chair of the Fine Arts Department of Boston College (where he also codirects the Film Studies Program), has studied war as a major psychological catalyst for both individuals and society since 1970. His publications and television documentaries about conflict view film as a significant sociopolitical witness to the period in which it occurs. Some of his works include *Of Shamrocks and Stars* and *In the Shadow of the Reich: Nazi Medicine, Out of the Ashes: Northern Ireland's Fragile Peace, The Cross and the Star: Jews, Christians and the Holocaust, December's Dilemma: The Crèche, the Dreidel and the Star, Unexpected Openings: Northern Ireland's Prisoners, Prelude to Kosovo: War and Peace in Bosnia and Croatia, South Africa: Beyond a Miracle* (documentaries) and *The French Literary Filmmakers, The Italian Political Filmmakers* and *Costa Gavras: The Political Fiction Film* (books).

Susan A. Michalczyk completed her doctoral studies in Romance Languages and Literatures at Harvard University in 1986, with a dissertation on comparative literature and psychology. For the past ten years, she has taught the interdisciplinary curriculum of the Honors Program at Boston

College, where she is currently running a "Medicine and Literature" seminar. She has also recently coedited a book (with Jeffery Howe and Pamela Berger) titled *The Plume and the Palette*.

Sharon D. Downey is Professor in and Chair of the Department of Communication Studies at California State University, Long Beach. Her scholarly interests include the study of interpersonal, social, and international conflict, feminist rhetoric, and the mythic power of war and warriors in popular culture. Former editor of *Women's Studies in Communication*, she currently is director of the Peace Studies certificate program at California State University, Long Beach.

Karen Rasmussen is Professor in the Communication Studies Department at California State University, Long Beach, where she teaches courses in rhetorical theory and criticism and popular culture. Her research interests address the rhetorical dimensions of music, contemporary literature, TV and film, particularly films related to war and to the images of women in popular culture. Her essays have appeared in the *Quarterly Journal of Speech, Women's Studies in Communication, Western Journal of Communication, Communication Studies* and *American Communication Journal*.

Jennifer Asenas is a graduate student in Communication Studies at the University of Texas at Austin. She recently received her M.A. from California State University, Long Beach, where she wrote her thesis on post–Vietnam World War II films. Currently she is working on gathering narratives from World War II veterans concerning their impressions of the history told about them in popular culture.

Suzanne McCorkle received her Ph.D. from the University of Colorado at Boulder in 1978. Dr. McCorkle is currently Professor of Communication and Director of Conflict Management Services at Boise State University and was the 2002 winner of the Idaho Peacemaker Award from the Idaho Mediation Association for her research and service in conflict management and mediation.

Barbara Walkosz is an Assistant Professor of Communication at the University of Colorado at Denver. Her academic interests include the changing nature of civil discourse and social values in American society, and the politics of war as reflected through film analysis.

Index